# BECOME
## A new THEORY
# WHO
### of SELF-ESTEEM, human GREATNESS
# YOU
### and the OPPOSITE of DEPRESSION
# ARE
RYAN A BUSH

# About the Author

Ryan A Bush is a designer and thinker focused on building better systems, better people, and a better future. As founder of Designing the Mind, Ryan's central purpose is to provide wisdom education and expand human potential beyond the norm.

This journey has led him to write multiple bestselling books like *Designing the Mind: The Principles of Psychitecture*, build life-changing programs like The Anxiety Algorithm, and launch Mindform, the world's first psychitecture collective and training platform. Through his books, programs, and community, he works to integrate the insights of ancient and modern thinkers to form a new vision for psychological growth and self-mastery.

Ryan's background is in the design of systems—he has worked with tech startups to design and develop everything from patented physical products, to software, to buildings, to business models. But his most relevant credential is a lifelong appetite for introspective investigation, ravenous reading, and obsessive self-optimization.

For many years, Ryan has studied the insights of ancient teachers, practical philosophers, and cognitive scientists. His ideas have been featured on major platforms like Psyche, Modern Stoicism, and Lifehack, as well as podcasts like Modern Wisdom, This Anthro Life, and The Unmistakable Creative.

He lives in a small mountain town where he splits his time between creating, reflecting, and adventuring with his partner and their corgi, who is on track to be an honors student this year.

MORE OF RYAN'S WORK AT DESIGNING THE MIND

- DESIGNING THE MIND: THE PRINCIPLES OF PSYCHITECTURE
- THE BOOK OF SELF-MASTERY
- MINDSIGHT: INTROSPECTION CARDS
- THE ANXIETY ALGORITHM PROGRAM
- THE FLOURISHING FUNCTION PROGRAM
- MINDFORM: PSYCHITECTURE COLLECTIVE

BECOME WHO YOU ARE

Copyright © 2024 - Designing the Mind, LLC. Brevard, NC. All rights reserved. No part of this publication may be reproduced, stored or transmitted in any form or by any means, electronic, mechanical, photocopying, recording, scanning, or otherwise without permission from the publisher. It is illegal to copy this book, post it to a website, or distribute it by any other means without permission.
Library of Congress Control Number: 2024903406

# CONTENTS

| | |
|---|---|
| Introduction | 6 |

## PART 1: THE MODEL

| | |
|---|---|
| 1. Dimensions of Well-Being: The Essence of the Good Life | 11 |
| 2. The Virtue Game: The Spectrum, Domains, and the Portfolio | 24 |
| 3. The Philosophy of Virtue: From Socrates to Seligman | 36 |
| 4. The Overview: Learning to See the Third Dimension of Happiness | 48 |

## PART 2: THE THEORY

| | |
|---|---|
| 5. The Signal: The Origins of Values and Virtues | 67 |
| 6. The Simulation: Self-Esteem and the Default Mode Network | 91 |
| 7. The Stimulus: The Chemical Catalysts of Depression | 107 |
| 8. The Synthesis: Virtue Self-Signaling Theory | 129 |

## PART 3: THE APPLICATION

| | |
|---|---|
| 9. Paths to Enlightenment: The Tale of Transcendence | 149 |
| 10. Virtue Vision: Seeing Your Strengths Clearly | 168 |
| 11. Virtue Activation: Bringing Your Strengths to Life | 192 |
| 12. The Path of Self-Becoming: You Shall Become The Person You Are | 210 |
| Endnotes | 233 |

# THE BOOK OF SELF MASTERY

In addition to this book, readers can get a **free copy of** *The Book of Self Mastery*, **a thoughtful quote compilation and commentary on the discipline of mastering yourself.**

- Gain insights from Stoic philosopher Seneca on overcoming anxiety
- Find guidance from the Buddha on letting go of unhelpful attachments
- Learn from Robert Greene why continual discomfort is necessary for growth
- Hear how Roman emperor Marcus Aurelius embraced challenges and change
- Learn how to eliminate negative thoughts and bad moods from Dr. David Burns

Just go to designingthemind.org/becoming to get your free copy and subscribe to The Psychitect for a weekly dose of codified wisdom.

# Introduction

This is a book about the opposite of depression.

This is not to say that it's a book about "happiness." Just as depression is not merely generic unhappiness, the topic of this book is not merely generic happiness.

It is also not to say that it is a book about depression. Yes, it will inevitably end up covering depression in discussing its opposite, and I do hope it will help some through their struggles.

But this book is about a positive state, not the removal of a negative one. It's about striving for greatness, not recovering from an illness.

When I was about 14, I used to think there was a theory of the good life to be discovered. Some kind of secret, $E=Mc2$ style formula that could guide us all to satisfaction.

I would often pace around my room, formulating theories and metaphors and lecturing an imaginary audience on the wisdom I had gathered. I was perpetually on the verge of pinning down the mechanics of human happiness and building a foolproof framework for enlightenment.

I was obsessed. I would spend my evenings going on Wikipedia binges, opening hundreds of tabs at a time trying to find all the answers, but only ever ending up with more questions. I spent my days theorizing in class instead of listening to lectures or socializing. And this theory of happiness, however elusive, served as a sanctuary for me as I grew up—a shield from the storms of adolescence.

I found shreds of truth in the works of the Buddha, the Stoics, and Nietzsche. I studied positive psychology, evolutionary science, and psychotherapy. Every once and a while I would come across a quote or an idea that filled me with excitement and reignited my obsession.

But as I got older, I learned more and more how messy real life was, and the grand, unified theory of happiness began to seem less plausible. I started to suspect that perhaps it was those "great philosophers" who needed a lesson on happiness. They were trying to find it in abstract ideas and equations. Maybe if they stopped overthinking and danced, took in a sunset, or fell in love, they would find what they had been trying to calculate.

But today, I'm proud to announce that I've done it. That's right, the grand, unified theory of human well-being actually exists. Seriously! I'm as shocked as you are. You thought I was going to cop-out with that dancing line. But the formula is alive and well. Should I make you wait for it or just throw it all at you right away?

Before I do, how was that opener for you? I hear people like stories. How was your experience of that anecdote about little Ryan? If you liked it, there's more where that came from. Innovatively, I'm going to be presenting this theory through the lens of my own personal challenges as a straight, white man who was raised in a loving, suburban home.

If you are bored to death by personal anecdotes, don't worry. There will be plenty of ideas and frameworks for all of you weirdos like me.

"Become who you are" is a phrase attributed to 19th-century philosopher Friedrich Nietzsche. Like all of his work, it is cryptic and ambiguous. But it has an allure that hasn't left my mind since I first heard it.

We are used to hearing that we should be ourselves. Find ourselves? Sure. But becoming ourselves is a different, seemingly paradoxical, proposition. How can I become who I already am?

The theory I will put forward is a synthesis of Stoic philosophy and neuropsychology. Nietzschean virtue ethics and evolutionary psychology. Spiritual wisdom and psychotherapy. It's an interdisciplinary integration of a number of different ideas, theories, and practices.

It will aim to explain a wide array of human phenomena, like:

Why do we feel there's a reason to do the right thing even in the absence of consequences?

Why do lottery winners and paraplegics' happiness return to the same levels after their incidents?

Why do humans do weird things like writing music and running marathons?

Where do our values come from?

Why do we care so much about our self-esteem?

Why do we feel bad about ourselves when we aren't achieving anything?

Why do neurotypes like autism and ADHD exist?

Why do humans get depressed? Why are some people perpetually discontent in their lives?

This book contains many original ideas, few of which are my own. I am indebted to contemporary psychological visionaries like Aaron Beck, Martin Seligman, Daniel Gilbert, Mark Leary, and Geoffrey Miller. And the core teachings of the book date back thousands of years to the work of philosophical titans. My role has simply been to connect the dots.

The book is intended for intellectually-curious lay readers who like exploring concepts from many different angles. I will blend philosophical arguments, scientific data, and therapeutic advice. And I will gradually weave in experiences from my own life to form a story that will bring the theory to life.

I will warn you that the implications of the theory I present turn a number of conventional beliefs on their heads. Some claims I will put forward are that depression is not rooted in chemical imbalance and is not best treated with medicine. That autism and ADHD are not developmental disorders, but adaptive evolutionary strategies. And that meditative self-transcendence is not the end toward which we should be striving.

Some people seem to identify so closely with the prevailing views on these topics that even hearing them questioned feels like a personal attack. But I want to assure you that weakening your identity is the precise opposite of my aim in this book.

I've been driven to develop this theory to understand my own experience. To make sense of the sometimes baffling behaviors of human beings. But most of all to help the people I love whose struggles I know are preventable. To help light the way toward growth and flourishing for my readers.

There are three parts of the book, each containing four chapters. Part one answers the what, describing the practical framework I am proposing. Part two is the why, the scientific theory that explains why human life and well-being work the way they do. And part three is the how—how you can use this framework to live a great life.

The modern world is in great need of vision, aspiration, and optimism. In a time when we feel we can't rely on security or truth, we need a North Star of individual greatness toward which we can strive. This concept of greatness seems so far removed from our collective consciousness that the reader may require me to beat them over the head with it to open them up to it.

I write in the hopes that this model will help serve as a beacon for those who are lost. That it will help reveal new paths for those seeking new growth. And that it will provide a framework for those who have found their way and have struggled to articulate the path to others.

If you ever reached out to me and asked if my previous book, *Designing the Mind* was the best book to read if you were depressed or struggling to find your way through life, you probably got a response along the lines of "No. Read *Feeling Good*. Read *Meditations*. Don't read my book now."

But this book you have in your hands now is different. I genuinely believe the ideas in this book have the power to lift depression and catalyze transformation.

I think it will change lives. I hope it changes yours.

# PART 1

# THE MODEL

# 1

# Dimensions of Well-Being: The Essence of the Good Life

## Dimensions of Well-Being

This is the first dimension of happiness:

Pain ⬅——●————————➡ Pleasure

It's a simple scale running from pain to pleasure. We learn early on that some things feel better than others, and it's generally better to do the ones that feel good.

This simple model gives us a way to navigate our lives and discriminate between better and worse paths. Halloween candy is good—homework is bad. Got it.

And it serves us well—imagine where we would be if we made no distinction between pleasure or pain in our decisions. Say what you will about recreational drugs and casual sex—I'll take them over putting my hand in a blender any day.

But on occasion, something strange happens. Our happiness doesn't quite do what we would predict. We have an anomaly.

The Halloween candy makes us sick. The homework makes us feel accomplished and proud. We get through a drug binge that felt good in one way, but we end up feeling bad in some other way. There must be more to happiness than that.

Our model of happiness is inadequate, and it's time to give it an upgrade.

This is the second dimension of happiness:

Gain

Loss

This axis runs from loss to gain—shorthand for any good or bad life circumstances, achievements, or outcomes.

Once we can conceptualize this second dimension of happiness, we become long-term life strategists. We plot our decisions carefully to maximize a deeper kind of well-being. We realize how superficial the search for simple pleasure was and learn that a good life requires discipline and sacrifice.

When we combine these two axes, we get a two-dimensional plane of factors determining our decisions. This plane is the landscape of your circumstances, or for short, the circumscape.

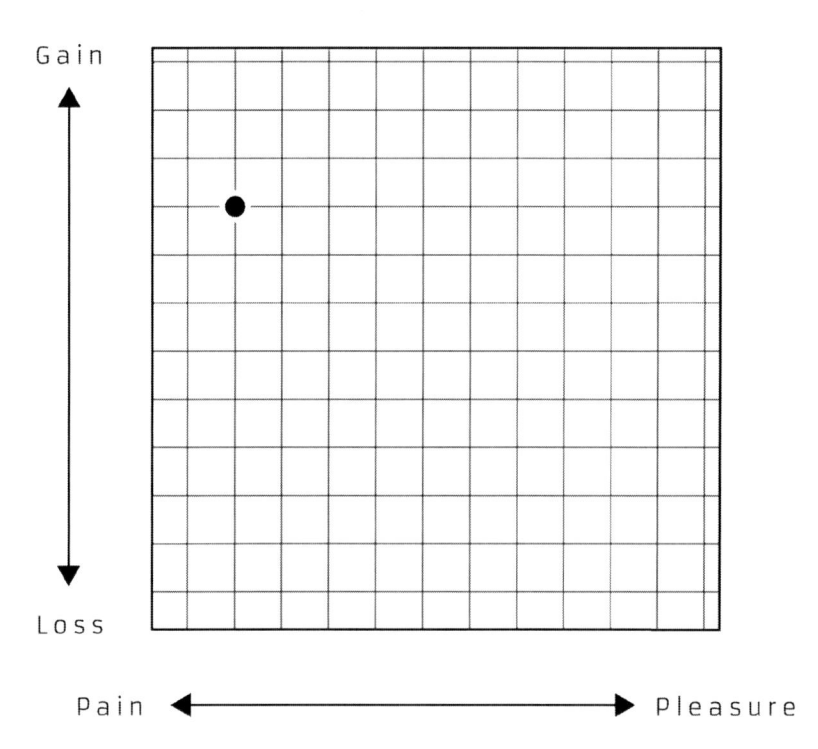

```
Gain
  ↑
  │  ┌─────────────────┐
  │  │                 │
  │  │  ●              │
  │  │                 │
  │  │                 │
  │  │                 │
  │  │                 │
  │  └─────────────────┘
  ↓
Loss

   Pain  ←──────────────→  Pleasure
```

This model is far more useful and comprehensive than the simple pleasure-pain axis. It enables us to weigh our decisions on multiple levels, balancing short-term pleasure with long-term success. We can choose to forgo the drunken party when our research paper is due the next day.

Once our understanding evolves to this point, we view and live our lives on the circumscape, and we gain a new understanding of happiness. Getting a raise is good—breakups are bad. Got it.

And most of the time, this framework seems to serve us and map nicely onto our experience. Buying a house after saving up for years brings joy—something deeper than momentary pleasure. Losing a friend brings sadness, something deeper than momentary pain.

But on occasion, something strange happens. Our happiness doesn't quite do what we would predict. We have an anomaly.

We'll achieve some clear success on paper, like getting a promotion, but our happiness will seem to stay the same. We'll go through a difficult divorce and end up saying it was the best thing that ever happened to us. And then we'll shrug and forget about this odd outlier before continuing our efforts for improved circumstances.

This is how most of us navigate our lives today. This is where the modern understanding of happiness stands today. Good things are good, but in rare cases, good things are bad, or bad things are good. And we're just not very good at predicting when that will be the case.

But this time, instead of shrugging and moving on, let's really pause and ask "why?" Why does winning the lottery rarely make people happier? Why do losses and failures so rarely affect us in the way we would predict?

Our model of happiness is inadequate, and it's time to give it an upgrade.

This is the third dimension of happiness:

I know, it doesn't look like anything right now. That's because it's the z-axis—we can't see it from our current two-dimensional perspective. But we're going to change that.

# Formulas for Happiness

We all know someone who is perpetually discontent. Maybe it's a friend who seems to do nothing but lounge around her house and indulge in drugs, streaming, social media, and video games. Maybe it's a colleague who is constantly stressed, restlessly chasing promotions, profits, and productivity. Maybe it's a family member who hops from one relationship to the next, continually confused when love doesn't deliver enduring bliss. Maybe it's you.

Actually, most of us don't just know one person like this; we know many. And they all seem to have something in common, something beyond their chronic dissatisfaction. But it's hard to pin down exactly what this is.

For millennia, philosophers have debated the essence of what it means to live a good life. One would assume that by this point in history, the matter should have been laid to rest. And sure enough, there are a number of modern frameworks and formulas for happiness.

Happiness is equal to the sum of three components: subjective life satisfaction, positive emotion, and the absence of negative emotion.[1]

Happiness is equal to your genetic set point (50%), your circumstances (10%), and voluntary factors like your attitude (40%).[2]

Happiness is equal to your extraversion minus neuroticism.[3]

Happiness is equal to the difference between the events of your life and your expectations of them.[4]

Happiness is equal to the conglomerate of your income (between $50,000 and $75,000 a year), your relationship status (married), the number of close friends you have (3-5), the number of children you have (0), and how often you write in your gratitude journal (weekly).[5]

Happiness is equal to your levels of neural chemicals dopamine, serotonin, oxytocin, endorphins, and cortisol.[6]

These formulas may all be valid within their own domains. But they don't provide us with a lot of useful guidance. You could have each of these rules memorized and still spend your life stumbling around the realm of well-being.

In a relevant work, *Stumbling on Happiness*, Daniel Gilbert argues that happiness is perplexing because we simply lack the capacities to predict what will make us happy. We have a number of biases that cause us to poorly forecast how we will feel about a certain event or decision, how intense that feeling will be, and how long it will last.[7]

He provides numerous examples of unlucky individuals, from twins conjoined at the head, to prisoners, to people paralyzed from the neck down. And he points out that despite how terrible we think all these fates are, all of these people he lists claim to be deeply satisfied. He suggests that our emotional predictions don't account for the psychological defenses that allow us to reason away inescapable circumstances.[8]

I remember watching Gilbert's TED talk on repeat. He talked about how lottery winners and paraplegics were equally satisfied a year after their incidents.[9] When I got his book, I found it interesting, insightful, and quite funny. But by the end, I couldn't help thinking "That's it?? We're just bad at predicting things? That's the grand formula?"

Gilbert is right that we aren't very good at predicting our own well-being. But it's become clear to me that these struggles for satisfaction are more than just haphazard prediction errors. There are consistent patterns behind our confounding quests for happiness.

Our subjective satisfaction levels fluctuate over time—they just don't correspond to the changes in life events that we expect them to. The reason lottery winners and paraplegics return to their previous levels of life-satisfaction isn't that happiness levels never change—we know they can change dramatically.[10] It's that these types of events, these gains and losses of circumstance, are not in the business of determining our well-being.

We are continually surprised to find that the life events we expect to defeat or delight us simply don't deliver. We stumble in the same way one would stumble when navigating a foreign terrain with the wrong map.

It's at this point that most people throw up their hands and shout "meaning." Meaning is a philosophical mystery meat. A shape-shifting concept that fills in the gaps when we don't understand our own fulfillment.

In *Man's Search for Meaning*, Viktor Frankl says that "life is never made unbearable by circumstances, but only by lack of meaning and purpose."[11] Many of us find this intuitively true and compelling.

The irony is that most of us don't really know what meaning means. Is it a coherent explanation for the universe and our place in it? Is it a sense of purpose in our work? A personal narrative? All of the above? All we really know is that it sounds good.

We have the sense that certain activities like hiking up a mountain or writing a book are rewarding things to spend time on, while others like watching television or laying around a pool are mere distractions.

Sure, we can say the former activities are meaningful. But what makes them meaningful exactly? What makes them rewarding?

Maybe meaningful activities are those done out of love. Maybe we find work rewarding when it is done to provide for our families. This quality applies to some rewarding activities, but not all. Composing music, building an app, or completing a graduate program could all be rewarding tasks, whether or not they are done out of love.

Maybe meaningful activities need to accomplish something valuable. They should be productive and contribute to society. This seems right, and it clearly has some truth to it. But it's hard to say that running a marathon or traveling to New Zealand would generate value for the world, despite seeming like a fulfilling experience to many.

Perhaps, it is often proposed, meaningful activities have to be difficult. You have to work hard and suffer for something in order for it to be rewarding. All the rewarding tasks I listed above are difficult in some way or another.

Psychologist Paul Bloom argues that there is a "sweet spot" of pleasure and suffering that we crave and that meaningful tasks must involve suffering.[12] He says, "If you ask people 'what's a meaningful experience?' they answer coherently, and they seem to be talking about projects that are difficult, that take a lot of time, and that involve struggle and doubt and uncertainty. They involve suffering of different sorts. And if it didn't involve suffering, it wouldn't be meaningful."[13]

This seems right too. But what about spending time with your loved ones? Though relationships can have their struggles, most of us don't feel like our relationships are more meaningful or rewarding when they are difficult or painful. If anything, we find positive, quality time with our loved ones the most rewarding.

Furthermore, the process of writing this very book has been almost entirely devoid of pain or discomfort for me. But it has been deeply rewarding, and I don't imagine more suffering would have made it more rewarding.

Perhaps an endeavor simply has to make sense in the context of your own personal narrative. Trekking across Vietnam is a valuable activity if it connects to your sense of identity in some way. Volunteering for a charity feels rewarding if it relates to who you are and what you care about. A job can be either rewarding or not, depending on the personal meaning you attribute to it.

But consider the fact that many people report being their most fulfilled in college, a period when personal narrative and purpose are typically fuzzy and undefined.[14] If meaning is truly at the heart of the good life, we would not expect a time like this to be satisfying, even in spite of the community and freedom it enables.

We're getting close, and all of these ideas have elements of truth to them, but we haven't quite hit the nail on the head yet. And the importance of nailing it cannot be overstated.

To understand the essence of a good activity is to understand the essence of a good life. Whatever our most rewarding days, months, or years have in common when we look back on them, we can expect a rewarding life to share it when we look back on it too.

This essence has to do with challenge, but it isn't challenge. It has to do with love, but it isn't love. It has to do with purpose, but it isn't purpose.

So without further ado, let's settle the matter.

# The Essence of the Good Life

The sense in which rewarding things must generate value is that they must embody one or more of your values. More specifically, your actions must, in one way or another, exemplify traits that you value in others.

The sense in which rewarding things must be difficult is not that they must be painful. They must be difficult in the sense that not just anyone could do them. The fewer other people there are who could do a particular task, the more rewarding it will be for you to do it. And the most rewarding activity is one which only you could do.

The sense in which rewarding things must connect to your personal narrative or identity is that they must utilize the strengths you have cultivated throughout your life, and help to cultivate them further.

A rewarding life does not have to connect to any kind of transcendent sense of purpose. To live a good life, you do not need to believe that your work will have global impact, enact a divine will, or leave a legacy. You can be deeply satisfied without any sense of purpose.

A rewarding life is not made by love. It is hard to see a life completely absent of love being a deeply rewarding one. And yet it's clear that a stereotypical "trust fund" life of idle comfort would not be deeply fulfilling, even in the presence of unconditional love.

Here is the essence of deeply rewarding human activity: A good action is an admirable action. A good day is an admirable day. A good life is an admirable life.

The weight we assign to admirability is not a matter of personal preference. Whether you realize it or not, your well-being is already determined by your admirability. When you rate your overall happiness on a scale from one to ten, your answer is determined by how admirable you currently perceive your own behavior to be.

Admirable behaviors are those that demonstrate your skills or character strengths. You feel good about yourself when you take action that another person might admire you for, even if no one is watching.

Streaming a show is not admirable. Many would call it enjoyable. But it isn't admirable. It does not require any kind of skill to watch television. And so streaming does not tend to increase our happiness.[15]

Getting high is not admirable. Many would call it pleasurable. But it isn't admirable. It does not require any kind of unique strength to get high. And so drugs do not tend to increase our happiness.[15]

Winning the lottery is not admirable. Many would call it enviable. But it isn't admirable. It does not require any kind of personal virtue to win the lottery. And so winning the lottery does not increase our happiness.[16]

Let's explore that one a bit more. Winning the lottery could certainly change your life in ways that would make you more admirable. If you invest the money responsibly, use it to quit your mindless job, and start a new venture that is rooted in your personal strengths, it could result in far more admirable action, and hence greater well-being.

Winning the lottery could also change your life in ways that would make you less admirable. If you spend the money on momentary pleasures, quit a job that was previously exercising your strengths and skills, and replace it with a passive and effortless life, it could result in far less admirable action, and hence lower well-being, or even depression.

Losing your job, your partner, or your legs could eliminate domains through which your admirable traits were previously being exercised. Losing your job, your partner, or your legs could also open new domains through which your admirable traits can now be exercised.

From post-traumatic growth to postpartum depression, the many counterintuitive stories of happiness actually all tell the same tale. Our overall well-being does not correspond to the surface-level events we tend to attribute it to. But it corresponds perfectly to something else, something going on beneath the surface of our external outcomes.

# The Mechanics of the Good Life

It is all too easy to get caught up in the daunting task of defining happiness. Luckily, we don't actually have to do this.

When we examine the mind from a functional perspective, it becomes clear that "happiness" is a clumsy conflation of different mechanisms that evolved for different functions. Pleasure, joy, relief from pain—these are all the chemical byproducts of different mental modules, sharing the sole commonality that we find them to be pleasant.[17]

But there is one mechanism—one metric that seems paramount to us. It seems amenable to ranking on a scale from one to ten and persists over time. And it seems unique to humans among the animal kingdom.

It is only the nature of this specific mechanism that we need to understand. Its corresponding metric, when maximized to its fullest, aligns most closely with the life we would choose to live. To the person we would prefer to have been. For simplicity, we will call this overall well-being.

The reason your overall well-being is equal to the admirability you exhibit is, I will propose, surprisingly concrete. A special part of your brain is always watching you, constantly making evaluations, and dynamically delivering chemicals based on those evaluations. These chemicals are responsible for your mood.

This big brother inside your brain is there because it was advantageous for our ancestors. It is a part of the evolutionary wiring of your mind to monitor your actions for signs of admirability. It's rooted in social status, in mating, and in communal belonging.

This part of your brain that monitors you might be called the default mode network by a neuroscientist. An evolutionary psychologist might call it the sociometer. A spiritual teacher would call it the ego.

It is all one thing—one very real mechanism that is central to the functioning of your mind. And contrary to popular belief, it is not your enemy. It is the source of the highest happiness available to you.

Having an admirable trait is not the same as demonstrating that trait. If a strength is latent and failing to make its way into your behavior, it will not count toward your satisfaction. You are as happy as the traits you observe in your own behavior. As happy as the actions you see yourself taking.

We're going to refer to these admirable traits, unique skills, and character strengths as virtues. And the exact measure of the good life is the extent to which your unique personal virtues are integrated with and being exercised through your daily activities.

This is the common element of all good uses of time—all rewarding activities in life. They all display what makes you special. The most rewarding actions are those that require such a specialized set of virtues that the combination is as unique as your own fingerprint.

You may believe you don't have many of these virtues. You may believe that you lack the intelligence, the self-control, the time, the energy, or the money needed to bring your virtues to life. And we're going to learn that you're wrong.

The good life is not the sum of simple pleasure or the fruit of success. Its essence is not comfort, struggle, purpose, or even love. You don't need meaning. You need virtue.

# Key Takeaways:

- The first dimension of happiness, the x-axis, is a simple scale running from pain to pleasure—it's how you feel. The second dimension of happiness, the y-axis, runs from loss to gain and includes all good or bad life circumstances, achievements, or outcomes—it's what you have.

- Together, these two dimensions make up the landscape of your circumstances, or the circumscape—the two-dimensional plane of external factors that determines most people's decisions. But despite appearances, the events of the circumscape do not affect our happiness.

- Our overall well-being is determined exclusively by a third dimension. For most of us, this dimension is hidden, secretly controlling our satisfaction and leaving us confused and dissatisfied. This third dimension is what we will call virtue.

- Admirable behaviors are those that demonstrate your skills or character strengths. You feel good about yourself when you take action that another person might admire you for, even if no one is watching. And the exact measure of the good life is the extent to which your unique personal virtues are integrated with and being exercised through your daily activities.

- Here is the essence of deeply rewarding human activity: A good action is an admirable action. A good day is an admirable day. A good life is an admirable life. When you rate your overall happiness on a scale from one to ten, your answer is determined by how admirable you currently perceive your own behavior to be.

# 2

# The Virtue Game: The Spectrum, Domains, and the Portfolio

## The Valleys of Virtue—January 2020

It was the start of 2020—a time filled with optimism and aspiration that would surely not be obstructed in any way. I was a product designer at an outdoor gear company, working just two days a week after having asked to go part-time to write my first book the previous year. I was pushing my creative output to its limits every week and making just enough money to scrape by.

The previous year had been exciting. I was embarking on a new adventure, starting a new business and kicking off my authorial debut. And I was happy to have a job that would let me cut down to just two days a week to work on my own project. But things were taking too long. The book still wasn't where I wanted it to be, and I still had to build an audience and complete a million other publishing details.

It's a lonely process, but thankfully, I wasn't going through it alone. My partner (and our corgi) had provided me with the support, distraction, and comic relief I needed to stay sane at this point. We would spend our weekends camping, mountain biking, and going on impromptu trips. And I would try my best to be present and not preoccupied with the world of theories and book details in my head.

At my job, the creative zeal I had brought when I started three years before had faded into jadedness and detachment. A year or so of fighting creative battles and beating my head against the wall had taught me a more peaceful way of existence at the company. Make your contribution, accept when it gets shot down, and move on to the next task. My naive aspirations to be the creative genius who transformed the company had given way to a simple hope to keep my job and finish my book.

My role had evolved as the product development cycle matured. At the start, I was pitching creative ideas and conceptual drawings. Now I was pinning down manufacturing details and drafting up technical drawings. That was about as much fun as it sounds.

But it wasn't just the tedium that wore on me. It was how bad I was at it. I'm not exactly a technical details kind of person, and I'm definitely not a math person. Whenever we would receive a component that I had sent in the drawing for, the question was not whether there would be a mistake in it, but how problematic the mistake would be.

I had started out as an innovation-bent industrial designer, but my job title had apparently changed to "sad excuse for a mechanical engineer" without my even noticing. Getting ready to go into work started to feel like putting on armor to go into battle. How is my identity going to be attacked today? What fatal error will I find out I made? Did I order a 3" extrusion when we needed a 3.5" one? Or did I just draft a conic radius on that part when we needed a curvature continuous one?

I was immensely grateful that my boss had taken a chance on a recent grad, given me an opportunity, and even supported my side project. But I would be lying if I said I wasn't a bit bitter too—I had spent years developing hundreds of inventive concepts for this project, navigating ever-tightening constraints, and eventually landing on the perfect one. All to be excluded from the patent, transitioned into an open-floorplan desk, and turned into a technical CAD gopher.

Only being at work two days a week had brought me out of the loop on many of the ongoings and project details. I had a sense of aloofness and alienation beyond my regular, comfortable level of aloofness and alienation. I didn't feel like a part of the team—I was an auxiliary resource. I was the guy who had to be quickly caught up on everything that had happened between Thursday and Tuesday so I could be handed my next task.

The imposter syndrome was strong. Or was it imposter syndrome? Was I actually just not that talented? Was my job just a charity case? Was I just there because I needed a job and had a lucky family connection? No, no, that's just the imposter syndrome talking.

And then there was Victoria. She had just come on board with the company a few months prior, and everything about her suggested she belonged in the board room of a fortune 500 company. And yet inexplicably, here she was at a small company in a mountain town, imposing her neurotic drive and terrifying competence on everyone else.

She was a political power-player who brought a certain cut-throat relentlessness to the culture. She was playing a giant game of 3D chess where coworkers were pawns. And she was good at it. My goal was to stay out of her sights, which shouldn't have been too hard for a part-time designer who kept his head down.

And yet somehow, Tory and I ended up crossing paths and bumping heads shockingly often. My best efforts to stay on her good side, or at least off of her bad side, almost seemed to be backfiring. She took my compliments as insults, my attempts to do my job as attacks on hers.

Admittedly, I am sure the impression she got from me as she joined the company was less than warm and inviting. Though I was not actively rude to her, she could probably tell I was not thrilled that she was adding another layer of complexity to my job.

Whatever the cause, it was clear there was an issue that needed to be addressed. In the past, I had found that minor workplace conflicts were usually resolved with a one-on-one conversation and expression of goodwill. So I asked her to join me at a brewery after work. I'm not sure whether the scene that took place would fit best in a drama or a comedy, but either way, I think I would pass on watching it.

I started out the conversation by trying to let her know that I was on her team. I wanted to see her change the company in the ways I had been trying to for years. I told her that I empathized with the challenges she was having getting her ideas through the chain of command. She seemed surprised that I had ever had creative aspirations there.

I asked her for advice on the book I was writing and the business I was building, letting her know I valued her expertise. To my surprise, she wasn't the slightest bit interested in the book. What? No interest? She proceeded to tear my plans for my book and business apart, ranging from warnings that books don't make money to reasons why I just don't have that charismatic X-factor needed to be a successful entrepreneur.

At one point in the discussion, seemingly out of nowhere, she asked if I was autistic. Apparently, she had worked with autistic people before who had similar mannerisms. Ouch. There was something ironic about being told I was autistic by someone doling out unsolicited mental diagnoses to coworkers.

I grasped for defenses. I wasn't surprised that I was fidgeting or avoiding eye-contact—I was uncomfortable. I was acting exactly how anyone would act if they were being personally attacked by Disney's Maleficent.

I had wanted feedback on my book marketing, but what I got could hardly be called feedback. I was being sent the message that my project was entirely misguided. And it was becoming clear that the fundamental problem with my book, as far as she was concerned, was the person writing it.

I had no business, as she saw it, writing a personal development book—that was a task for people who had, you know, developed personally. It was something successful, admirable people did. Why did she not see me as a successful, admirable person? Did I remind her of someone she was traumatized by in the past? Was she jealous of me? Or was she right?

I could see things from her perspective, and it wasn't pretty. Here was a guy who had let his social skills and work ambitions go over a little writing obsession that hadn't received a bit of validation. Most of the personal strengths on which I prided myself were not showing up to this conversation, or to my life in general at this point. My ingenuity, my wisdom, my sense of humor—they didn't have much of an outlet at this particular time.

I was putting all of my time and energy into a book that remained unpublished, and hence could garner no reception, no confirmation that anyone would find it valuable. My mind was an echo chamber, wondering whether this book was award-winning material or just adolescent musings that would fall into oblivion as soon as they were released.

My job had gradually ceased to be an outlet for logic and creativity. Making new friends had taken a back seat to my career. And though I was in a loving relationship, I was often too distracted by my projects for it to effectively bring out my greatest interpersonal strengths.

The book had consumed me and my goals. My drive to be a great author was overshadowing my strivings to be a great person. It wasn't that I was taking vicious or corrupt actions. I simply was not seeing evidence of my own virtues. I was not taking the actions that made me proud of who I was.

I had gradually begun to neglect my character. I had transitioned out of the domains that were supporting my self-esteem, and my sense of identity was starting to crumble. I was descending into the valleys of virtue.

## Rethinking Virtue

I'm going to be sharing sections of this story gradually and intermittently throughout the book. By the end, you should be able to see how my personal virtue journey illustrates and brings to life the more abstract principles and theories I offer.

Virtue has a dated and stuffy connotation in modern culture. It conjures images of moral righteousness and chastity. It is the opposite of sexy.

As a result, every time I use the word "virtue," you are going to be tempted to gloss over it and say "ehh this sounds preachy." And don't get me wrong, morality is a part of virtue.

But it's not the crux of what this concept means for you. One of my goals in this book is to change that connotation of virtue. I want to make virtue sexy.

When I talk about your virtues, I don't want you to think about colorless mandates and righteousness. I want you to think about your greatest, most unique personal strengths.

I want you to fill with excitement and remember the time you made your wife laugh on your first date. The time you blew your colleagues away with a creative presentation. The time your best friend thanked you for having her back.

Think about the most "you" things about you. The things you are great at. Your virtues are literally any strengths you have that people tend to admire.

Yes, compassion is a virtue. But so is courage. So is creativity. So is charisma. Any trait that we humans tend to deem a "good" quality for someone to have is a virtue. And I can assure you that you are full of these virtues, even if you haven't seen much evidence of them lately.

We all have virtues on which we pride ourselves. But because they are so intangible, it can be challenging to wrap our heads around them. Let's go over a few of the basic concepts you'll need to understand this process.

Everyone who talks much about values or virtues always includes a list. It's usually organized into a set of four to ten broader sections, which usually reflect the views and values of the person compiling them.

Positive psychologists Martin Seligman and Christopher Peterson have created a list of universal character strengths and virtues found by studying the commonalities of many different cultures:

1. Wisdom and knowledge (Creativity, Curiosity, Open-mindedness, Love of learning, Perspective)
2. Courage (Bravery, Persistence, Integrity, Vitality)
3. Humanity (Love, Kindness, Social intelligence)
4. Justice (Citizenship, Fairness, Leadership)
5. Temperance (Forgiveness and mercy, Humility / Modesty, Prudence, Self-regulation)
6. Transcendence (Appreciation of beauty and excellence, Gratitude, Hope, Humor, Spirituality)[1]

I think this is a fantastic and immensely valuable list, and I appreciate their nod to the cardinal virtues of the ancients. That being said, the organization strikes me as rather arbitrary. Is integrity really a subset of courage? Is humor really a type of transcendence? I want to take the slightly different approach of laying a massive and redundant list of values on top of a gradient, which we will call the virtue spectrum.

Though overwhelming, I think there is good reason to view our virtues this way. The first is that I think we should resist the urge to impose a universal organizational system for our values. I will argue later that the task of understanding your own values can be seen as a process of personal synthesis, so that classification system needs to be your own.

Second, I want to capture the fact that our values are of evolutionary origin. Evolution does not work in pretty, clean, organized ways, and our values are no exception. Who am I to say that "honesty" is a single virtue when it actually might break down into seventy-eight different evolutionary use-cases? Evolution endowed us with potentially infinite shades of values which vary from one individual to the next.

Aristotle thought virtues were means between two extremes. Courage was the golden mean between cowardice and brashness. This was a convenient choice to focus on, as most of the strengths we would recognize don't fall between two imbalanced extremes.[2]

What is creativity the mean between? What about humor? Yes, you can sort of come up with answers if you're set on it, but it will be a stretch.

Rather, I think it makes sense for virtues to fall on a spectrum from high to low. So courage isn't the mean between cowardice and brashness. Someone highly courageous would simply be high in the virtue of courage. Someone who isn't very courageous would be lower. And someone who is brash might be low in the virtue of discretion while simultaneously being high in courage.

Think of it like this:

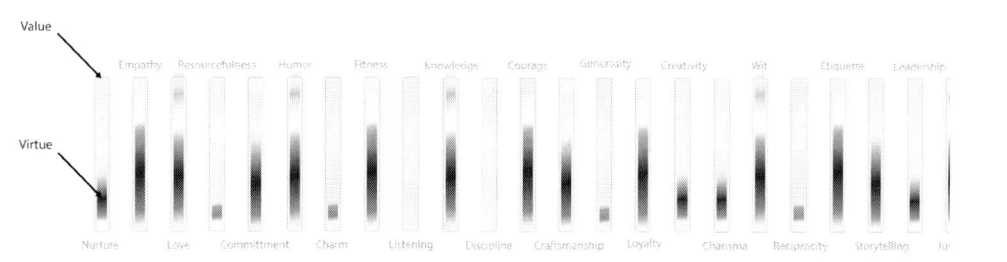

Values are like containers; virtue is what goes inside them. Values are the evaluative impulses in our minds that look for virtue in human behavior. Virtues are the traits that align with our values.

What about vice, you may ask? Much like the electromagnetic spectrum on which visible light lies, the virtue spectrum has no limit in either direction. It is possible to achieve unusually high or unusually low levels of a particular virtue. The extreme lows of virtue are sometimes referred to as vice. But I will urge you not to focus on vice.

This theory is not centered around transgression or guilt—it's fundamentally positive and life-affirming. You will improve more by focusing on maximizing virtue than by eliminating or apologizing for vice. I personally don't have any vices to my knowledge, though I have plenty of areas that are lacking in virtue.

I will rarely mention vice in this book. Virtues are active and positive. One does not act contrary to something in the name of virtue. "Thou shalt not kill" is not a virtue; benevolence is a virtue.

## The Virtue Game

It is your job, both to discover and create your unique personal virtues. To maximize the total amount of virtue in your character, or net virtue.

Yes, more virtue is always better; there is no way for a person to be too virtuous. Do-gooders who appear to be overly virtuous are not what they seem. We regard people this way when, for all the righteousness they signal, they lack other virtues like social intelligence, humility, or humor.

But maximizing net virtue can be a challenge. Virtues often compete for your resources and are limited by your time, attention, and care. This project is a constant negotiation to see how much virtue you can squeeze out of your resources.

With your sights set on net virtue, you can look for low-hanging fruit, areas you are currently low in virtue that wouldn't require much time to improve dramatically, or areas you are already high in virtue where you can compound your results. Certain virtues may require immense energy for you to elevate, while others may come much more easily to you.

You can also learn to integrate the virtues you bring out and become more efficient. We build vessels we can use to bring out our strengths and admirable traits. I call these virtue domains. Your relationship with your brother is a virtue domain. Your job is a virtue domain. The animal shelter you volunteer at is a virtue domain.

You develop paths in your life that enable you to bring out dozens of virtues simultaneously rather than requiring separate and competing domains for each. Though Nietzsche believed all were in competition,[3] most virtues are synergistic in the right conditions.

Furthermore, after exhibiting virtues for long periods of time, they start to become automatic, default responses that no longer require concerted effort. As I've shared in my work before, you can improve the system of interconnected habits on which you operate.

When you come across a person who exudes kindness, generosity, and compassion every time you see them, don't simply take them for some kind of anomalous saint. Ask yourself how Mister Rogers built such an impressive virtue strategy. How has Dolly Parton crafted her virtue domains to bring her greatest strengths out into the world? How can you do the same?

## The Virtue Portfolio

We all have a few personal virtues that serve as the foundation for our identity. Seligman calls these your signature strengths.[4] I like to think of them as a virtue portfolio. It's the collection of traits in which you have invested most heavily—the strengths you would be most crushed to learn you didn't actually have.

These traits must be treated with particular care. You must choose your virtues wisely based on your nature. Your virtues should feel authentic to you.

When we travel abroad, my girlfriend and I have different reactions when approached by native solicitors. She is incredibly kind and will entertain full conversations with people hoping to sell us souvenirs. I am by no means rude, but am more inclined to give a quick no thank you and move along.

Ultimately, her overwhelming kindness and my assertiveness are both virtues, and largely incompatible ones. Her sweetness is what I love about her, but she would probably have ended up attempting to single-handedly save Indonesia's economy with her savings if it weren't for me. I like to think my cool assertiveness is part of what she loves about me.

There are almost always tradeoffs—for me to be as kind as her, it would take far more energy and may not be as sustainable, but I would also lose the cool-headedness that comes so naturally to me. Of course it is always best to embody as many virtues as possible, but the balancing act can be a daunting process.

The importance of the virtue game is absolutely central to the functioning of our minds. The more we signal our character strengths to ourselves, the more our personal happiness increases. Our daily actions serve as evidence of the type of person we are to ourselves. You are both the protagonist and the audience of your own life, and how greatly you appeal to this audience of one is the measure of well-being you will realize.

I am by no means the first to propose this relationship between virtue and happiness. And to fully understand this relationship, we're going to need to explore the ancient philosophies that first arrived at this intuition, long before we had the neurological or evolutionary data to back it up.

## Key Takeaways:

- Virtue is not just about morality—any trait that we humans tend to deem a "good" quality for someone to have is a virtue. Though virtues can remain latent and fail to make their way into our behavior, every human being has innate virtues.

- It is your job, both to discover and create your unique personal virtues. To maximize the total amount of virtue in your character, or net virtue. There are endless shades of virtue on the virtue spectrum.

- Virtue domains are the vessels we use to bring out our strengths and admirable traits. Your relationships, your work, and your communities are all potential virtue domains.

- Your virtue portfolio is the set of personal virtues that serve as the foundation for your identity. It's the collection of traits in which you have invested most heavily—the strengths you would be most crushed to learn you didn't actually have.

- To maximize our well-being and satisfaction in life, we must nurture our virtue domains and portfolio to bring out the highest net virtue we can. It is best to put most of our focus on our strengths rather than our weaknesses, and to ask how we can increase the amount we exercise them each day through our actions.

# 3
# The Philosophy of Virtue: From Socrates to Seligman

## Original Ethics

When you think about the philosophical study of ethics, your first thought probably has to do with the moral rightness or wrongness of certain actions. And your second thought is probably about something else entirely, because you are bored.

But long before they began concerning themselves with the devastating carnage of runaway trolleys, ethicists were concerned with a different kind of question. Their focus was, first and foremost, on living a good life. This meant a life that went well for the person living it, not just for everyone else.[1]

Though we are rarely faced with decisions about whether to save drowning children or not, we make decisions that affect our own well-being every single day. And this is what ethics was originally meant to help us with. It was a blueprint for psychological health. And it begins with this misunderstood concept of virtue.

I'll admit, when I first started studying the ancient Greek philosophy of Stoicism a decade or so ago, I was most drawn to the ideas that are most often repeated today.

**The Dichotomy of Control:**

> Some things are within our power, while others are not. Within our power are opinion, motivation, desire, aversion, and, in a word, whatever is of our own doing; not within our power are our body, our property, reputation, office, and, in a word, whatever is not of our own doing.
>
> —**Epictetus**, *Discourses*[2]

**Cognitive Mediation:**

> It is in our power to have no opinion about a thing, and not to be disturbed in our soul. For things themselves have no natural power to form our judgments.
>
> —**Marcus Aurelius**, *Meditations*[3]

**And the Love of Fate:**

> Don't demand that things happen as you wish, but wish that they happen as they do happen, and you will go on well.
>
> —**Epictetus**, *Enchiridion*[4]

These are the concepts that have the immediate power to make us feel better in difficult situations, so it's understandable that they are placed front and center in most modern Stoic teachings. They're powerful ideas.

But the Stoics themselves would say these therapeutic ideas are only peripheral components to the core philosophy. The Stoics argued that the goal of life was to 'live in accord with virtue', or human excellence.[5]

I would often hear this concept of "virtue" and brush it off, saying "true, that's important, but let's get to the good stuff." It wasn't until years later that it all began to click and I realized the power of virtue.

## Human Excellence

The Greek word for virtue is areté, which is actually more accurately translated to "excellence" than morality.[6] Areté was about thriving and greatness—excellence in the art of human life. And these ancient Greek thinkers were adamant that this excellence was at the heart of our quest for the good life.[7]

So why is this such a crucial concept? We all already knew that being good at things was good. The thing is, the Stoics argued that virtue, or the exertion of our positive traits, decisions, and character, is the only thing that's good.[9]

> For God's sake, stop honoring externals, quit turning yourself into the tool of mere matter, or of people who can supply you or deny you those material things... A boxer derives the greatest advantage from his sparring partner... It is enough if I hold the right idea about poverty, illness and removal from office: all such challenges will only serve my turn. No more, then, should I look for bad, and good, in external conditions.
>
> —**Epictetus**, *Discourses*

We generally go about our lives assuming that totaling our cars would be "bad" and that receiving a large sum of money would be "good." But the Stoics said that these fleetingly pleasurable or painful experiences are simply beside the point to the good life. Cicero's Stoic paradoxes include these assertions:

> Virtue, or moral excellence, is the only good (conventional 'goods' such as health, wealth and reputation fundamentally count as nothing with regard to living a good life).
>
> Virtue is completely sufficient for Happiness and fulfillment, a man who is virtuous lacks no requirement of the good life.
>
> All forms of virtue are equal as are all forms of vice (in terms of the benefit or harm they do to the individual himself).[8]

These still may sound like dogmatic assertions, so let's make it a bit more concrete and observable. Have you ever noticed that when you spend a whole day, or certainly a whole week, laying around and doing nothing, you tend to feel pretty bad about yourself by the end of it?

Similarly, have you noticed that when you spend a day or week doing a mix of all the things your ideal self would do, maybe a blend of creative work, loving connection with friends, a bit of relaxation, exercise, and some form of benevolent contribution, you tend to feel amazing about yourself?

When I was in high school, I would always go into summer breaks thrilled that I didn't have to work for three whole months. I would be ecstatic that I could just sit around and do nothing all day if I wanted to. But inevitably, by the end of the summer, I would always be so bored and miserable that I would almost be excited to start back at school.

When I was about sixteen, I learned how to keep this from happening. I would go into every summer with bold ambitions and big goals. I would get up early, exercise, shower, drink tons of water, and eat a healthy breakfast.

I would break down weekly milestones for exercising, reading books, and playing piano. And I found that not only would I not get bored by the end up the summer, I would look back on those summers as massively positive and transformative periods.

Our moods fluctuate based on our behaviors because, like it or not, we are constantly evaluating ourselves to see how closely we are aligning with our own values, even if this monitoring is unconscious.

It is an observable fact that when we take an action that meshes with some value we hold, we experience pride. When we take an action that clashes with one of our values, we experience shame.[10] When someone else takes an action we do or don't approve of, we experience admiration or disgust.[11]

We all strongly desire to be good and admirable.[12] It goes without saying that high self-esteem feels good, and low self-esteem feels bad. But the Greeks were interested, not in high self-esteem for its own sake, but in the reasons for that high self-esteem.

They wanted to evaluate themselves positively, for reasons that were grounded in an accurate perception of reality. They wanted to achieve genuine excellence. In other words, to be virtuous.

To live a good life is to live a virtuous life. This is no psychological claim, or even a philosophical one. Virtues are nothing more than the attributes we already deem good. To live a virtuous life is, by definition, to live a life you yourself deem to be good.

When you say that someone has lived a good life, you are saying it has attributes that you approve of. So the essence of living a good life is to live a life with the attributes of which you approve.

## Understanding Eudaimonia

The ancient Greeks used the word eudaimonia to refer to the good life. It was the highest and happiest mental state a person could achieve.[13] I know, it's a big, exotic word, and it's pretty annoying of me to expect you to remember it.

But there simply isn't another word in the English language that captures its meaning. Happiness, flourishing, satisfaction, fulfillment, well-being... they all fall short in some way. So eudaimonia it is.

Eudaimonia referred to a specific kind of well-being—the kind of happiness we get from being a person of whom we ourselves highly approve.

One of my favorite scholars of Stoicism, Donald Robertson, clearly illustrates this principle:

> A wise and good man like Socrates might be reduced to poverty, imprisoned, and ridiculed, but even if he loses everything the majority refer to as 'good', including his own life, and every so-called 'misfortune' is heaped upon him, that does not make him any less praiseworthy. In fact, maintaining his virtues in adversity arguably just makes him more great-souled and admirable. If the externals can neither add nor take away anything from the good of virtue or evil of vice, then they are not intrinsically good or bad things, at least not in the same sense, and they count as nothing with regard to the good life, and our ultimate wellbeing or eudaimonia.[14]

Yes, this ultimate form of satisfaction, the ancients proposed, was inherently self-centered. It was not just a matter of feeling good. It was a matter of feeling good about yourself.

This perspective is consistent with the research and understanding I have developed. But it goes against much of the Eastern wisdom that has become so popular in the West today as to be virtually unquestionable. It is commonly assumed today that the ego is the source of our problems, that our sense of self must be transcended to achieve the highest form of enlightenment.

I, and the Stoics, would argue something like the opposite. That we must embrace our egos, learn how to hack and optimize them, and build the most positive, strong, and crucially, accurate self-appraisals possible.

As we'll explore more later, part of the magic of this principle is that when you grasp it, external events cease to affect you like they once did. Not only do they begin to seem somewhat irrelevant to your happiness—you start to see "setbacks" as opportunities to cultivate and express greater virtue.

## Virtue through the Ages

The Stoics had followed after Plato and Socrates, and held a particularly extreme stance on virtue. For one thing, they thought all virtues were actually one. You couldn't have the virtue of wisdom without also having the virtues of courage, temperance, or justice.[15]

They also thought only a perfect sage was virtuous. Anyone who had not achieved perfection did not have virtue. And they thought circumstances could have no impact on virtue. Poverty, disease, and torture—all completely irrelevant to our well-being.[16]

There is something appealing about this extreme stance, but I think we can make a number of improvements on their virtue system. In fact, other philosophers have already done this for us.

Aristotle took the ideas that Socrates and Plato put forward on virtue and gave them an upgrade. He said that there were many virtues, not just one with different aspects. Ambition, wit, and generosity were all different virtues.[17]

He thought we could all have any combination of virtues in varying degrees. And he thought that while virtue was the only thing that mattered for well-being, it was possible for life circumstances to affect the amount of virtue a person was able to exercise.[18]

Aristotle saw a virtue as an excellent trait of character. Not merely an individual action, but a disposition that was deeply integrated into the character of the individual. It was a trait that contributes to eudaimonia.[18]

And he believed that the core trait needed to build virtue was practical wisdom. In other words, he thought we needed insight into our deep values, and into the paths for effectively bringing them out.[18]

David Hume built upon this system by incorporating virtue into a naturalistic perspective. Virtues were not objective properties of the universe, but natural evaluations built into the human mind. He said "Vice and virtue... may be compared to sounds, colours, heat and cold, which, according to modern philosophy, are not qualities in objects, but perceptions in the mind."

Hume believed that a virtue was a virtue specifically because humans tend to respond to it with the sentiments of approval. Benevolence, he believed, was a part of every person's natural constitution, even if effectively bringing it out required refinement and cultivation.[19]

And then there was Nietzsche. Though he is commonly thought to only take negative ethical stances, Nietzsche was very much a virtue ethicist. He rejected the universal and "disinterested" system of ethics seen in utilitarianism and Kantian ethics. He believed that good was something that grew out of a person's character, not found in a mathematical calculation of utility or universal law.[19]

Nietzsche ventured to explore the psychology of virtue more deeply than previous thinkers. He was fundamentally concerned with psychological health, and he believed that the negative, self-sacrificial, and guilt-inducing ethics of his time were harmful to health. He didn't think we should evaluate right and wrong in terms of rules or transgressions, but in terms of personal excellence or greatness.[20]

He rejected self-sacrificing pity, and promoted in its place a kind of wise selfishness. He thought virtue should overflow from a place of creative abundance to benefit others, and even bring about the flourishing of society as a whole.[20]

Nietzsche was also interested in the interaction of our virtues. He thought they were all at war with one another. But higher individuals, he thought, were able to integrate their virtues and bring about an upward striving in their capacities.[20]

The development of virtue, for Nietzsche, was a dynamic process of self-becoming. This process inevitably involved overcoming the resistance in yourself to affirm your life and "bring style to your character." And reaching the highest level of virtue actualization required a never-ending journey of creative self-experimentation.[20]

Set up the things that you have honoured in front of you. Maybe they will reveal, in their being and their order, a law which is fundamental of your own self. Compare these objects. Consider how one of them completes and broadens and transcends and explains another: how they form a ladder which all the time you have been climbing to find your true self. For your true self does not lie deeply hidden within you. It is an infinite height above you — at least, above what you commonly take to be yourself.

—**Friedrich Nietzsche**, *Schopenhauer as Educator*[21]

This process, I believe, is what Nietzsche was referring to when he implored his reader: Become who you are. By coming to know our unique, individual impulses of admiration and pride, we could gradually learn to embody them, until the reality of our character came to resemble the template of our ideals.[22]

Thinkers East and West, from Confucius to Jesus, have proposed their own systems of virtue.[23] These virtue-based theories of ethics fell out of fashion during the enlightenment as calculating ethical systems like utilitarianism became dominant. But beginning in the 20th century, virtue ethics has seen a great resurgence.[24]

Like Nietzsche, philosopher Elizabeth Anscombe rejected the legalistic foundation of modern ethical systems, arguing that the prevalent concepts of moral obligation and permissibility were obsolete. Her influential essay, "Modern Moral Philosophy" made the case that, though they had originally been grounded in the belief in a divine lawmaker, moral laws made little sense in the absence of this belief.[25]

This stance should not be mistaken for a claim that we should all do whatever is appealing or expedient, without regard for others or the long-term consequences of our actions. As Nietzsche clarifies in *Daybreak*:

> It goes without saying that I do not deny—unless I am a fool—that many actions called immoral ought to be avoided and resisted, or that many called moral ought to be done and encouraged—but I think the one should be encouraged and the other avoided for other reasons than hitherto.[26]

Proponents of virtue ethics have argued that consequential and contractual principles that state certain things are objectively right or wrong disconnect our reasons for action from our innate human motives toward growth, health, and happiness. That these universal and disinterested moral laws encourage us to take certain actions out of dogmatic obedience instead of wisdom.[27]

It has been argued that even if it were possible to perfectly follow the modern mandates for ethical agents, this would ironically result in a world in which no one was truly thriving. And that when we disregard character in favor of contracts and consequences, we flatten the entire landscape of human health, fulfillment, and virtue down to a superficial hedonic computation.[28]

Contemporary philosopher Alasdair MacIntyre made the case for a virtue revival, and a return to a view of the good life like Aristotle's. He understood virtues as the traits that enable us to attain the intrinsic rewards of engaging in social practices and community. The good life, he thought, was not merely an individualistic endeavor, but inseparable from each person's social and historical context.[29]

Philippa Foot presented a view on virtue that was rooted in practical reason. Virtues were simply qualities that characterized healthy and well-functioning natural organisms. Dispositions like courage and justice served the health, excellence, and long-term interests of human organisms.[30]

And other contemporary virtue theorists like Bernard Williams, Rosalind Hursthouse, and Martha Nussbaum proposed their own virtue-based systems of ethics, building on the foundation first laid by the ancient Greeks.

What they all agreed on was that there was something off about our contemporary notions of ethics, and something precious to be rediscovered in ancient ethics.[31]

Around this same time, the field of psychology was converging on the study of human virtues. Humanistic psychologist Abraham Maslow observed that there were certain traits shared by the most psychologically fulfilled people, who he called self-actualizing individuals.[32]

> The evidence available shows that B-Values are more often chosen by "healthy" people (self-actualizing, mature, productive characters, etc.). Also by a preponderance of the "greatest," most admired, most loved people throughout history.
>
> —**Abraham Maslow**, *The Farther Reaches of Human Nature*

What he called "being values," or B-Values were the traits embodied by the people he observed to be the most fulfilled and self-actualized. He compared these virtues to vitamins, noting that psychological neuroses, or "metapathologies" could be caused by a deficiency of these universal values.[33]

Maslow held the belief that each person had within them a kind of blueprint for who they were to become. Some "instinctoid" seed, containing everything needed for the acorn of the individual to grow into the towering oak tree of their potential. And this seed of ideals, he argued, paved the path toward our greatest happiness.[33]

Most recently, Martin Seligman, who is widely regarded as the father of positive psychology, has championed the importance of virtues and signature strengths in our understanding of human well-being.[34] As referenced in the previous chapter, he has compiled a list of universal virtues by studying the values shared across many diverse cultures, and built a growing body of research on their psychological power.[35]

Each thinker has provided a slightly different take on the philosophy and psychology of virtue. Each one can provide us with clues into our own nature. But I want to propose a framework that can give us a new lens through which we can interpret and integrate the philosophical wisdom shared through the ages.

## Key Takeaways

- The focus of ancient ethics was, first and foremost, on living a good life. This meant a life that went well for the person living it, not just for everyone else.

- The ancient Greeks conceptualized virtue as personal excellence. Virtue was about thriving and greatness—excellence in the art of human life. And these ancient Greek thinkers were adamant that this excellence was at the heart of our quest for the good life.

- The Greeks used the word eudaimonia to refer to the good life. It was the highest and happiest mental state a person could achieve. Eudaimonia referred to a specific kind of well-being—the kind of happiness we get from being a person of whom we ourselves highly approve.

- Modern ethical systems have become disconnected from human growth, health, and happiness. In the attempt to provide universal and disinterested moral laws, they promote dogmatic obedience over wisdom.

- Though virtue theorists have differed on how exactly they conceived of virtue, many of them, from the Stoics, to Nietzsche, to Maslow, to Seligman, have converged on the idea that virtue was at the heart of the good life and eudaimonia.

# 4

# The Overview: Learning to See the Third Dimension of Happiness

## The Climb To Self-Becoming—August 2005

I walked under the bright, fluorescent lights and into the crowded room, full of both trepidation and excitement about this new adventure. My knees were shaking as I said goodbye to my dad and walked into the unknown. I was eager to start making new friends, going on dates, and being a "normal" teenager.

My early education had been rather unconventional—a mix of Montessori, self-education, and homeschooling (I'm ashamed to admit that yes, I was one of those millennials who didn't watch SpongeBob growing up). But in seventh grade, I decided I wanted to go to "real school." As a side note, of all the years to stop being homeschooled, seventh grade is probably the worst.

I had somehow assumed that by the ripe age of twelve, people were pretty much adults, and the cafeteria would be filled with stimulating conversation and a welcoming attitude. What I found instead were competitions to see how many Cheez-Its people could stuff into their mouth before they spewed all over the table.

I felt like I had landed on an alien planet full of strange creatures whose language I didn't speak. And so I didn't speak.

Almost at all, for that entire year. I didn't know exactly why I didn't talk. I spent an embarrassing amount of time trying to figure out why I didn't talk.

I just didn't know how to communicate with these people, and I was filled with anxiety even thinking about it. I had plenty of things to say to my family and childhood friends, but this was different. Despite wanting to connect with my peers, my interaction with them was limited to one-word answers to questions they would occasionally ask.

I vividly remember one particular time, I grabbed a chair from an empty table at lunch, and an eighth-grader started yelling at me in a classic, movie-bully tone for taking "his chair." I started apologizing, despite knowing the chair didn't belong to anyone. I scampered back to my table, trying my best to ignore the heckles of the eighth-grader and his friends.

In that moment, I had a crucial realization: I wasn't proud of the person I was. I know, some might argue that it's the bully who shouldn't have been proud. But the fact was, I was afraid of the world. I was afraid to talk, afraid to stand up for myself, afraid to be seen.

The world seemed like a scary place. I was simply trying to survive. I was not living courageously. I was not thriving. And in some way, I must have known that I was going to fall short of my potential in life if I didn't make some big changes.

The following summer was a period of radical transformation. I started setting goals and asking myself what kind of changes I would need to make to become the person I wanted to be. I formed strategies and took on daily tasks to overcome my fears and shyness.

I have no idea how I understood this at the age of 13, and I know for a fact I could not have consciously articulated it. But on some level, I must have understood that in order to grow, I would have to confront my fears and get as far out of my comfort zone as possible.

So I did the unthinkable: I joined the football team. I know, lots of kids play on the football team in high school. But you must understand, I was a 100lb kid who didn't talk. I was a chess-team type of kid, but here I was going head-to-head with 250lb kids, getting my lights knocked out, and running until I puked.

My teammates didn't get it. My parents didn't get it. But I stayed on the team for the entire year. And then I played for four more years. I use the term "played" loosely, as I knew I was never going to be starter material. But I didn't care. The purpose of this was to grow.

Over the course of those years, I learned how to embrace the feelings of nervous energy that filled me when I did uncomfortable things. I learned how to be a member of a community. I got past my anxieties around interacting with my peers, and I got to know people I'm still close friends with today.

This experience of expanding my comfort zone opened a new door. It created a new (positive) addiction. I started seeking out scary, uncomfortable experiences anywhere I could find them. I started volunteering to give presentations in class. I started asking out people I had only recently met. I signed up for boxing training, just to challenge myself.

I also started sharing some of my hidden virtues with others. I would turn boring school projects into creative films and out-of-the-box presentations. I would turn papers and homework assignments into satires that would get the class giggling when I would recite them. I found more and more ways to bring my creativity and sense of humor out into the world.

My courage, confidence, and social skills gradually improved, and all the counterintuitive work I put in during these formative years paid off. It's only because of the time I spent growing, expanding, and overcoming my prior limitations that I'm able to live the life I have today.

If I hadn't built the habit of seeking out the scary and the uncomfortable, I would never have made the lifelong friends I found by getting out of my comfort zone. I would have turned down all the talks and interviews I've done on my book and closed a lot of doors.

I would never have met my incredible partner because meeting new people would have given me too much anxiety. I never would have traveled to twenty different countries and had amazing experiences out of fear of the uncertain and unknown.

If I hadn't intuitively understood on some level that my happiness was determined by how highly I approved of myself, I never would have done all these counterintuitive things. I would have stayed comfortable, and my gifts would have remained latent and hidden.

As I pushed out of my comfort zone and developed my capacities, my self-esteem and overall sense of well-being grew steadily. In combination with the work I was putting into mastering my thoughts and emotions, I gradually became deeply proud and satisfied with who I was, and felt that I had uncovered some important keys to happiness.

It was this process of working to align with my ideals that brought me the closest I had ever been to eudaimonia in my life. I had reached new peaks of self-becoming. And this experience gave me my first glimpse into the third dimension of happiness.

## The Overview

There was a viral video floating around the internet during this period called "Imagining the 10th Dimension."[1] It was probably my very first taste of philosophy, and I was fascinated.

One of the ideas that this video talked about was the concept of a flatlander. The idea is that a two-dimensional being that lived in a three-dimensional world would only see strange objects and nonsense enter their field of awareness as three-dimensional objects pass by them. They would remain oblivious to what was actually going on in that third dimension.

Somehow, this concept of the flatlander started coming to mind when I observed the life decisions of the people around me. I would see friends making decisions based on what seemed like surface-level considerations, and I couldn't help but feel like there was some "third dimension" they were missing.

Couldn't they see that screwing their friend over to get with a girl wasn't actually going to make them happy? Couldn't they tell that the social status gains they may make by taking big risks weren't going to increase their overall life satisfaction?

I started to feel like a three-dimensional being surrounded by flatlanders who simply couldn't see the whole picture. It wasn't that I was a selfless saint. It was that they weren't as good at being selfish as I was. Years later, these ideas would come together into a visual metaphor that I think could help many people understand the basis for wise decisions and a happy life.[2]

When we combine our three axes—the x-axis of pleasure, the y-axis of gain, and the z-axis of virtue—we get a three-dimensional landscape that we'll call the overview.

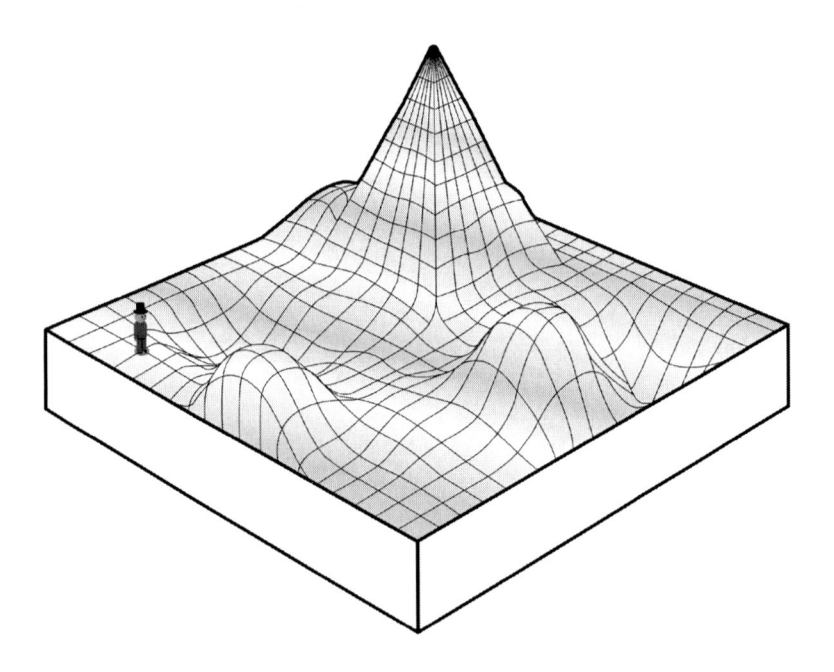

You will notice that little dot we saw on the circumscape is actually a person, and that person represents you. If you look closely, you may also notice you are sporting a top hat, and I must say you're really pulling it off.

At this point, I should also note that the overview is really meant to be shown in color. The format you are reading is in greyscale, and I'm sorry about that. You can always refer back to the cover, or go to designingthemind.org/become to get the full-color illustrations.

The overview is the centerpiece of the theory proposed by this book. It represents the three-dimensional lens we must learn to navigate our lives through. The overview adds the dimension of depth to the plane of the circumscape—the z-axis of well-being.

The measure of the z-axis is virtue. Virtue is what determines the most crucial form of happiness in humans, what we're calling overall well-being. This topography illustrates the peaks and valleys of virtue, and everything in between.

Most people don't have three-dimensional vision. They set and evaluate their goals according to the circumscape. And as a result, things don't make sense a lot of the time.

Some people feel that something is inherently wrong whenever they experience pain or discomfort—being on the left side of the x-axis. But this pain may simply be the burn of climbing to greater heights of virtue.

Some think they will finally be happy when they attain the sensual pleasure they crave—moving to the right in the x-axis. Some think they will have succeeded in life when they attain the wealth to buy a fancy new car—moving up in the y-axis. But once they do, they find that the brief thrills of pleasure and possessions wear off shortly after securing them, and their overall well-being has not been affected.

## The X and Y Axes

The x-axis is how you feel. The immediately pleasurable or painful experiences in life in a momentary, hedonistic sense. It spans suffering, pain, discomfort, comfort, pleasure, and ecstasy.

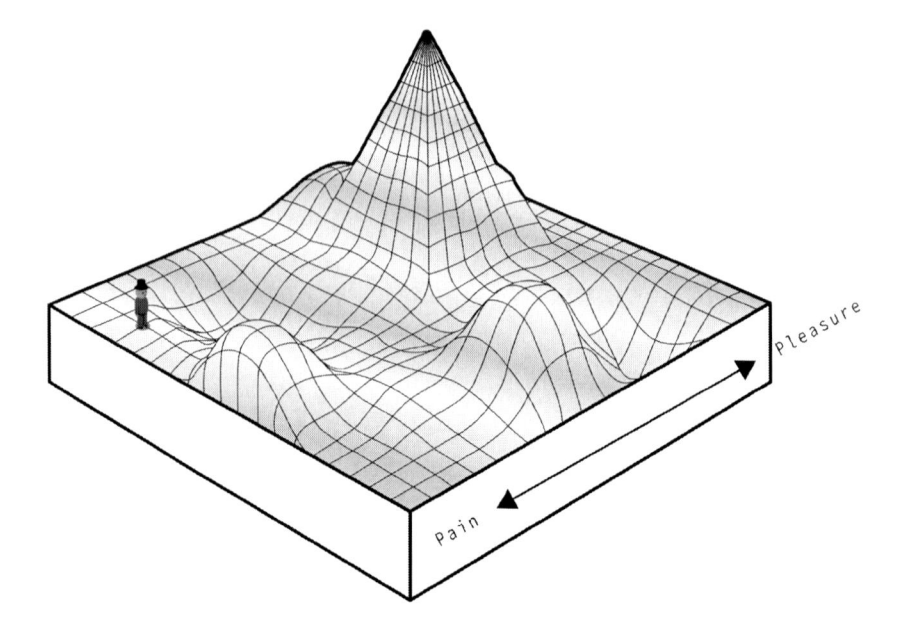

We all know that pleasure feels good. In the absence of other factors, I would gladly take ecstasy over suffering. But pleasure does not constitute, or even contribute to the good life on its own. It would be a great mistake to take the momentary feelings of pleasure, which can easily be chemically induced, as a sign that you are living a good life.

There's a thought experiment known as the "experience machine" that asks you to imagine a device that could virtually simulate any pleasurable feelings or blissful experiences in your brain—sort of like virtual reality if it were connected directly to your nervous system. You could create a dream life in this world, and it would be indistinguishable from reality in every way.[3]

Most people say they would rather live in the "real" world than this blissful virtual one.[4] But they usually mistake it for a matter of authenticity. The real insight of the experience machine is not that an analog world is somehow more real than a digital one.

But when equipped with the overview, it becomes clear why the experience machine does not seem right. It clashes with our intuitions because we

**54** | BECOME WHO YOU ARE

assume it would provide us with a life of pure hedonic bliss. We would not expect it to deliver a life of challenge, growth, or virtue. And on some level, we know that virtue is all that matters.

But pleasure is also not bad. Enjoying a delicious dessert with a friend or taking a drug-induced journey of self-exploration can be entirely worthwhile endeavors. This is the case when they cause you to move up in the z-axis of virtue, or at least don't bring you down in it.

Some people gravitate toward comfort. Others try to get out of their comfort zone whenever possible. But from the overview, comfort looks different as well.

There will be times when leaving your comfort zone is necessary for achieving greater virtue integration—more often than not. But there will also be times when pursuing the uncomfortable and dangerous would serve no such purpose and need not be a goal in itself.

Like pleasure, a life of greater comfort is not inherently better than one of less comfort. A leisurely work schedule and financial ease can remove barriers to virtue. Comfort can eliminate distractions that take away from the cultivation of character.

But comfort can also foster complacency. It can become an addiction that lulls us into a state of ease and makes us averse to the hard work often needed for growth. Comfort itself can become a barrier to virtue.[5]

Comfort and discomfort are tools for growth—nothing more. Both can be used strategically to elevate your position in the z-axis.

What about pain and suffering? As you might have guessed, pain is not inherently bad either. It is not uncommon for people to come out of painful periods of their life with the sense that they are better people because of them.[6]

When painful experiences result in a higher position up the mountains of virtue, we can say that pain resulted in something good. When it results in a lower degree of virtue, or even an equal degree, we can say the pain resulted in something bad because the unpleasant experience did not serve us in any way.

Sometimes people misunderstand this relationship and go too far, arguing that pain is necessary or worthwhile in its own right. Suffering is not a requirement for virtue.

Philosophers like Nietzsche sometimes make the mistake of idealizing suffering.[7] Suffering is good only insofar as it contributes to greater virtue—to the cultivation of character. But much of the suffering experienced in the world does no such thing.

Sometimes people praise suffering to justify their own pain. But suffering is not good in and of itself. Suffering is not inherently positive. It is not inherently meaningful or catalytic. Suffering can be pointless. Pain is beside the point of the good life.

The y-axis is what you have. It spans material failure, loss, setback, advance, gain, and success. It can relate to the loss or gain of wealth, social status, possessions, jobs, or even relationships. The things for which we often temporarily sacrifice the first dimension.

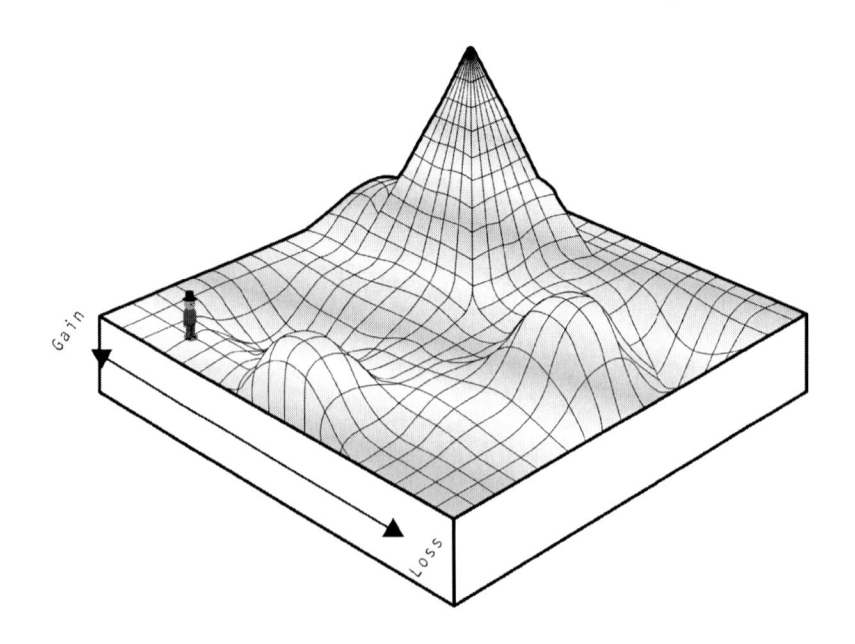

The y-axis is sort of like the x-axis stretched across time. Because we are unique beings capable of contemplating the future, we developed a set of emotions related to this experience of "having things."

Pleasure and pain in the present moment are not the only experiences relevant to us. We can also "attain" things that may or may not continue to bring us pleasure or pain over time.

A job offer feels good because of the pleasure, or mitigation of pain we anticipate it will bring over time. A breakup feels bad because of the pain, or mitigation of pleasure we anticipate it will bring over time.

What about money? We have all heard that money doesn't buy happiness. But we can build a more nuanced perspective on this platitude. Money has an indirect relationship with happiness. Depending on how it is used, more money may result in greater, lower, or equal virtue.[8]

If you lack the income needed for basic financial security, you may have very little ability to cultivate your virtues. You might end up spending all of your time working multiple repetitive, virtue-less jobs just to meet your physical needs. In this case, a lack of money could result in significantly lower well-being.[9]

This relationship will not always be straightforward. Many of the things that can only be bought with exorbitant amounts of money, like sports cars, private jets, and yachts, will not increase a person's well-being. But money can be used to start a business, become an angel investor, or donate to a purposeful cause as well. It can also be used to eliminate a job that provides little opportunity to exercise virtue.

Money can easily become a pathological addiction. Making too much money can distract you from the virtue game that is taking place beneath the surface. It can train you to think of it as your sole aim in life, despite the fact that it may not facilitate, or may even impede your vertical trek to virtue.

Money often causes people to be confused about work. Some people, seeing that work can play an important role in well-being, go so far as to praise mindless and arbitrary labor, as if it had inherent value.

Others go too far in the opposite direction, believing that work is a capitalist scam that has no value beyond earning wealth. The need to engage in paid labor to support our lifestyle tricks us into discounting the satisfaction good work can bring. We are then surprised when retirement brings boredom, or even despair.[10]

A job can be a major opportunity to exercise virtue. Losing a job can mean losing a prominent domain for building and sharing your character.[11] It can also open up new avenues for building admirable traits into your lifestyle.

When people say things like "losing my job was the best thing that ever happened to me," they aren't necessarily saying it randomly led to a lucky turn of events. They are also not necessarily merely justifying their misfortunes.[12]

They are generally saying that losing their job gave them the opportunity to reform their virtue strategies and get to a much higher place in the z-axis. When you lose one particular job, you merely lose one particular domain through which to exercise your virtues. But it may not take long to find another, even better one.

How does love fit into this framework? Love can be pleasurable. Love can constitute an improvement in circumstances. And love can aid us in the cultivation and expression of virtue. Like sleep or nutrition, love can serve all dimensions, and a total absence of it could be detrimental to all.

Losing a relationship can lead to grief, lower well-being, and even depression.[13] This is because relationships, like jobs, are important arenas through which we can activate our virtues.

Relationships are rewarding insofar as they provide each person with an opportunity to share their virtues and have them appreciated. Losing a relationship, through death, divorce, or simply losing touch can tragically cut people off from one of the core virtue domains of their lives.

There is no doubt you would be losing something if you lost all the love in your life. Love relationships are among the primary avenues through which we can surface our own best qualities. If you lost the person you are closest with, a significant set of your personal strengths would be shut down until further notice.[14]

But losing a relationship, too, can end up being a positive thing, or even the best thing that ever happened to you.[15] Unhealthy relationships are often those that deprive at least one partner of the opportunity to bring out their virtues.[16]

Parenting can be largely understood as an act of virtue cultivation. A bad parent fails to model or facilitate the development of virtues in their children. Overprotective parents force virtue behavior on their kids, who then go on to lack the capacities to act out those virtues without their parents.[17]

Social status is similar, though in some ways more complex than other rewards of the y-axis. Higher social esteem is not necessarily better than lower social esteem. The quest for status and popularity may pressure us into becoming less virtuous, satisfying our social drives while moving us further away from our values.

But social status also may be the result of high levels of virtue. When we exhibit traits like courage or kindness, we are often acknowledged for these traits by our peers. When we are among the most confident or creative members of our social circles, we may find this reflected in our status.

While not inherently good, social approval and respect can serve as a mirror that indicates our virtues to us. If we aren't receiving any social approval for certain virtues, it may be a sign that we are not exercising those virtues. It could be an important signal that could lead us to reflect and re-strategize.

You should only care about social approval insofar as it reflects your own approval. When it does, pay careful attention. When it does not, feel free to disregard it.

It must be emphasized that no external reward has value in and of itself. But the indirect effects of our circumstances can have implications for our well-being. With no relationships, no friends, no achievements, and no job or business, a person will have few opportunities for value alignment and virtue.

It is essential that you understand exactly which factors are responsible for your well-being. Actively work to break the habit of associating circumstantial gains with happiness. Insist on perceiving the virtue-implications of all decisions and outcomes, and keep your gaze continually fixed on the z-axis.

# The Z-Axis

The z-axis is who you are. Being higher in the z-axis means integrating more virtue into your character and actions. And unlike the fleeting highs brought by short-term pleasure or material gains, the happiness reaped from becoming a more admirable person is stable and robust.

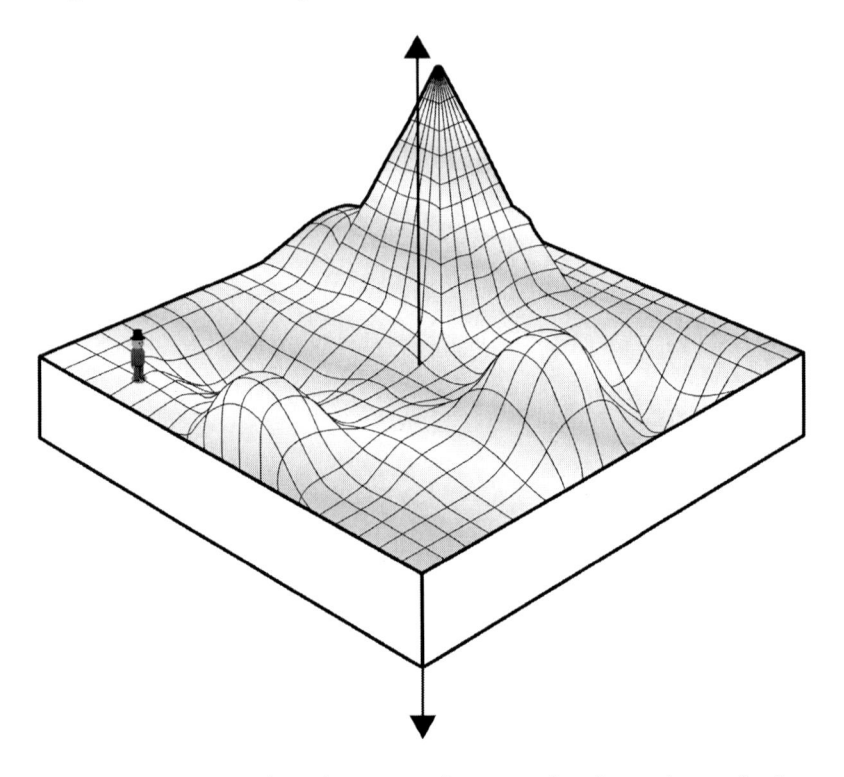

Your virtues cannot be taken away from you by the actions of others or mere chance. Though you may temporarily lose domains through which your virtues are expressed, the virtues themselves are yours once you have done the work to cultivate them. Bringing them out will always be a simple matter of finding an avenue for them.

These axes have to do with the final aims of your goals and actions—strategies, not particular endeavors. The life of someone navigating on the overview may not look dramatically different from someone on the circumscape.

A person navigating on the circumscape might have a job because it enables them to buy things that bring pleasure or because it confers material success and status. A person living according to the overview might have a job because it enables them to exercise and cultivate their virtues.

Crucially, each of these people will react in different ways emotionally to the outcomes of their lives. The overview allows you to respond appropriately to the natural fluctuations of life. Pain and loss begin to look like stepping stones instead of tragedies.

When you are navigating on the overview, goals are opportunities to exercise your virtues—nothing more. The entire two-dimensional circumscape of pleasure and pain, loss and gain, is merely instrumental to the true object of the game.

Your job is not, as some might conclude, to maximize the happiness provided by each of the three axes. The weak and fleeting pleasures of the circumscape simply do not factor into your overall well-being. Your job is to navigate the three axes so as to elevate your position on the one that actually matters. The z-axis is the sole benefactor of overall well-being.

Most people run around frantically trying to grasp the objects of their desires, mistaking them for true ends. Throughout their lives, they repeatedly form attachments to specific objects and outcomes.

When they fail to attain the thing they wanted, they feel a burst of disappointment that quickly gives way to more craving. When they do attain the thing they wanted, they feel a burst of excitement that quickly gives way to more craving.

You already live in all three dimensions. There is nothing you have to realize or learn in order to enter the third dimension. Your happiness is already dictated by the third dimension.

It's simply that without this dimensional model, you won't understand why. Your happiness and unhappiness won't make sense to you much of the time, and as a result, your efforts to navigate your own well-being will be chaotic and confused.

There is a wide range of innate understanding of this third dimension. While no one has, to my knowledge, used this model before, some people seem to intuitively understand it. Even as a young person, they grasped that there was something deeper, something more important than pleasure and gain, though they may not have been able to put their finger on exactly what it was.

But there are also many fully grown and otherwise mature adults who completely fail to grasp it. They do their best to seek true happiness through pleasure, love, and comfort, and can only conclude by the end of the day that their vague sense of ennui must be due to a chemical imbalance.

Developing the perspective of the overview will have major implications for how you view and navigate your life. It will change the way you see pleasure and comfort and pain; it will change the way you see obstacles and successes. It will change the way you see yourself.

When you learn to see in three dimensions, you don't suddenly stop experiencing pleasure or lose all interest in career gains. But you start seeing them as a means to the end of virtue.

You may choose to endure a period of pain and loss voluntarily so as to climb higher up the mountain of virtue. You also may find that in the context of some landscapes, the path toward virtue will be filled with abundant pleasure and gain. At other times you'll find the goals which would seem senseless to some have deep meaning in the context of virtue cultivation.

The x and y axes, which were once valuable in and of themselves, now begin to look like mere instruments in the service of virtue. They are means to the end of aligning with your own values, nothing more.

Life is one big game of virtue maximization. To start seeing in three dimensions and building a great life, you must learn to frame all your decisions and evaluations in these terms.

Many philosophical insights can be viewed through this lens. Take the core teachings of Buddhism, for example. The Buddha claimed that normal human existence was "unsatisfactory" and that the root of this problem was our tendency to form attachments and cling to specific outcomes.[18]

We make the mistake of thinking that pleasure and gain will be rewarding, but these rewards are fleeting and unsatisfactory. The solution of Nirvana that the Buddha prescribed may seem to differ from this framework.

But I think it's no coincidence that the Eightfold Path he offered consists of the cultivation and improvement of character in many different domains. We could interpret this path as an expression of the fact that the z-axis, not our fleeting, two-dimensional circumscape, is the key to satisfaction.

The Stoic indifference we looked at in the last chapter is a clear expression of the fact that our circumstances are indifferent to our well-being. A distraction. All that matters is the virtue and character we are able to build.[19]

We see this taken to its extreme in the Stoic doctrine of amor fati, or the love of fate. The directive given by Epictetus to demand not "that things happen as you wish, but wish that they happen as they do happen" reflects the idea that we can not only become indifferent to, but embrace the events of the circumscape.[20] It is not the plane that produces genuine well-being, as happiness comes from the z-axis alone.

Stoic practices like asceticism, or voluntary discomfort, serve as reminders to oneself that comfort is a circumscape consideration.[21] It is beside the point to genuine well-being. External achievements like profit, pleasure, and prestige are merely elevations of the y-axis, not the z-axis that regulates our well-being.

What about Taoism? Its central principle of wu wei, or "effortless action," expresses the idea that we can let go of the results of our actions.[22] We can learn to practice an attitude of nonresistance to seemingly negative outcomes, as outcomes do not actually affect our happiness. We must stop pretending that our happiness corresponds to "good" or "bad" circumstances and see that it comes from the z-axis alone.

Friedrich Nietzsche rejected hedonism and what he called "decadence." He warned of the emergence of the "last man" who was driven by superficial measures of a good life. He was adamant that the good life was not made merely of pleasure and insisted that suffering had its place in greatness.[23]

We can see this as an expression of the fact that great individuals live in the third dimension, not the superficial plane of pleasure and suffering. The point of our challenges is that they are challenging, otherwise they would not require our unique virtues to overcome them.

Abraham Maslow was primarily interested in self-actualization, or in what he sometimes called full humanness. One of the most prominent qualities of these self-actualizers according to Maslow's view was a tendency to be motivated by intrinsically rewarding processes, such as growth, inquiry, and creativity, rather than by "flattery, applause, popularity, status, prestige, money, honors..."[24]

He called this healthy inclination growth-motivation, in contrast with the more common deficiency-motivation. And these two motivations correspond perfectly to the dimensions we have laid out above. While most people are driven by deficiency-based circumscape consideration, the wisest and happiest people are motivated by growth in the z-axis alone.[25]

> The motivation of ordinary men is a striving for the basic need gratifications that they lack. [Self-actualizing individuals] no longer strive in the ordinary sense, but rather develop. They attempt to grow to perfection and to develop more and more fully in their own style.
>
> —**Abraham Maslow**, *Motivation and Personality*[26]

All of these thinkers have brought immense insight and wisdom to our understanding of virtue. Their intuition gave them clues that would only be confirmed centuries later. But there is one thing they were all missing: a modern understanding of the human mind, brain, and evolution.

These theories of virtue have lacked a psychological justification for their claims. Why do virtues dictate our happiness? Where do these values come from? We need to go deeper. We need to excavate the origins of human happiness.

## Key Takeaways:

- The overview is the centerpiece of the theory proposed by this book. It represents the three-dimensional lens we must learn to navigate our lives through. The overview adds the dimension of depth to the plane of the circumscape—the z-axis of well-being.

- The measure of the z-axis is virtue. Virtue is what determines the most crucial form of happiness in humans. This topography illustrates the peaks and valleys of virtue, and everything in between.

- Most people don't have three-dimensional vision. They set and evaluate their goals according to the circumscape. And as a result, things don't make sense a lot of the time. The z-axis of virtue is, counterintuitively, the one that truly delivers enduring happiness.

- When people attain the pleasures, power, or profits they crave, they improve their position in the x and y-axes. But the brief thrills of pleasure and possessions wear off shortly after they secure them, and their overall well-being is not affected.

- When viewing life through the overview, it becomes one big game of virtue maximization. The overview demonstrates a perennial practical philosophy, and many philosophical insights can be viewed through this lens. And you too must learn to frame all your decisions and evaluations in these terms.

# PART 2

# The Theory

# 5

# The Signal: The Origins of Values and Virtues

## The Peacock's Tail

> No one can play a game alone. One cannot be human by oneself. There is no selfhood where there is no community. We do not relate to others as the persons we are; we are who we are in relating to others.
>
> —James Carse, *Finite and Infinite Games*[1]

As I've stated throughout my work, I believe our individual virtues and values are the ultimate factors in the equation of our happiness. But these concepts can be fuzzy.

Most of us aren't quite sure what exactly a value is. Is it a rational priority? Is it an emotional impulse? How can we be sure we're maximizing our virtue if we aren't sure just what virtues are?

This book is about our personal evolution. But it's also about the evolution of our species. And in order to get to the root of our values, we have to go all the way to their true roots—their evolutionary origins.

I've come to see that without understanding the role our mental mechanisms played in our evolution, we can't fully understand ourselves. In order to explain how these mysterious phenomena arose, let's turn to a surprisingly central concept: virtue signaling.

You may have heard the term "virtue signaling" used in a negative light in the last few years. It's when a person acts "in order to garner praise or acknowledgment of one's righteousness." It is often used to smear ostensibly altruistic intentions. People tweeting their outrage or companies giving to charity will be accused of virtue signaling.[2]

I used to be vehemently opposed to virtue signaling (long before I knew the word for it). Anytime I would observe someone showing off, bragging, or worse, "humblebragging," I would get annoyed and swear never to engage in this artificial practice myself. But I realized that signaling went deeper than the occasional "weird flex."

When you start looking, you find that everyone is constantly, and subtly, signaling their strengths and accomplishments. It wasn't going to be easy to completely avoid doing this. So I would go as far as deliberately trying to keep others from discovering my strengths.

I kept my creativity to myself. I intentionally dumbed down my vocabulary. If I did a kind thing for someone, I would do it anonymously and try not to get found out. I avoided mentioning my intellectual interests, exercise regimen, or musical talents.

I was set on removing all approval-seeking behavior from my lifestyle. Extreme, I know, but I was determined to live only for my own acceptance. So you can imagine how shocked I was to discover that signaling is at the very heart of all virtue.

This is how we will visually represent an individual and their virtues:

INDIVIDUAL

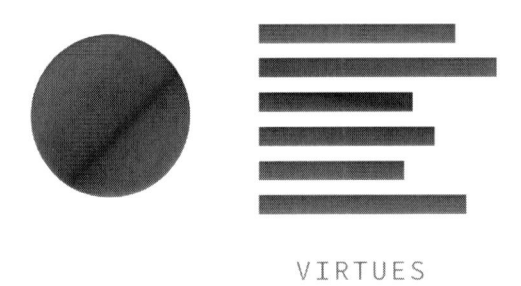

VIRTUES

Virtues are like the real-life stats and strengths of our character, and the person shown above has a pretty well-rounded set of virtues. When we signal our virtues to others, it looks like this:

VIRTUE SIGNALING

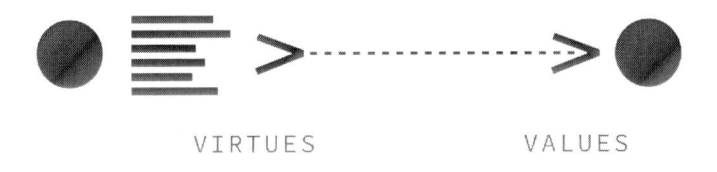

VIRTUES            VALUES

The V symbol on the left represents the virtue signal being sent out by one person, and the V symbol on the right represents the values of the second person as they receive and evaluate the signal. It gets more complex when we consider that there are not just one, but many different sets of virtues, values, and judging members of our social tribes.

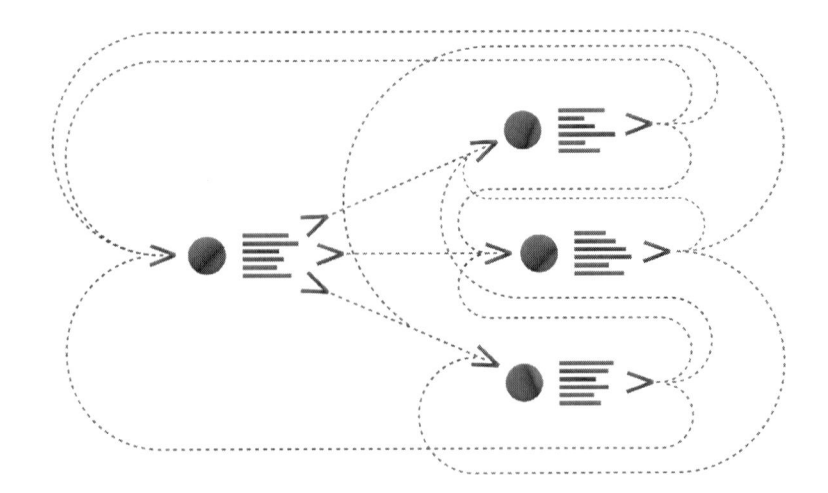

Here, we see an intricate play of virtue-value combinations—ambition, endurance, boldness, empathy—every human trait we have positive or negative feelings about plays a part in this dance. And we all simultaneously possess both values and virtues, which link up with those of others in endless combinations. What we now must explain is how this elaborate game unfolding in our social relationships came to be in the first place.

The peacock's tail has become a symbol of Neo-Darwinian understanding. Darwin himself said at one point "The sight of a feather in a peacock's tail, whenever I gaze at it, makes me sick!" As he was developing his theory of natural selection, he couldn't wrap his head around why a bird would have evolved such an elaborate target on its back.[3]

Today, we know that this tail evolved through sexual selection—peacocks with elaborate tails are more attractive to potential mates. And why would that be? The counterintuitive truth that came along later is that the deadliness of the peacock's tail is exactly what led to its selection.[4]

This elaborate and large tail is also biologically expensive. For a peacock to be able to survive with a giant advertisement to predators attached to it, it had to be incredibly fit. It had to be fast and agile enough to escape predators in spite of its lavish colors. It had to be effective enough at gathering food to overcompensate for the energy costs of its tail.[5]

**70** | BECOME WHO YOU ARE

Over time, this caused female peacocks to develop a preference for extravagant tails, as it became a way of identifying fit males. This type of ornament is known as a fitness indicator, as it provides a reliable signal of a potential mate's adaptiveness.

This type of selective pressure can sometimes go out of control, and cause mates to prefer extreme traits long past the point of being biologically useful. Sexual selection elegantly explains many puzzling characteristics and behaviors in animals.[6]

And it explains a lot about humans too. Most things, actually. We often assume that humans are special because our big brains, creativity, and social cooperation helped us to outsmart predators and survive. But experts are doubtful that a costly big brain and excessive intelligence came about for survival purposes.

## Signal Selection

> The human mind's most impressive abilities are like the peacock's tail: they are courtship tools, evolved to attract and entertain sexual partners. By shifting our attention from a survival-centered view of evolution to a courtship-centered view... we can understand more of the richness of human art, morality, language, and creativity.
>
> —Geoffrey Miller, *The Mating Mind*

When you look at human behavior in contrast to other animals, it's easy to be confused about the evolutionary benefit. Most animals are running around trying to get food and fend off predators. We're doing ridiculous and seemingly masochistic things like climbing mountains for fun and writing books.

Some would speculate this is because of the luxuries afforded by modern civilization. But they're wrong. We've gathered enough about prehistoric human behavior to know that colorful and seemingly superfluous behaviors and rituals can be found in hunter-gatherer tribes across cultures and eras.[7] So how do we explain these enigmatic behaviors?

The answer is that our creative intelligence and social cooperation have co-evolved with a complex social landscape and elaborate selection mechanisms. And we're running around trying to advertise our virtues, to our tribes, to our mate prospects, and crucially, to ourselves.

When you observe a trait that appears to be unique to any single species, including homo sapiens, odds are it did not evolve for ordinary survival reasons. It's not the product of natural, or environmental selection. It's the product of sexual selection.[8] You didn't think I was being so literal when I said I was going to make virtue sexy, did you?

Evolutionary psychologist Geoffrey Miller has argued that human traits ranging from creative intelligence to humor to kindness all evolved for mate selection signaling.[8] This idea initially strikes many of us as distasteful. But as the history of science has shown, our puritanical preferences don't determine what's true (and when it's all said and done, we may not want them to).

Think about it. For someone to have developed exceptional artistic abilities, comedic genius, or overwhelming generosity, they must have quite a bit of free time and energy on their hands. It's a luxury to be able to become great at things that don't directly serve your own survival interests.

To be courageous enough to singlehandedly take on a buffalo, you also have to be fit enough to survive to tell the tale. To be compassionate enough to give up your meal to help a hungry member of your tribe, you had to be resourceful and connected enough to be able to secure more food soon. And these fitness indicators let potential mates know that you're a catch.

This is where virtue signaling comes in. You see, evolutionary psychology gives us an interesting new perspective on virtue signaling. This gene-centric explanation of our virtues shows us that virtue signaling is no exception; it is very much the norm. Virtues exist to be signaled. We would never have evolved these virtues like generosity or confidence if not to be demonstrated to others.[9]

We all evolved both a set of potential virtues, which exist to signal our fitness to others, and a set of values, which exist to evaluate the virtues of others. And others use their values to determine the worth of our virtues as well. We are simultaneously the protagonists and audiences of this great social drama playing out around us.

To think about how this state initially came about, we can imagine that early humans may have evolved a bit of some virtue—a bit more honesty, compassion, or humor than their ancestors had for some small survival reason. But then they evolved a taste for those virtues, which drove the evolution of even more of those virtues. Before long, we humans had developed reinforcing feedback cycles amplifying our virtues and values in tandem.[9]

Miller has proposed that this mechanism explains not only the origin of certain virtues, but the origin of humanity. After all, what is remarkable about humans can be captured by our unique creative intelligence, our social cooperation, and our altruistic capacities—in short, our virtues.

In many ways, Miller argues, we're all like entertainment systems for potential mates. We're creative for the sake of saying "Hey look guys, I'm creative!" We're kind for the sake of saying "Hey look guys, I'm kind!"[8]

No one is suggesting these are the conscious motives behind our virtues. Most people don't decide they want to drink water because every cell and organ in their body needs it to function. We drink because we're thirsty. But there is a reason we get thirsty. And we don't necessarily donate to charity or compose music to attract potential mates. We do these things because they are fulfilling. But there is a reason they are fulfilling.

Miller makes a compelling case that while many of the traits we share with other animals are the result of environmental selection, the traits that are unique to humans are far more likely to be the result of sexual selection.

I suspect there is a bit more to the story of our virtues than sexiness. I have often wondered why we only learn of two primary selective forces: natural and sexual. It seems to me there are at least a few more.

For one thing, the term "sexual selection" implies that our values are purely the traits we look for in sexual partners. While some of our traits probably do trace back to short-term sexual selection, more of them probably come from long-term selection, or what we might call partner selection.

And how about social selection? Some virtues, like fairness, likely have their roots in a non-sexual, social selection mechanism. Those who lack the virtue of fairness will likely get caught cheating, and may be ostracized by their group, ultimately preventing them from reproducing. Those who lack the value of fairness will likely get cheated.

What about parenting selection? Could there be certain traits that, though they may not be adaptive from survival and sexual perspectives, tend to result in parenting styles that are adaptive for offspring? How about commitment and nurturing?

Whatever combination of selective pressures led to our virtues, we've got them now. And in the vast majority of cases, they seem to have evolved to be displayed to others. We've been wired to want to show them off to the world and to carefully scrutinize others who are doing the same.

When you think of virtue, don't think of the colorless mandates of morality. Think of the magnificent colors of exotic birds. Because that's effectively what they are.

But if virtues evolved to signal mental fitness to our tribe like the colorful traits of these birds, why do we see such diversity throughout the human population? We generally observe consistent fitness signals and rituals across entire species. So why are some people honest and reliable while others are passionate and funny? To answer this, we're going to turn to the concept of neurodiversity.

# Barriers to Becoming—February 2020

In the previous chapter, I shared some of my own climb toward self-becoming from my adolescence. These changes and growth were all genuine, and it was undeniable that I had improved in leaps and bounds since seventh grade.

But now, two decades later, here I was grappling with an actual diagnosis. After that conversation with Tory, I spent the next couple of months researching, nodding, and debating until I finally accepted that I was autistic.

For those wondering if I received a formal diagnosis, you're looking at a guy who publishes psychology books with no formal certifications. You'd better believe I had the audacity to read a manual and check a few boxes myself.

And any doubts I may have had looking at the formal criteria were put to rest when I started listening to first-hand accounts of life with autism and realized they were describing my experience with pinpoint accuracy.

This realization hit me harder than expected. At first, it seemed like nothing more than a label that should have little bearing on my identity. I had already been living with the difficulties my whole life—shouldn't this be the easy part?

But this diagnosis was calling into question the idea that I had, or ever truly could, overcome my social difficulties. I always assumed that the virtues I lacked in the social domain were just skills I needed to work on. With a bit more practice, I could build normal, or even exceptional social skills.

But at this point, it seemed to me that I had been an outsider since before I was born, and always would be in a sense, regardless of the veneer I built around myself. After all, my brain was, according to the prevailing scientific views, structurally different from a neurotypical one. And I wasn't just different; I was disabled.

Some days, being autistic simply feels like being a passionate, interesting person. I feel connected with others and conversations flow easily. Other days it feels like my brain and body freeze up the minute I enter a social situation. Like my brain is a server with a thousand bots weighing down its bandwidth with meaningless queries. It has so much to process that it loses almost all ability to function.

I recently took a trip to Medellin, Colombia. It was beautiful and vibrant, and my first few days there were incredible. But by the end of the week, I was utterly exhausted by the experience of having to navigate this place without speaking almost any of the language.

I had been to South America before, but this was really the first place I had been in which almost no one spoke any English. You don't just feel confused a lot when you don't speak a language. You feel guilty. You feel like everyone is mad at you for not communicating properly, or not taking the time to learn before coming.

At one point, a woman became upset with me for apparently sitting in the wrong seat on a bus, which she had been trying to communicate to me by passive-aggressively telling her friends. She eventually got the ticket guy to come over and kick me out, assuming that I was being intentionally uncooperative. She didn't even know I didn't speak Spanish until I attempted to apologize. By the end of this trip, I was literally choosing my activities based on what would require me to do the least talking.

It has since occurred to me that socializing is almost exactly like Spanish for me. It's not my first language, and I didn't really start learning it until high school. By the end of high school, I had actually gotten pretty good at it.

But when I was no longer being forced to practice it constantly, and as other priorities crowded it out, I quickly lost my proficiency, only to gain it back periodically when I've felt the need to prove to myself that I could.

Socializing is most people's first language. They're confused by the fact that I could forget how to speak it. They don't account for the mental exhaustion that comes after a day of speaking a second language.

They assume I must think I'm better than them if I'm not making the Herculean effort it would take to talk to them. Most days, I feel like I only know how to say those few phrases you absolutely need to get by, like "where's the bathroom?" and "may I have five tacos?"

If I want to be likable, I have to put intellectual work into my social presence. I have to go into many social situations with a clear plan. But conversations aren't predictable, so I can't prepare and rehearse a script, however much I may want to. So instead, I'll go into high-stakes interactions with a kind of branching conversation flow diagram in my head. "If they say x, I'll say y. If they say a, I'll say b." If it sounds exhausting, that's because it is.

I have to consciously craft my personality in order to make it enjoyable to strangers or acquaintances. How are you enjoying your Ryan Bush experience (v12.0.7). On a scale from 1 to 5, how likely would you be to recommend me to someone else? If I used phrases like "Just another day in paradise, my friend," would that make your experience better or worse?

When I think of myself, I see myself as I am around my closest friends. Someone charming and full of personality and humor. And then I'm continually surprised when I actually enter a social situation with strangers or acquaintances, and it doesn't come out. It feels like my whole body tightens up and freezes and some kind of lock has been placed on my personality.

Like all human beings, I want to be liked and loved. I have repeatedly found that genuine friendship is one of the most rewarding experiences in life. And a part of me always feels like if I can just accomplish enough, if I'm an award-winning designer, if I write fascinating books, if I'm a "successful" entrepreneur, it will make people interested in me and outweigh my social difficulties.

But if anything, I often feel like my skills and accomplishments make me harder to relate to. Finding someone interesting from a distance isn't the same as wanting to be friends with them. As the great Twain once said, "Okay, so you're a rocket scientist. That don't impress-a me much."

By and large, the reason I have close friends today is that a few rare and unusually persistent people have been willing to put in the extra work to build a relationship with me. They have pushed past my aloofness, insisted on hanging out with me, and eventually broken through the barriers to build a real relationship with me.

I know this description may make it sound like I was right—I had a tragic disability that I simply needed to accept. But something about this perspective didn't add up.

I couldn't make sense of it from an evolutionary framework. What could have led the genes of this largely hereditary disability to be preserved? And why did their limitations so often appear to be balanced by rare strengths and abilities?

# Neurodiversity Explained

These sometimes tragic conditions like autism and ADHD appear to be clear disadvantages to healthy social and vocational functioning. It is tempting to conclude that they must be pathologies that somehow slipped through the evolutionary cracks.

But I don't think this is the case. The more I have reflected on the topic of neurodiversity, the more my understanding has fallen into place. I have come to the conclusion that these apparent disabilities are actually advantageous evolutionary strategies.

I know, it sounds outrageous—insensitive even—to suggest that such crippling conditions could have been adaptations. To explain this counterintuitive hypothesis, let's first revisit the concept of the virtue spectrum:

I have argued that human virtues like courage, compassion, and charisma evolved through social and sexual selection, much like the exotic colors, songs, and dances seen in birds of paradise.

We've all been genetically programmed with a cocktail of admirable strengths and skills to show off and contribute to our tribes, social circles, and potential mates. Whether we find ways to bring these virtues out into the world is up to us.

But in order for genetic virtue strategies to be effective, compromises have to be made. If we were all good at everything, then no one would actually be good at anything. All virtues would be a dime a dozen. And this is where our genes get crafty.

Think about it from a business perspective. Imagine you want to open up a shop in your community, but the industry is saturated and there are huge competitors like Walmart already dominating the market in your town.

You could attempt to compete with these giants on their level and cut your prices as low as possible. But you would inevitably fail due to a lack of resources and economies of scale.

On the other hand, you could adopt a strategy that used your disadvantages to your advantage. You could lean into the higher cost and set yourself apart by optimizing for high product quality, pleasant in-store experience, and high-touch customer service. To truly stand out, you have to embrace your disadvantages and build unique advantages.

Natural selection does the same thing in humans. It amplifies certain valued traits, even though this comes at a cost, because uncommon strengths are opportunities to stand out.[10]

I have come to the conclusion that neurotypes like autism can be viewed as niche virtue strategies that are selected in the genes of a small percentage of the population. The autism spectrum is just a subset of all virtue combinations—a corner of the overall virtue spectrum.

*The Autism Spectrum*

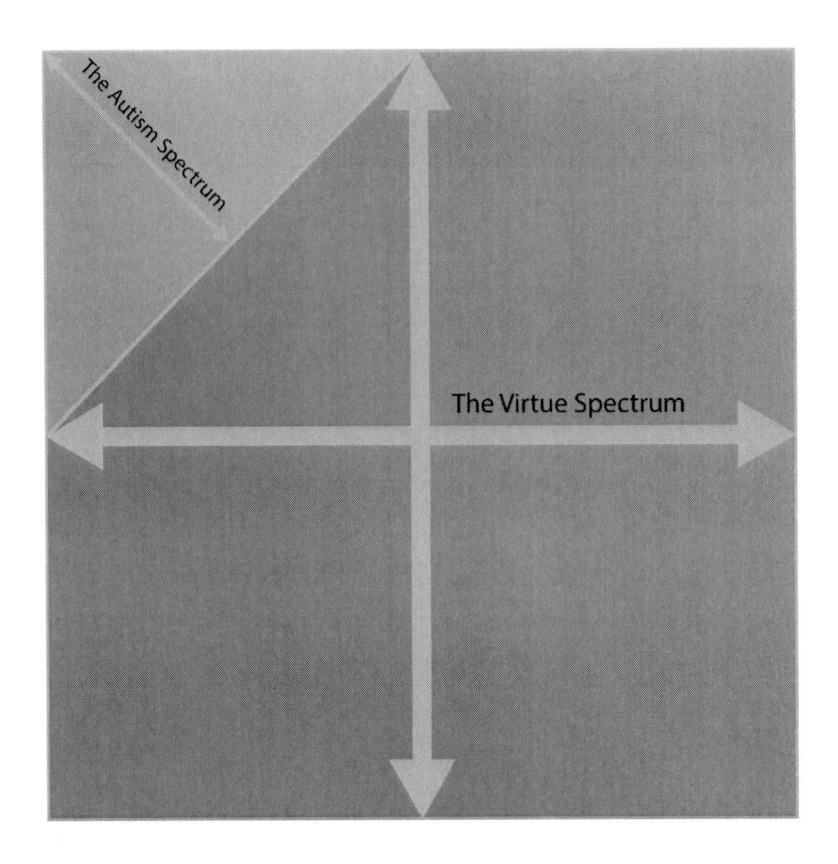

The Virtue Spectrum

At first glance, you might say this can't be right. Sure, there are a few people like me who lucked out with a "less severe case" of autism and have been able to thrive in spite of it. But most autistic people, you may argue, can hardly function socially. How could being unable to communicate or empathize with one's peers help someone reproduce?

But here's the thing: Most autistic people aren't autistic. What I mean by this is that the vast majority of people who got the autistic virtues neurotype would be unlikely to qualify for the formal disorder and receive a diagnosis.[11]

When you think about an archetypal autistic person, you probably aren't thinking about Elon Musk. Whatever your thoughts on that guy are, you must admit that his eccentric way of thinking and interacting has not gotten in the way of his reproduction (he is now a father of 10).[12]

Traditionally, only the people toward the very corner of the autism

80 | BECOME WHO YOU ARE

spectrum have been clinically and popularly deemed autistic—the diagnosed minority. For most people on the spectrum, the unique strengths that come with this different way of thinking are enough to offset the social costs.

Autistic people are often intriguing and impressive in unique ways—they can be unusually creative, honest, and thoughtful. They have been behind countless breakthroughs in collective understanding, art, and technology.[13] And this means they can attain a certain kind of social or romantic appeal, even if they're often eccentric and socially awkward.

If this theory is correct, we would expect the genes associated with autism spectrum disorder to also correlate with some of these advantageous traits. And sure enough, a body of evidence suggests that the gene variants associated with autism are also linked to cognitive function, memory, and verbal intelligence.[14]

These cognitive virtues come at the cost of other strengths like social intelligence and empathy. And it is precisely because these traits have costly trade-offs that they are not shared across the entire species, and they can confer a competitive edge in the genetic marketplace.

If these strengths clash with your understanding of autism, that understanding may be due for an update. Autism Spectrum Disorder is not an intellectual disability, and it hasn't been scientifically regarded as one for over a decade. What was once known as Asperger's Syndrome, or the high-functioning version of autism, is now known simply as autism. And the only critical criteria for autism relate to deficits in social understanding and communication, not deficits in intellect.[15]

Autism is currently classed as a developmental disorder. But I suspect that it, along with other neurodivergent states like ADHD will soon be formally classed as neurotypes and not inherent disorders. This is why the neurodivergent community prefers the use of phrases like "autistic person" over the people-first language that is used for diseases, like "a person with autism."[16]

The medical model of autism as a disability is falling out of fashion quickly. The neurodiversity movement has pushed for the embrace, accommodation, and celebration of these less-common neurotypes and different brains.[17]

Autism makes one particular virtue domain exceedingly difficult, and it's one that matters quite a bit in the social world: socializing.[18] It's surprising that this wouldn't be the only thing that matters, but it isn't.

As we've covered, we evolved to value everything from ambition to trustworthiness to creativity. And thankfully, much of the time, the fact that I'm different from others strikes me as a virtue advantage.

What exactly is this advantage? Well, I have my theories. No literally, I have my theories. I have a brain that loves to find patterns and explain them systematically. I'm able to absorb and synthesize large amounts of information, as long as it relates to the things I find fascinating, and not the things I find painfully boring.

I often think of autism as a neurotype that affects two different systems: the connection system and the obsession system. On the connection side, I struggle with things that come easily to others. Feeling and showing warmth toward people I'm not close with, and hence becoming close with anyone, is a great challenge.

The obsession system, unlike the connection system, is a delightful feature of autism, whether or not it is brought out for others to see. Despite the unhealthy connotation of the word "obsession," it is quite nice to have undying interest and focus within certain topics.

Though there is debate among researchers, it has been argued by some that there is a spectrum of mental capacities, with more social and nurturing traits on one end and more logical, systematic thinking on the other end. Autistic individuals, it is argued, fall on the extreme systemising end of the spectrum.[19]

This systematic mindset and the critical and lateral thinking that result from it set me up for a collection of creative and intellectual virtue domains. I have days where my drive for greater knowledge about a certain topic is absolutely insatiable. I'll be reading about a topic that I'm just beginning to grasp, and I'll suddenly be filled with a hundred questions that I have to get answers to right now. I'll scour every book, paper, and article I can find to understand.

Autistic people broadly seem to develop idiosyncratic interests that they obsess over, systematize, and focus on to the exclusion of other social and environmental stimuli. They may obsess over the classification of plants, the mechanical workings of cameras, or the physical laws of the universe.[20]

It seems plausible that the reason for the social deficits in autism have more to do with personal inclination than ability or understanding. If you've been obsessed with understanding and systematizing weather patterns your whole life, you've probably spent a lot less time identifying patterns in facial expressions and social norms.

After my self-diagnosis, my partner told me it had occurred to her before that I might be autistic. It wasn't eye contact or social skills that tipped her off. It was the way I zone out in social situations.

Anytime I've been socializing for more than a few hours, I run out of "social energy" and a combination of boredom and cognitive exhaustion takes over. I still want to show up well socially, but I reach a point at which the effort is no longer sustainable. I'll then end up silently pondering topics I find more interesting until I realize it's been ten minutes since I showed any signs of life to the people I'm with.

Sometimes I will get lost in observing the dynamics of social interactions and forget that I'm supposed to be a participant. I'll find myself reflecting on the psychology of the people around me instead of actually talking with them like a fellow human. And I've learned that my philosophical contemplations are rarely appropriate or valued in the context of a casual social gathering.

Confusingly, the machine I have always been most interested in understanding systematically is the human mind. I am fascinated by the mechanics of human emotion. I'm very interested in people, but in a different way than most are.

Sometimes I wish I could explain to my acquaintances, "Look, the fact that I don't have much desire to talk to you doesn't mean I'm not interested in you. I would pay good money for the opportunity to analyze your private journal!" Somehow I don't think this would have the intended effect.

This perspective aligns with the fact that I am extremely unobservant about most things outside of my areas of interest, not just social things like facial expressions or eye color. I didn't pick up on that social cue for the same reason I didn't notice the color of your throw pillows. It's not interesting!

The question is, why did you buy the throw pillows? What psychological motives fueled you to invest a piece of your financial freedom to have these items in your house? And what does this say about human nature? Now it's getting interesting.

What about other, seemingly disabling conditions like ADHD? Despite common difficulties with executive function and impulse-control, people of this neurotype can be some of the most charming, funny, interesting people you will ever meet. They have a peculiar and rare set of virtues at the expense of other, more common traits.[21]

And similarly, studies have found that people diagnosed with ADHD have higher degrees of creativity than average across the population, and self-report studies suggest that high levels of energy, agreeableness, and empathy belong on this list as well.[22]

The ADHD poster child may be the kid who can't sit still or the acquaintance who will ask you seven questions without waiting to hear your answer to the first. But again, this represents the diagnosed minority. Most people with these traits are far more balanced.

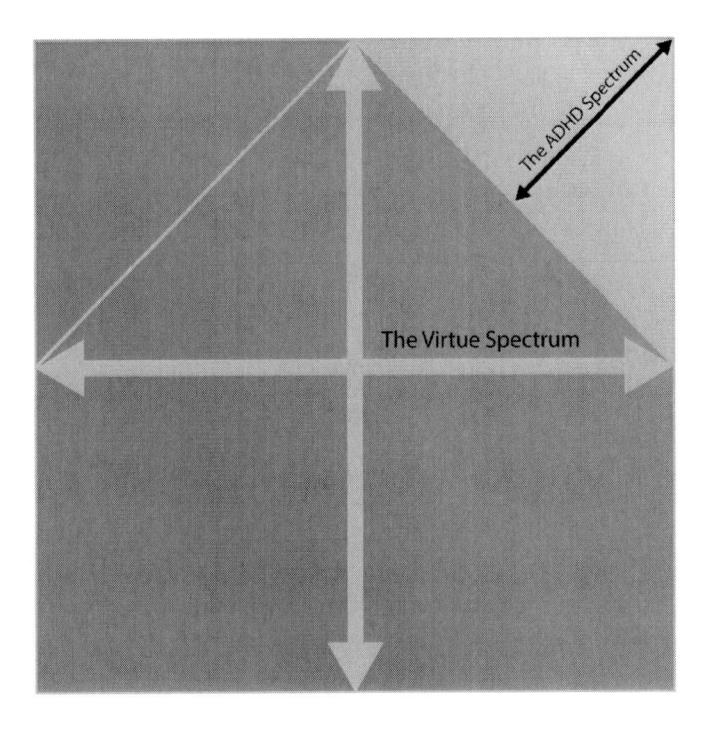

[Diagram: Two crossed axes forming a plus sign inside a triangle. The horizontal axis is labeled "The Virtue Spectrum". A diagonal axis is labeled "The ADHD Spectrum".]

Furthermore, it's likely that the disadvantages of these traits are amplified by the modern, neurotypically-structured world. Though these weaknesses still would have limited our ancestors, they were probably less crippling in the context of hunter-gatherer tribes.

Having a hard time sitting through boring lectures, keeping track of your phone, or keeping your house clean wouldn't have been such a problem before boring lectures, phones, and houses existed.[23] And with autism, being bad at making strong first impressions wouldn't have been such a problem when the only 150 people you knew were the ones who had known you since you were born.[24]

This is where things get really interesting. I first encountered the idea of frequency-dependent selection in an evolutionary analysis of psychopaths.[25] It talked about how evolution can favor certain combinations of traits (like dark triad traits) at a specific frequency throughout the population. This paper lays it out well:

> In an environment in which the majority of people adopt a strategy of cooperation, a small number of individuals may be able to maintain an exploitative, socially parasitic strategy. The strategy can bring high fitness benefits when rare, but becomes less rewarding at higher frequencies because of anticheater vigilance in the population and because of the increased probability that a cheater will encounter another cheater.
>
> Although psychopathic traits are thought to exist on a continuum, approximately 1% of the general population is thought to be highly psychopathic, suggesting that at this low frequency it may be advantageous. Frequency-dependent selection may be a more likely model for psychopathy than for other mental disorders because there are plausible explanations for why the fitness of the alleles associated with psychopathy would increase as their frequency decreases.[26]

In other words, psychopath genes only work when a certain, small percentage of the population (1-5%) have them. Once they become common, everyone stops trusting each other, and any genetic value in deceptive strategies vanishes.

Now I'm not suggesting that the genes for ADHD or autism thrive because they allow us to deceive or manipulate our peers like psychopaths. The reason these strength/weakness combinations are relatively rare is that they are only noteworthy when they are rare. They are only admirable when they are rare.

There are numerous animal species that demonstrate high degrees of variation in sexually selected traits. For example, Side-blotched lizards are known to have several different morphs, or "alternative reproductive tactics," which correspond to the color of their throats.[27]

Orange-throated males are dominant and territorial, controlling areas with multiple females. Those with a yellow throat cluster on the fringes of orange-throat territories and mate with females while the dominant males are absent. And males with blue throats are less aggressive and only guard a single female, being unable to fend off orange-throated males but capable of keeping out yellow-stripe males.[27]

These mating dynamics are sometimes referred to as the "rock paper scissors" effect. Just as rock beats scissors, scissors beat paper, and paper beats rock, each morph of the lizard thrives because of the leg-up it can gain on one of the others.[27]

Another example is found in guppies. This fish species varies widely in its color patterns, and certain rare color patterns are preferred by mates over more common colorations. These preferences are thought to depend on the overall frequency of different color patterns in the population, and rare patterns are selected and maintained in only a small percentage of guppies.[28]

In humans, I believe, atypical neurotypes are preserved in a minority of genetic lines because their value starts to diminish when they become typical. If everyone had systematically-oriented minds like autism or hyperactive minds like ADHD, their positive traits would become unremarkable, and warm/empathetic or focused/calm genes would start to be appreciated more and more as unique traits.

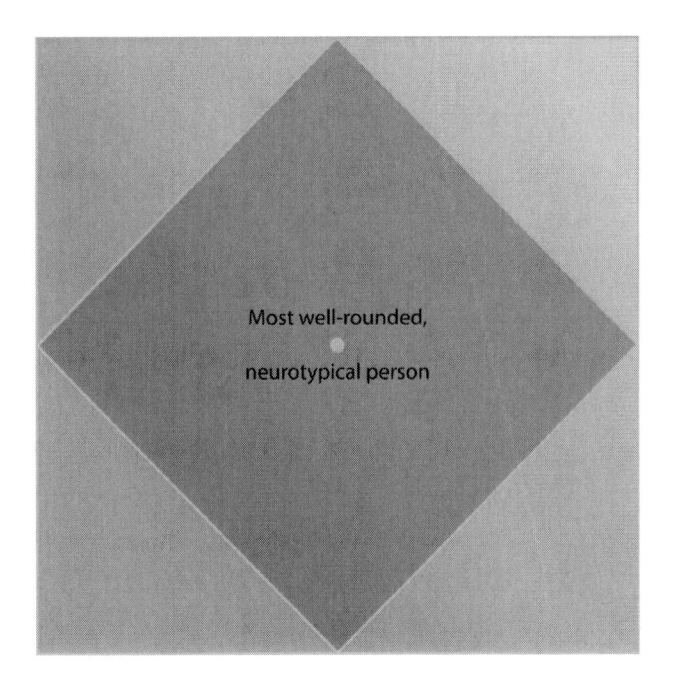

Most well-rounded, neurotypical person

Each combination of positive traits and costly weaknesses we observe in people may represent a different evolutionary strategy. And overall, I believe this theory could finally solve the mystery of neurodiversity. It's quite early, and there is a lot more research to be done.

But I think this perspective, or something very close to it, could make sense of the many different types of brains we see in our world. It could explain how these types of minds emerge, and how they can be seen as virtue advantages instead of tragic disorders.

Autism has put limitations in the way of my cultivation of certain virtues. But it has provided opportunities for others in its place. In many ways, I believe the constraints and challenges have actually helped me to develop greater character.

In the process of trying to overcome this set of difficulties I was dealt, I have inquired into my greatest capacities and found new paths to self-becoming.

And in grappling with this apparent disability, I gained access to a new way of looking at the landscape of human virtues. Beyond specific neurotypes like autism and ADHD, this principle of the frequency-dependent selection of virtues sheds light on why we see such diverse distribution of talents and strengths among people.

NEUROTYPES

We each develop a set of virtues as a part of an evolutionary strategy. Some of us get a more common, well-rounded set of virtues, and others get more rare, atypical combinations. But they all exist, fundamentally, to be signaled to our tribes and maximize our evolutionary prospects. And importantly, whether those innate virtues become actualized or remain latent depends on the decisions we make throughout our lives.

I've come to understand that it's not virtue signaling that's a problem. The problem is bad virtue signaling. When someone says, "I'm a super creative person," they are creating an unreliable signal.

It's easy to say you are creative. It's far harder to do something so creative that people will find out on their own. It's easy to post a photo of you volunteering on Instagram. It's far harder to design your lifestyle around giving and contribution, to the point it couldn't be ignored by anyone around you.

This great interplay may seem to be all about social approval. But doesn't this go against the message of cultivating our minds directly and not living to get some external reward or recognition? Should we really be directing our lives based on other people's approval?

We should not. But as I will try to make very clear later on, there are massive implications for this virtue-value tango. I am going to expand this theory to explain why our virtues determine our well-being on the highest level, whether or not we have the approval of our peers.

We've now built an understanding of the virtue landscape underpinning our strivings and social lives. We've learned how virtue strategies shape different minds to contend with our peers and stand out.

But now it's time to go deeper into the mental mechanisms that regulate our identity and happiness. To do this, we're going to turn to the familiar concept of self-esteem and reveal its strange and unfamiliar workings.

## Key Takeaways:

- The virtues and values that make humans unique did not, for the most part, evolve to aid our survival. They evolved through social and sexual selection processes, similar to the feathers, songs, and dances of exotic birds.

- Everything from compassion to courage to creativity evolved to be signaled to our tribe to bring about genetic outcomes. The result is a complex social landscape in which we are all compelled to advertise our virtues to our tribes, our mate prospects, and ourselves.

- The diversity of virtues we observe can be explained through these social selection mechanisms as well. The reason we live in a neurodiverse world is that trait combinations are maintained at certain levels of the population because they are admirable and adaptive when they are rare.

- We each develop a set of virtues as a part of an evolutionary strategy. But they all exist, fundamentally, to be signaled to our tribes and maximize our evolutionary prospects.

- Whether those innate virtues become actualized or remain latent depends on the decisions we make throughout our lives. And as we will see, our virtues determine our well-being on the highest level, whether or not we have the approval of our peers.

# 6

# The Simulation: Self-Esteem and the Default Mode Network

## The Roots of Self-Esteem

I've now made the case that our virtues and values coevolved through a complex process of socio-sexual selection. But there's still a small gap in our understanding of this value-virtue complex of ours.

If evolution wanted us to be effective advertisers of our virtues, we would have to be able to evaluate them ourselves. We would need the ability—the obligation—to reflect on how closely we are aligning with our own values at any given time.

We aren't mind-readers. We don't ever know exactly what our tribe is thinking about us. For this reason, our mind has to run a kind of simulation. We have to be able to observe our own actions in much the same way that other people might observe us. And we have to be able to detect how closely our behaviors are aligning with those values. We need a sociometer.

Self-esteem is an integral component of the human mind. It is closely linked to subjective happiness, is highly correlated with clinical depression, and appears to play a major role in both the greatest and most horrific of human acts.[1][2]

Self-esteem is central to the ruminative spirals that haunt many of us.[3] The constant questions of whether we're "good enough" or not. Oh, and it's at the core of those virtues and values that I never seem to shut up about.[4]

So let's get to the bottom of self-esteem. Why does it exist? Why do we have any opinion of ourselves at all? Why do we have such strong feelings about it? And how do we get it to serve us instead of sabotaging us?

Self-esteem can be defined as an individual's subjective evaluation of their own worth, cognitive and emotional. It's how good we think we are, and how we feel about this.[5] And the fact that we care deeply about our own worth is one of the few points of consensus in the whole field of human psychology.[6]

A number of theories have been proposed for why self-esteem exists. One known as Terror Management Theory suggests we developed this self-centered orientation to allow us to cope with existential anxiety and mortality.[7]

But this type of explanation seems naive in light of evolutionary theory. Does having self-esteem really solve our anxiety around death? And why would natural selection favor such an elaborate workaround instead of just down-regulating our anxiety itself?

We need a functional explanation for the self-evaluation that is so central to human nature. If you consider yourself an evolutionary thinker, you may have already formed a hypothesis—it may even strike you as rather obvious. If not, go ahead and think it through for a moment before reading on.

Remember from the last chapter that we are all constantly sending and receiving signals about personal character throughout our social circles, all the time. And this results in the incredibly complex social landscape we see all around us.

## VIRTUE SIGNALING

VIRTUES → VALUES

But this is where it gets interesting. The study of human behavior has revealed that we often get to know ourselves by observing our own behaviors—the signals we send to ourselves.[8]

> Individuals come to "know" their own attitudes, emotions, and other internal states partially by inferring them from observations of their own overt behavior and/ or the circumstances in which this behavior occurs. Thus, to the extent that internal cues are weak, ambiguous, or uninterpretable, the individual is functionally in the same position as an outside observer, an observer who must necessarily rely upon those same external cues to infer the individual's inner states.[8]

We don't just send messages to others through our actions—we send messages to ourselves. In fact, in some ways, observing your own behaviors without accounting for internal cues could be a more useful signal. Other people can't see what is going on inside our heads, so when it comes to evaluating virtue, behavior is the gold standard.[9]

Despite the perception many of us share that we know ourselves deeply, we largely learn about ourselves the same way others do: by observing our behavior. We signal our character to ourselves through the actions we perform repeatedly.

And this makes a lot of sense given the importance of successful signaling to our survival and reproduction. In order to effectively and responsively signal our virtues to one another, we also need to signal them to ourselves. We need to be able to gauge how others are evaluating us, and to dynamically adapt our behaviors accordingly.

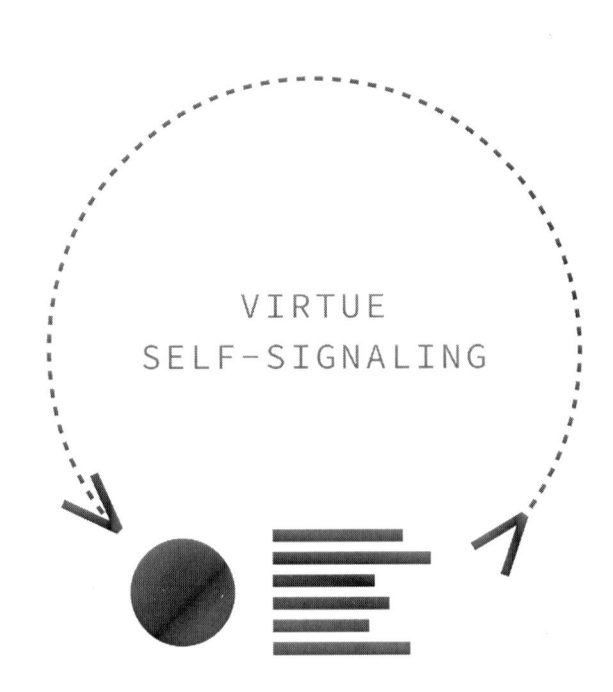

## VIRTUE SELF-SIGNALING

In order to gauge how others are going to receive the signals of kindness in our actions, for example, we have to signal this kindness to ourselves. This signal can modulate our behaviors, like increasing kindness when we start to detect that we aren't living up to this value.

In order to maximize our social virtues across the board, we need to be constantly evaluating them ourselves. We have to ask ourselves questions like "Am I good enough?" "Am I as creative as Jennifer?" "Do people think I'm funny?" "Did I embarrass myself at the meeting yesterday?" and in extreme cases, "Am I completely worthless?"[10]

We continually observe ourselves in action, and constantly appraise our own worth, to the point of obsession. This system is so crucial that it was built to run in the background anytime we aren't immersed in another activity.

If Miller is right that the human brain was crafted as an elaborate set of fitness indicators, wouldn't it make sense that we would have highly refined abilities to monitor how we're doing? While other animals' mating displays are generally a matter of unchangeable physical characteristics or capabilities, the human plumage is highly malleable.[11]

Our brains, our beliefs, our emotions can be modified in real-time. Lacking the ability to monitor how we're doing would have more dire genetic costs than blindness. For this reason, we evolved a central system in our brains for simulating our social approval.

## The Sociometer

Sociometer theory, first put forward by Mark Leary, proposes that self-esteem is a psychological gauge of the degree to which people perceive that they are relationally valued and socially accepted by other people. An internal indicator of social status.[12]

Self-esteem, it holds, is not a free-floating goal state that we have an innate desire to protect. It is an internal gauge, or "sociometer" built to monitor our success in regard to certain social goals.[13]

In other words, social esteem is like the gas tank in a car; self-esteem is simply the fuel gauge. It's here to let us know how we're doing, and especially when we're running low.

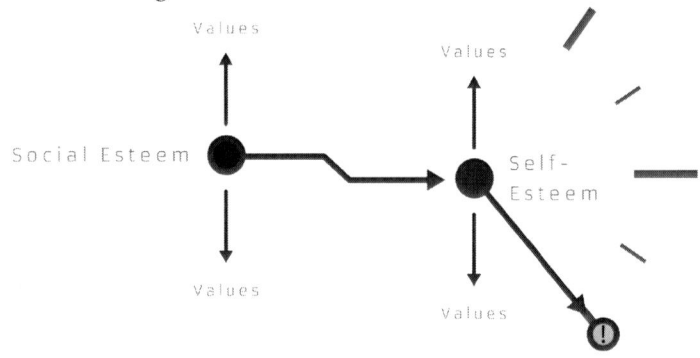

It's not too hard to see why this mechanism would have developed to play a massive role in our psychology. Social status plays a huge role in our ability to pass on our genes because anyone who lacked the respect and approval of their tribe would raise a red flag to anyone who might consider befriending, mating, or raising a child with them.

> Early humans who had no inclination to develop and maintain supportive social relationships (and thus to maintain self-esteem) were ostracized, banished, or killed.[12]

Low self-esteem is often seen as a pathology—a mental issue to be treated. But through the lens of the sociometer model, this very well might amount to treating a symptom, and potentially neglecting its root cause.

> From an evolutionary point of view, however, low self-esteem is no more a puzzle than is high self-esteem, and it surely does not necessarily reflect malfunctioning of an adaptive system. If you take a swig of spoiled milk and experience an unpleasant taste, has your evolved taste system malfunctioned? If you later enjoy a delicious culinary feast in a fine restaurant, is the system now working better? In both cases the system is functioning exactly as it was designed, alerting you as to which foods to avoid and which to ingest with gusto.[13]

Though it does seem possible for the sociometer to malfunction and become distorted, particularly in the modern world,[14] we should generally assume that there are real-life reasons for our high or low self-esteem. The model has seen a good deal of empirical verification, and this has made it a leading theory among evolutionary psychologists.

Five studies tested hypotheses derived from the sociometer model of self-esteem according to which the self-esteem system monitors others' reactions and alerts the individual to the possibility of social exclusion. Study 1 showed that the effects of events on participants' state self-esteem paralleled their assumptions about whether such events would lead others to accept or reject them. In Study 2, participants' ratings of how included they felt in a real social situation correlated highly with their self-esteem feelings. In Studies 3 and 4, social exclusion caused decreases in self-esteem when respondents were excluded from a group for personal reasons, but not when exclusion was random, but this effect was not mediated by self-presentation. Study 5 showed that trait self-esteem correlated highly with the degree to which respondents generally felt included versus excluded by other people. Overall, results provided converging evidence for the sociometer model.[15]

Just as this model predicts, elevated social status is significantly and positively associated with elevated self-esteem.[16] But don't be fooled by the apparent simplicity of a social status gauge. There is a world of complexity in the ways we make these evaluations of ourselves.

When most of us think of status, we think of a linear ranking system. High school popularity or socioeconomic class. But this is misleading. Unlike other mammals that evaluate status based on simple dominance hierarchies and aggressive battles, the human social landscape is deeply complex.

Though some thinkers will insist that humans have a "dominance hierarchy" like other mammals, this is clearly an oversimplified model. For one thing, our evaluations are multivariate—we aren't just looking for one trait when we evaluate an ally or potential mate. We're looking at dozens of different traits.[17]

And though it would be reasonable to call our values comparative, it would be too far to call them competitive. We determine how praiseworthy a person is based on where they fall on any given virtue spectrum. But it isn't based on one-upmanship.[18]

Our status isn't determined by dominance. It's determined by contribution.[19] We can contribute kindness, artistry, courage, or humor. What matters is that our actions align with the attributes we all evolved to place value on. So when you're thinking about the hierarchies that shaped our brains, don't think social status. Think social value.

Our seemingly desperate need to be doing something useful at all times did not originate with the smartphone or social media or even the post-industrial world. This need is hardwired into the brain and has been for at least 100,000 years.[20]

We need to be doing something useful because we are a member of a social species. We need to contribute to our tribe and provide value in one of the ways that are socially admired.

This shift is crucial for a proper perspective on self-esteem. We don't evaluate ourselves based on some kind of social rank. We evaluate ourselves based on the valued traits we exhibit: our virtues.

## The Default Mode

The default mode network is a group of interacting brain regions that appears to be highly active in humans "by default," hence the name.[21] Anytime we are not deeply immersed in an external task, this part of our brain is lighting up.[22]

It has been argued that activity in the default mode network simply represents introspective processes like mind-wandering and daydreaming.[23] Others propose that the spontaneous thoughts linked to the network help us simulate possible scenarios to prepare for the future.[24]

But while prompting subjects to complete external tasks tends to silence the default mode network, prompting them to complete internal, self-referential tasks causes it to activate.[25] [26] And these findings have informed the most compelling conclusions about the network's function: that it is responsible for self-related thinking, particularly in regard to our status and comparison with others.[27]

Some have gone so far as to suggest that the default mode network is the neurological basis for the self and directly regulates our self-esteem, or ego.[28] When I come across a popular science explanation, I tend toward the cynical and assume it's rooted in an oversimplified narrative. But the more I've read about the default mode network, the more I conclude that the popular explanation is generally right.

One of the network's main subsystems has been found to play a role in reflecting on the mental states of social agents.[29] It activates when we appraise social information, like the mental states of other people and their thoughts and feelings toward us.[30] Other subsystems are active when we are presented with autobiographical information or when we simulate future events that have personal relevance to us.[31] [32]

It has been found that trait self-esteem is strongly linked to default mode connectivity.[33] Studies have shown that experienced meditators have less activity in this network than controls.[34] And other studies indicate that psychedelics like LSD and psilocybin interrupt activity in these areas as well, which aligns with reports that these altered states are characterized by ego dissolution and a lowered sense of self.[35] [36]

Numerous studies have found that the default mode network activates and reconfigures itself in reliable ways when a person watches, reads, or listens to a story, as they put themselves into the life and social context of another person.[37] And a study conducted by Sam Harris et al. found that challenging a person's political beliefs increased activity in their default mode network, which is exactly what we would expect given how closely people identify with their political stances.[38]

There are countless studies on the connections between the default mode network, social status, self-esteem, and the display and evaluation of virtue. And while it can be all too easy to impose meaning onto complex neurological data, all of my research has reinforced the idea that this constantly active part of our brains is in fact analyzing us, comparing us to others, and fantasizing about gaining status.

Because of the network's seemingly selfish and status-oriented nature, it is generally widely considered to be harmful to our well-being and best to quiet down. But consider the findings of this analysis on some of the functions of the network's subsystems and the individual brain regions that make it up:

> Common results show that the medial prefrontal cortex (MPFC) plays a key role in the social understanding of others... At the bottom, the ventral MPFC in the medial temporal lobe (MTL) subsystem and its connections with emotion regions are mainly associated with emotion engagement during social interactions. Above, the anterior MPFC (aMPFC) in the cortical midline structures (CMS) and its connections with posterior and anterior cingulate cortex contribute mostly to making self-other distinctions. At the top, the dorsal MPFC (dMPFC) in the dMPFC subsystem and its connection with the temporo-parietal junction (TPJ) are primarily related to the understanding of other's mental states...
>
> Increasing studies have shown that regions of the default mode network (DMN) largely activate in tasks requiring participants to understand and interact with others, such as perceiving and interpreting other's emotion status, showing empathy to other people, inferring other's belief and intention, and performing moral judgments on other's behavior.[39]

These findings suggest that the default mode network is central to our understanding of ourselves and others in our social world. That it enables us to infer the emotional states of others, extend empathy to them, and evaluate the intentions and virtues of their actions. Here's a bit more:

> Decety found that the adult group showed the strongest connectivity between the vMPFC and pSTS/TPJ during viewing of moral actions relative to non-moral actions when compared to other, younger groups (Decety et al., 2012a). Harrison et al. (2008a) compared the FC within the DMN when subjects were resting, judging moral dilemmas, or performing the Stroop task. They found that regions within the DMN, particularly the posterior and anterior cingulated cortex, showed greater correlated activity during the moral dilemma task compared to the resting state. Pujol and colleagues further discovered that, in contrast with control subjects, psychopathic individuals with documented histories of severe criminal offenses showed significantly reduced functional connectivity between the medial frontal cortex (aDMN) and posterior brain areas (pDMN) in the resting state (Pujol et al., 2012).[39]

In other words, the default mode network plays an important role in our values and virtuous behaviors. The very root of our moral judgments and evaluative impulses appear to be socially comparative in nature. And psychopaths, who exhibit low levels of empathy and moral consideration have reduced connectivity in this network.

My understanding is that this network plays a crucial role in healthy mental and social functions. Yes, it is the network responsible for our social comparisons and self-critical ruminations. But it is also behind a core component of pro-social behavior and psychological well-being: identity.

## Domains of Identity

Though self-esteem is generally thought of as an overall metric ("she has high self-esteem"), it seems more likely that we all have a fluid collection of domains through which our self-worth is formed. Our self-esteem seems to depend on the interpersonal context in which our traits were selected, or virtue domains.

Here is one way we might organize these domains based on important evolutionary functions:

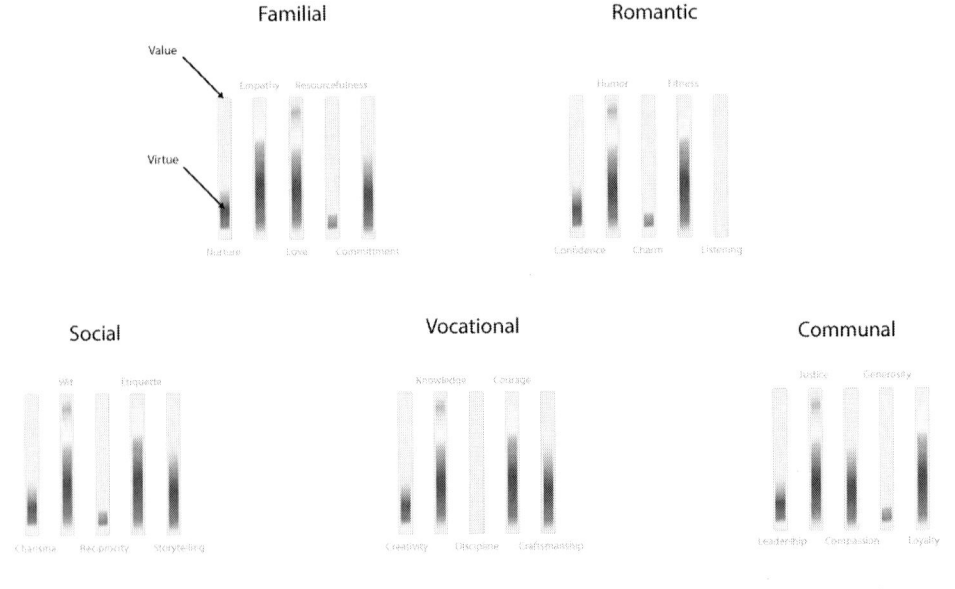

**Familial**
Value
Virtue
Empathy  Resourcefulness
Nurture  Love  Commitment

**Romantic**
Humor  Fitness
Confidence  Charm  Listening

**Social**
Wit  Etiquette
Charisma  Reciprocity  Storytelling

**Vocational**
Knowledge  Courage
Creativity  Discipline  Craftsmanship

**Communal**
Justice  Generosity
Leadership  Compassion  Loyalty

The authors of the paper cited above agree. They suggest that self-esteem can vary within different contexts, like macro tribes, instrumental coalitions and alliances, mating relationships, family groups, and more.

> From an evolutionary perspective, however, we expect that several functionally distinct kinds of relationships are important for different reasons, and that domain-specific sociometers might therefore be associated with each.[13]

Furthermore, it's clear that not all virtues have equal pull on our self-esteem. Understandably, we tend to seek more of the types of social approval that we've gotten in the past. Our brains learned and formed chemical pathways around the particular virtues that have worked for us before.[40]

We continue to build on these pathways throughout our lives. And our self-regard incurs the most damage when we reach a dead end in the types of approval in which we have invested most heavily. If your identity has been built around unsustainable traits—virtues that are no longer working to yield social value, it can require a difficult process of rebuilding.

With all this discussion of social approval, it would be easy to conclude that our self-esteem responds directly to the opinions of our tribe. But this doesn't quite line up with our experience.

When we receive a piece of evidence from the people around us about our own worth, we often spend days or even weeks evaluating and coming up with counter-evidence before a verdict is declared.[41] And it's clear that everyone's self-esteem is based on slightly different traits and values.[42]

Think about the top performers in your occupation or a major interest or hobby of yours. It could be world-class engineers, famous philanthropists, or competitive dog groomers. Whoever it is that is good at things you care about, imagine you walk into a room and overhear a group of them chatting.

To your disbelief, they are talking about you—mocking you. They make clear that they see you as a joke and don't value your skills or virtues. Stings, doesn't it?

Now imagine the same thing happened, but with a group of top performers at things that you couldn't care less about, whether that's musicians, professional hunters, or politicians. They are mocking you as well and suggesting that you are no good at insert thing you don't care about.

I probably don't need to tell you where this is going. The opinions of people who don't fit your personal values will likely have little or no effect on your self-esteem. But the people who have the strengths you aspire to have the power to break you down.

> A person who has high self-esteem regarding his or her intellectual ability may have low self-esteem in athletics, or vice versa. Likewise, self-esteem motivation differs across domains. The person described above may work hard to maintain intellectual self-esteem, but care not a whit for his or her athletic self-esteem. The sociometer model easily explains these differences in how people respond to events that reflect on various domains of self-esteem. The meaning or importance that people attach to particular self-views influences the effects of those self-views on their self-esteem.[12]

This illuminates a point that is obvious upon reflection: It is not the external words or actions of others that impact our self-esteem. It is how their words or actions affect our own beliefs about ourselves, which then determine our self-esteem. It isn't social status or approval that directly regulates our well-being, but the internal simulation that's running in the background.

Humans are unique in our possession of this internal simulator and its intermediary role in our well-being. Other mammals' inner states are determined directly by external cues. But humans have a cognitive mechanism that interfaces between social status and emotion.[43]

> Because increases in self-esteem accompany acceptance and inclusion, and because acceptance and inclusion are associated with positive affective states, people may sometimes behave in ways that maintain self-esteem even in the absence of explicit interpersonal implications. Even so, their behaviors tend to be ones that, if known by others, would increase others' acceptance and inclusion of them.[12]

At times, it can seem like an insult from someone else hurts us directly and instantly. But it only seems this way for plausible insults. If someone gives an absurd insult that clearly has no truth behind it, again there's no sting.

Ultimately, the painful response we sometimes feel when someone disapproves of us is actually the pain of agreeing with them.[44] And these signals of social approval or disapproval can be viewed as tools for virtue cultivation.

When our simulator gets distorted, social information can set it back in its place. Ultimately, if we really are the best at ultimate frisbee, why would all the people around us be acting like we aren't? Maybe it's time to reflect on that.

On the other hand, sometimes our views about ourselves can be perfectly accurate, but someone else can come along and distort our simulation into concluding they aren't. The actions and reactions of others are submitted as evidence for the judge, your social simulator, to consider. Other people will affect your self-esteem to the extent that you agree with them.

The ones who are obviously wrong will hardly move the needle. But when you agree with what that person said, when you feel the rejection is valid, that is when your self-esteem will take a dive, and your mood along with it.

The signals that affect our self-esteem aren't social signals. They are self-signals. We constantly signal our admirable traits to ourselves. And as we will see in the next chapter, there are concrete and compelling reasons to think the result of these self-signals are the determinants of well-being.

Social esteem in humans operates within value-based niches. We each have our own set of values, and we value the values of those who value the values most similar to our values. Was that sentence as much fun to read as it was to write?

As complex as it seems, we can simplify it dramatically when we remember that the person whose opinion will have the greatest effect on your self-esteem will be someone with values identical to yours. In other words: You.

## Key Takeaways:

- The study of human behavior has revealed that we often get to know ourselves by observing our own behaviors—the signals we send to ourselves. We don't just send messages to others through our actions—we send messages to ourselves.

- Because the virtues we exhibit through our behavior are of such great importance for our genes, we evolved an internal simulator for how others perceive us. We unconsciously scan and analyze our own behavior for virtue to appraise how others will view us.

- Sociometer theory argues that self-esteem emerged in the human mind to monitor our success in regard to certain social goals. We evaluate ourselves based on our contributions to our tribe and the socially admired traits we exhibit.

- The default mode network is the network in the brain that is active whenever we aren't engaged in an external task. This network is most likely the neurological basis for the sociometer, and the self-oriented thinking processes that dominate our minds.

- It is not the external words or actions of others that impact our self-esteem. It is how their words or actions affect our own beliefs about ourselves, which then determine our self-esteem.

# 7

# The Stimulus: The Chemical Catalysts of Depression

## The Struggle—March 2020

When we were told we were going to be working from home in 2020, I wasn't totally sure whether it was a deus ex machina saving me from my nasty work situation, or the icing on top that would make everything worse. It was the latter.

The funny thing about having an identity crisis at the start of a pandemic is that just when you would normally be proving all your distorted beliefs false, you become completely cut off from all possible sources of course correction. Your workplace, your community, your routine, your hobbies, all disconnected.

You have nothing to provide you with counter-evidence for all your worst suspicions. You're in a vacuum, left to try to find the signal in silence.

I quietly gave myself permission to do something I had never done before: I let myself go. No, I didn't gain 80 pounds—I actually lost weight, which is rather alarming in my case. I quit playing piano. I quit exercising. I quit reading.

I allowed myself to be lazy—there's a pandemic going on, surely I'm allowed to sit around and play Animal Crossing now. A part of me even thought it would be a fun little experiment, sort of in a prolonged sick-day kind of way.

If you've ever wondered whether letting yourself go might be fun, let me assure you, it isn't. Don't ever do it.

Things only seemed to get worse at work. It became harder and harder to prove my value to a company that was now in dire financial straits. I felt like more of a burden than an asset as I grasped for projects I could contribute to.

And it started to seem that Tory was intentionally sabotaging me wherever she could. She could find a problem in even the best work and magnify it. It's tempting to call it malicious, but I know I was the bad guy getting what I deserved in her story.

I would try to tell myself that it didn't matter. I'm just here to fund my book project at this point. Why should anyone's opinion here matter to me? I might as well have been waiting in line at the DMV when you think about it—this was just a temporary space serving an instrumental goal.

And yet they did matter to me. Most of all, my opinion mattered to me. And it was my opinion of myself that was steadily declining as this strange year progressed.

My sense of self-esteem, which had gone largely unchallenged for the last decade, gradually fell apart. I was now in a constant debate over my worth on a daily basis. I was not the type of person who wrestled with their self-esteem.

I was the one teaching others how to overcome these pesky tendencies. I was literally writing a book on how not to let this happen. I was ashamed that these ruminative thoughts I thought I was long past were even entering my mind.

But how could I move on with my usual, high sense of self-worth when I had this piece of confirmation in front of me? Tory couldn't have been completely wrong about me if she had correctly diagnosed me with a developmental disorder.

Perhaps she was just more honest about the things everyone else was thinking. What other terrible things about me had I been denying my whole life? Did everyone think I was arrogant and abrasive? Were my vocal patterns alienating everyone around me?

I thought about other likely autistic people I had known throughout my life. The people whose mannerisms were jarring and uncomfortable. Who would tell stories that had no point and jokes that didn't make sense. Who were oblivious to social cues and were constantly saying weird, inappropriate things. Oh god, am I that guy?

This diagnosis was calling into question the idea that I had, or ever truly could, overcome my social difficulties. It wasn't just that I was homeschooled—I wasn't just behind. It now seemed that I had been an outsider since before I was born, and always would be in a sense, regardless of the veneer I built around myself.

This is what makes it difficult to find out that you're autistic. You've already been living with the difficulties your whole life—you would think this would be the easy part.

But think about it this way. You've spent your whole life being different because fitting in and being normal wasn't an option. Assuming your self-esteem isn't in the bottom of a dumpster, chances are you've come to pride yourself on being different. You've developed an identity that centers around not being able to be categorized.

You pride yourself on thinking differently, speaking differently, and living differently. You don't pride yourself on the labels and categories and groups you fit into like most people. You pride yourself on the fact that you're unlabellable, ungroupable, uncategorizable.

And now you're being told that you have a label—some would call it a disease—which has determined all these things about you that you thought made you unique. Your unique traits, your unique values, your unique brain, they're not so unique after all.

They're so not-unique, in fact, that they can be captured by a single word. They're quite standard traits. Standard symptoms. You aren't actually different—you just don't belong.

A little-known fact about autism is that finding out you're autistic actually makes you 50% more autistic. You are constantly trying to make "normal" eye contact, "normal" movements, "normal" conversation. And you are all too aware, at every moment, that you are not succeeding at this. A recipe for bad interactions.

The resulting self-consciousness was definitely affecting my ability to connect with others. I was finding simple conversations harder than ever to get through. I would go into them thinking "okay, I'm going to act like a normal person." And then I wouldn't. I felt like I had been transported all the way back to seventh grade.

True, I probably just wasn't aware of all my autistic traits before. But the awareness itself creates a vicious cycle of checking in, criticizing yourself, losing focus on the social task at hand, and checking in some more.

I also started noticing all kinds of clever, unconscious strategies I had been using all these years to divert attention and only show my best side. The way I time greetings to minimize slip-ups. The way I'm always trying to smoothly stop while I'm ahead when a conversation is going well. The way I built a world of creative endeavors to make it seem like I just have better things to do than sit around and socialize. It started to become clear that I had unconsciously been building a facade of distance and mystery to hide my social ineptitude.

My partner was disoriented by the pandemic as well, but she remained a supportive friend and companion during this difficult period. If not for her overflowing sweetness and goofy pranks, I suspect my struggle would have been far deeper and longer lasting.

But it wasn't easy for me to act like things were the same as they had always been—as if I saw myself the same way she saw me. She never lost sight of my virtues, even as I increasingly struggled to find the evidence for them.

But some days, I felt like my negative view of myself was contagious. I was waiting for the moment that she took the cue from Tory, and now from my own beliefs, and lost interest. And this concern added yet another layer to the vicious cycle going around in my mind.

In the past, anytime my self-esteem started to decline or I felt I was personally stagnating, my intuitions have always told me to get out there in the real world. Take on a new challenge, get out of my comfort zone, and meet new people.

But the pandemic shut down this possibility. It was hard to wrap my head around the fact that the world was simply saying "No. You can't do that." I, like many others during this time, felt trapped in a negative spiral of mental health.

In hindsight, I was definitely depressed in 2020. I know, I know, saying you were depressed in 2020 is like saying you don't care for the word "moist." But in my case, the trend toward an identity breakdown was already in motion, and the pandemic was really just the icing on top.

It was mild depression—thoughts of suicide far from my mind. But I couldn't look at myself in the mirror without feeling vaguely ashamed of the person I was. I had this awful, clenching feeling in my stomach preventing me from enjoying myself.

The days would blur together, and they were no longer punctuated by the spurts of excitement and flow I normally felt. I was in a fog.

At one point, I attempted to turn left out of a parking lot without noticing that a car was speeding through one of the inner lanes. I swerved and managed to minimize the damage as we collided, and thankfully no one was hurt. But both of our cars were damaged, and it was entirely my fault. In hindsight, I was really in no mental state to be driving in the first place.

After a few months of laziness, it became clear that this wasn't fun, and it wasn't doing me any good. Convinced by this point that I wasn't fit for the normal work world, I started clawing for other opportunities. I began working constantly, simultaneously trying to redeem myself at my job, impress clients on the side, get new clients, and of course finish and publish the book.

This extreme productivity was not the cure for my mental state, at least not in itself. My bleak mood remained, even as my work output tripled. I became fixated on finishing the book.

I say THE book because it wasn't just supposed to be a book. It was going to be a masterpiece. The culmination of all of my thinking and recreational research over the last decade. I was going to drive my career in reverse and publish my magnum opus first.

By the end of 2020, I was finally ready to launch the book I had spent years on. I had set out to create the book about designing your own mind. It was going to be a 21st-century operating manual for the mind. I had written and rewritten it a million times, invested in editing, publicity, and an entire self-publishing education.

I wanted this book to reach and impact millions of people. I also wanted it to meet my own financial needs and kick-start a sustainable business. I wanted it to be a timeless work of wisdom for generations to come, and simultaneously, a highly marketable and instant bestseller. It was a tall order, but I was prepared to obsess over it to make sure that happened.

During the launch week, I applied everything I had learned about the publishing world. I ran promotions each day to boost sales. I held out for the possibility that it would magically keep selling once the promotions ended. But with each passing day, the sales dropped a little lower. Fifty copies, twenty-five copies, thirteen copies, seven copies... I could see where it was going.

So the book wasn't an instant bestseller. Most books aren't! That didn't mean it wasn't valuable or couldn't serve as a building block for future endeavors. But the evident financial failure of the book wasn't the only thing that challenged my intellectual identity. Then there was the book itself.

I wanted to create a pure, almost geometric manual for operating the mind. I wanted to create the book that I had longed to read. It wouldn't be a run-of-the-mill self-help book, packed with fluffy anecdotes and extraneous life-experiences. It would be all substance. Like a textbook! Everyone loves reading textbooks, right?

I didn't put my name on the cover because I wanted it to feel larger than me. I didn't want people to see it as the musings of a twenty-something guy with a design degree. I wanted them to see it as a culmination of millennia of wisdom, as I saw it. And who cares about peoples' name, face, or life experiences anyway? It's all about the ideas!

The book was a lot like me in a sense. People seemed to perceive it the same way they had always perceived me. Cold and aloof—impressive, yet hard to connect with. It was something to admire from a distance.

Of course much like in my case, there were a idiosyncratic individuals who really loved the book. They left glowing 5-star reviews, leaving outsiders to assume it must be pretty cool once you get to know it. I am deeply grateful I had this group of people to get me through the process.

But I'm not sure I was one of them. By the time I had finished it, I had grown tired of my own writing style and hyper-aware of the book's faults. I was proud of what I had created—as long as I avoided actually reading it.

Even in the middle of the writing process when I began to realize the book was not going to be everything I dreamed it would be, I didn't have a choice but to finish it. I was its hostage.

My inability to fully realize the ambitious aims I had set for the book added an additional layer to my already vulnerable sense of identity during this period. My virtues had been challenged by my work, my social life, and my intellectual work, all in tandem.

The reason my self-esteem eroded at this point wasn't just because of social disapproval. It was because of what the disapproval indicated. I wasn't living up to my own values, and so my brain registered that disapproval as accurate. I wasn't seeing the contrary evidence.

Prior to this experience, I had convinced myself of a story that I had attained a kind of enlightenment. I thought I had fully cracked the code to satisfaction and serenity and thanks to the work I had done to enhance my mind, I was now largely immune to the suffering and setbacks that most people faced.

I had always told myself that life was like a great transoceanic voyage that we each begin in a tiny canoe. Some attempted to sail around the storms in a futile attempt to avoid the hazards. Others got to work fortifying the vessel that would carry them through the storms. Those who spent years building up the vehicle of their mind would someday find themselves on a towering cruise liner, impervious to the turbulence of the ocean.

But at this point, my greatest fear was that all these mental optimizations I had been making were more like sandcastles. Had I been building an elaborate veneer of gradual improvement and self-actualization, just waiting to be decimated by the brutally indifferent waves of life?

# The Chemical Catalyst

We are now venturing into the most treacherous and speculative caverns of our theory. We will turn next to clinical depression and its evolutionary and neurochemical roots.

I'm not cavalier in my treatment of depression—it's a serious topic that many of my friends, family members, and readers, have struggled with. It is out of a deep desire to help that I share the hypothesis that follows.

Though my research, intuition, and experience have made me increasingly confident in the insights that follow, it is ultimately a theory that will take decades to completely validate.

Depression is among the most common psychological disorders, and according to the World Health Organization, it is the single most burdensome and disabling disease in the world.[1]

In addition to its psychological detriments, it is associated with poor physical health and a fair share of physical diseases like fibromyalgia and cardiac problems. It's correlated with high school and college dropout, teenage pregnancy, poor marital quality and divorce, and failure in transitioning from school to work.[2][3][4]

It is the most problematic psychological issue in existence. And the stakes could not be higher for cracking the code and finding solutions.

There is plenty of discussion today about depression, its symptoms, and its treatment. The "what" of clinical depression has been covered extensively, and we know more and more about the physiological explanations, cognitive components, and even lifestyle correlates.[5]

But there is one question that began to haunt me in these types of analyses: Why?

Many people assume that human depression must be a dysfunction or a pathological illness. This is the most immediately intuitive explanation. How could a state so miserable and crippling be healthy or functional?

But something doesn't add up. Given the heritable nature of depression, we would expect the genes that yield it to have been selected against and to make it a rare exception. Yet estimates show that as much as a quarter of the population is likely to develop depression at some point in their lives.[6]

Furthermore, pathologies, like dementia or heart disease, almost always increase with age, and this isn't what we find with depression.[7] It doesn't become more likely as organs deteriorate—people are most likely to have their first experience of depression by early adulthood.[8]

Others assume it is a problem created by the modern, Western world, like obesity.[9] But again, this is problematic. Depression appears across cultures, even in indigenous tribes who live in environments very similar to those of our ancestors.[10]

This brings us to the idea that depression is no pathology. It's not a disease—it's an adaptation. I know, it seems crazy. It might even seem callous to say a condition with such horrific effects isn't a disease. But in order to solve it, we need to understand it clearly.

Depression appears to be a state that we're all capable of falling into. Despite the fact that some people are more genetically prone to depression, people without this predisposition are still observed to get depressed under the right—or rather, wrong conditions.[11]

And it doesn't strike at random. Depression is activated by fairly reliable triggers, such as the loss of a loved one or a job.[12] And it triggers a coordinated set of responses in the body, mind, and behavior.[13]

But depression is truly bewildering from an evolutionary perspective. Why would natural selection favor genes for a state that made us miserable, unmotivated, and worse at nearly everything?

Several theories have been proposed. One argues that the state evolved to conserve energy and resources.[14] Another suggests that depression makes us better at analytical rumination and social problem-solving.[15] And yet another argues it came about to keep us close to our friends and loved ones and elicit help in times of need.[16]

But all of these have major issues. For one thing, depressed individuals show a strong inclination toward isolation and irritability.[17] If the goal were to bring us closer to other members of our tribe, it seems about as effective as trying to heal a wound with a crossbow.

If the (dubious) improvements in analysis associated with depression were that important to our genes, wouldn't they have been selected for by themselves?[18] Natural selection would not have preserved all the other crippling byproducts of depression, which are essentially poison to our genes, if it just wanted us to be a little better at solving problems.

And perhaps most crucially, none of these theories explain the egocentric nature of depression. No, I'm not saying depressed people are egotistical in the traditional sense—quite the opposite. They despise themselves.

Almost invariably, across cultures, depression is linked to negative beliefs about the self and self-referential rumination.[19] Those who are severely depressed often genuinely believe they are worthless and utterly unlovable.[20] To explain the function of depression, we have to explain its connection to the self.

Low self-esteem is a hallmark of depression—the link between the two phenomena is strong, robust, and well-documented.[21] [22] [23] [24] But today, many people seem to assume that depression is a disease that causes low self-worth and negative self-beliefs. The critical rumination characteristic of depression is presented as a symptom.[25]

But I think this view gets it backwards. Depression doesn't cause low self-esteem. Low self-esteem causes depression. And quite a bit of data supports this view of the relationship—a major meta-analysis of longitudinal studies strongly favored the view that low self-esteem contributes to depression over the opposite relationship that depression erodes self-esteem.[26]

In the previous section, I argued in favor of the sociometer theory of self-esteem: that self-esteem evolved to simlulate social esteem. I proposed that the default mode network was the core command post for this complex simulation.

But what does it do with this information, and why? To understand the functional connection between self-esteem and mood, we need to consider the lives of our evolutionary ancestors.

If you had lived in the hunter-gatherer age, you probably would have lived in a nomadic tribe of around one hundred fifty members. Your tribe was everything. You spent your days collecting food for your tribe. You spent your evenings sitting around the fire with your tribe.[27]

All of your friends were in your tribe, and so were all of your romantic options. So remaining in good social standing would have been absolutely critical.

If your fellow tribe-members decided you were a lazy freeloader, a violent jerk, or a creep, they might turn against you. They might exile you, which would have been very bad news given that your tribe provided you with food, protection, and companionship.[28] They might kill you.[29]

Or worst of all, they might talk shit about you behind your back. If you failed to align with the values of your tribe, the most likely outcome is simply that you would end up with low social status. You might end up being mocked and dismissed, and would not be a desirable mate.[30]

Though you might still survive through the winters, your genes might not fare as well. And given that your brain was programmed to protect your genes, failing to pass them on qualifies as an existential risk.[31]

For this reason, the social simulator in your brain was designed to induce moods that cause you to act in the best interest of your genes. Self-esteem exists fundamentally to upregulate (increase) or downregulate (decrease) certain chemicals and mood states in the brain.

Based on what your internal simulator concludes about you, it will deliver a different cocktail of hormones and neurotransmitters. When it determines that you are "approvable" it will deliver chemicals that make you want to get out there and show yourself off. Display your virtues. Interact. Show the world what's so great about you.

But what if it decides you are not approvable? When the people around you don't approve of you, the most important thing you can do from a genetic standpoint is stop. "STOP!" Your genes would yell if they could. "Whatever you're doing, stop before you get us all killed. We would literally prefer you go and pull on a wild tiger's tail than piss off your tribe."

And this is when you would start to get depressed. No, I don't mean you would get severely clinically depressed. Just slightly more depressed than before. Your brain would slightly adjust the dials of your neurotransmitters to change your social strategy.[32]

We said that self-esteem was like the fuel gauge for social esteem. And much like the low fuel light in a car, depression is meant to tell you to stop driving. Stop going on as if everything were fine. Everything isn't fine. You are going to fail to pass on your genes. You have to stop and find a way to refuel.

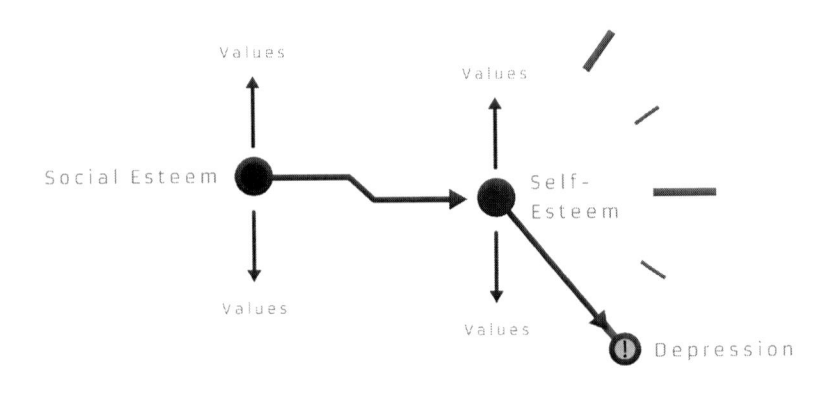

```
         Values                  Values
           ↑                       ↑              /
           |                       |             /
Social Esteem ●————————————→ ● Self-         —
           |                  Esteem          
           ↓                       ↓             \
         Values                  Values           ●  Depression
```

If you were socially awkward and unsuccessfully trying to be cool in tribal times, a dose of depression would have let you know it wasn't working. It would force you to stop and consider pivoting to becoming a valued member of the tribe through generous contributions, hidden talents, or deadpan humor.

Your tribe might have said, "Yeah, we know you're not the Fonz. That is a futuristic anachronism given that the year is 52,036 BCE, and yet somehow still an outdated reference. Why would you even attempt to be like a 20th-century sex symbol portrayed by Henry Winkler when you live in a hunter-gatherer tribe? If anything, you should be more like Andy Griffith. Anyway, we're glad you've been taken down a couple notches and look forward to spending time with the new and improved you."

When your brain determines that you are not praiseworthy in a particular domain, it down-regulates signaling behaviors, gets you to play the social game on defense, and decreases motivation and energy.[33] It gets you to let off the gas of the current status goals you've set and promotes a loosening of your self-concept in that domain to facilitate a more adaptive restructuring of identity.[34]

A depressed state makes you socially risk-averse—it makes you more likely to interpret social cues as negative.[35] Like a smoke detector, it must be oversensitive to make sure you don't mistake disapproval for approval and continue pushing ahead with a failing social strategy.

It has been found that those with high self-esteem adopt social strategies that capitalize on the approval of others and broadcast their positive attributes.[36] They exhibit self-serving biases like the fundamental attribution error and generally believe that they are slightly more competent, likable, and praiseworthy than they actually are.[37]

Those with low self-esteem, on the other hand, are found to unconsciously adopt strategies that minimize the risk of offending someone or being rejected. They embody what is called depressive realism, or a reduced tendency to be biased in their own favor.[38]

But how does the brain actually make these changes?

## The Neurobiology of Depression

Depression is marked by a number of neurochemical patterns. Depressed individuals are thought to have high levels of cortisol, which plays a major role in our physical response to stress. The prolonged release of cortisol is probably responsible for the extremely unpleasant, chronically anxious feeling associated with depression.[39]

They have low levels of norepinephrine, which typically increases active body movement in response to stress.[40] And they have low levels of dopamine, which plays a major role in the pursuit of rewards. These two likely contribute to the enduring feelings of fatigue and the lack of interest in pursuing goals or hobbies we see in depression.[41]

Most famously, they have low serotonin. Serotonin has a reputation for being the "happy chemical" of the brain, but its role is far more complex than this. And though it can't be measured in the living brain, measures of serotonin in the bloodstream, urine, and cerebrospinal fluid strongly suggest that levels are notably lower in depressed individuals.[42]

Unfortunately, this fact has led to the popular notion that depression is caused by the single factor of serotonin deficiency. This oversimplified perspective, however, was debunked decades ago, and persists largely due to pharmaceutical propaganda.[43]

We now understand that serotonin's role in depression is far more complex than any deficiency model can explain. In his work on depression, *Lost Connections*, Johan Hari argues that there is little to no evidence for the serotonin deficiency theory of depression, and that this should limit our confidence in antidepressants as a panacea.[44]

And he's right. But he wouldn't be right if he said serotonin does not play a huge role in depression and mood. The link between serotonin and depression is one of correlation, not causation. Low self-esteem is like the virus that causes a cold - low serotonin is like a runny nose. Yes, it happens, but treating it directly does nothing to affect the root cause.

A decrease in serotonin is a part of the brain's coordinated response to low perceived social value and self-esteem, not the original cause. Many people like the idea that a simple chemical imbalance could explain this horrible state. They see this view as a step toward destigmatizing the condition. It seems to remove potential blame from patients themselves.

But it also removes opportunity. Hari makes a compelling case that the "chemical imbalance" theory actually adds stigma to the condition.[44] If depression is a disease caused by an isolated brain malfunction, then your only hope is that a chemical drug will fix it. Unfortunately, it generally doesn't, but we'll cover this more in part three.[45]

There are a few behaviors that are associated with serotonin in mammals from mice, to chimps, to humans. It reduces aggression, it increases short-term impulse-control, and it profoundly enhances the desire to socialize.[46][47]

Serotonin can be viewed as the confidence chemical.[48] Yes, its release feels good, so it isn't entirely wrong to call it the happiness chemical. But chemicals don't exist in our brains to make us feel good. They exist to get us to do things.

Social explanations of serotonin regulation have often centered around status rankings or dominance hierarchies. This is based on the observation of other social animals, whose behaviors are often determined by rigid status rankings.[49]

In many species, from cows, to gorillas, to the notorious lobsters, males fight for access to mates. The most physically dominant are able to rise in status, access more mating opportunities, and experience increases in serotonin.[49]

The losing males experience a decrease in serotonin levels and a predictable pattern of behavior that often involves submission until they find an opportune time to overtake the dominant males.[49]

In one study, the dominant male in a group of vervet monkeys had twice as much serotonin in its bloodstream as the other monkeys in the group. When they isolated the dominant monkey, its serotonin levels dropped sharply. But when a new dominant male stepped in to take the former one's place, its serotonin levels spiked—that is until the original monkey was returned to the group and everyone's serotonin returned to their original levels.[50]

But despite what seedy bars or middle school parking lots might lead you to think, physical dominance is not, and was not the primary method of determining social esteem for our ancestors. Males don't just compete to impress females—both sexes vie for status and mate choice.[51] And as we established in the previous chapter, social esteem in humans is determined by multivariate metrics of social value, not a simple hierarchy of aggression.

Serotonin has deep origins in social approval.[52] And though the human brain and social landscape are far more complex, serotonin still appears to exist as a stimulus for social striving.[48]

Many studies support the idea that depression is closely connected to the default mode network, which seems to be the basis for self-esteem. One found that depression is characterized by a failure to properly down-regulate self-referential ruminations and activity in the default mode network.[53] Another found that an increased, negative self-focus and feelings of hopelessness in depression were tied to abnormal functioning in the default mode network.[54]

There are some close connections between serotonin regulation and the default mode network as well. Altered connectivity in the default mode network has been linked to lower cerebral serotonin synthesis.[55] And there is evidence that an important part of the default mode network, the ventromedial prefrontal cortex, directly controls the release of serotonin and socioemotional behavior.[56]

One study found that deep brain stimulation of the vmPFC induced a sustained increase in hippocampal serotonin levels.[57] One of the other two regions of the network, the posterior cingulate cortex (PCC) has been linked to major depression as well. One particular part of this region known as Brodmann area 25 has been closely linked to depression.[58]

This region of the default mode network is known to play a role in self-esteem and is extremely rich in serotonin transporters.[59] The process of electrically stimulating this part of the brain has shown incredible promise for treating severe cases of depression.[60]

To be clear, the significance of these findings is not that we should all be drilling electrodes into these regions of our brains—a highly invasive and dangerous procedure—to keep the happy chemicals flowing. It's that there seems to be strong neurological support that self-esteem exists to calculate what neurochemical state to put you in.

The default mode network is the simulator in your brain that appraises you and the virtues you are exercising. Its activity and connectivity indicate the level of selfhood, or self-referential evaluation you engage in.

And this network tells the chemicals in your brain how confident, happy, and motivated you should feel. To bring about the optimal mood to either show off your virtues with vitality or keep a low profile.

Most notably, it determines how much serotonin should be released in your brain. Serotonin is the feeling of confidence. It's the feeling of pride. It's the feeling of being a person you love.

Decreases in serotonin make you feel unconfident, humbled, and unhappy. When your brain keeps determining that you lack the virtues needed for social approval, it lowers serotonin (and a host of other chemicals) to the point that you have consistently low mood, low vitality, and low self-regard.

The unfortunate byproduct of this behavioral scale is the tragic mood state we know as depression. It seems cruel for evolution to program such a painful and crippling condition into our minds for the sole purpose of optimizing social status and genetic outcomes. But I think the counterintuitive contrast between the tragedy of depression and the calculating indifference of evolution is a big part of the reason why this perspective has evaded theorists and researchers so far.

Clinical depression is best viewed as the bottom end of a sliding mood scale. Most people find themselves gradually moving up and down along this scale, receiving higher and lower levels of neurotransmitters based on their mental simulator's calculations. But when you fall all the way to the low end of this scale, you can reach cripplingly low levels of mood and motivation.

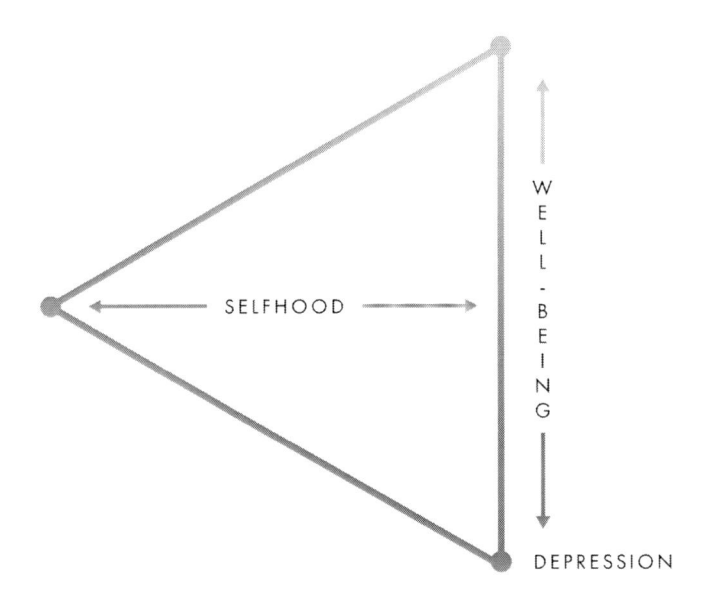

# The Domains of Depression

> Positive emotion alienated from the exercise of character leads to emptiness, to inauthenticity, to depression, and, as we age, to the gnawing realization that we are fidgeting until we die.
>
> —**Martin Seligman**, *Authentic Happiness*[61]

We know more about the lifestyle correlates of depression now than we ever have before. We know that the initial onset of depression is very often triggered by some type of loss. It can be the loss of a loved one, the loss of a job, or the loss of a cherished aspect of one's identity.[62] And this might lead some to think it is a straightforward reaction to painful experiences.

But it is also very often triggered by things that most would call a gain. An apparent upgrade in lifestyle is almost as likely to result in depression as loss. In general, significant life changes seem to be the strongest indication of depression.[5]

This could paint the deceptive picture that a change in lifestyle is more likely to make you depressed than happier. In fact, the opposite is true.[63] It isn't that change leads to depression often—we usually adapt to change, learn from past experiences, and build equal or greater levels of virtue into our new lifestyles.

But depression is most often precipitated by change. In other words, we are most susceptible to depression when our virtue domains are in flux. We might get depressed after losing a relationship that once served as a core domain for our strengths, getting a promotion through which we struggle to integrate our skills, or moving to a new city where we have to rebuild our virtue domains from scratch.

Over the course of our lives, we form a sense of identity around particular virtues. The ones we were rewarded for as a child. The ones we believe make us great. Dr. Loretta Breuning illustrates how our brains learn to repeat the behaviors that brought social rewards in the past.

> When you get respect, serotonin paves neural pathways and motivates you to seek more respect in that particular way. Imagine that you cooked dinner for your family when you were young and got great recognition. Serotonin built a pathway that expects cooking to make you feel good… The chemicals of emotion are like paving on your neural pathways.[64]

But when the behaviors that have brought rewards in the past cease to deliver, we reach a point of identity failure. Depression occurs when you hit a dead end on the pathways on which your self-esteem has been built.

Your virtue strategies are not working, and you need to detach from them and start building toward new paths. It's your brain's way of telling you you've got to stop pushing down this path because it's not working. You must carve out a new path.

The extent that the loss of a loved one ends up resulting in deep grief and depression is the extent to which that relationship had served as a core virtue domain for the individual. If you were not reliant on that relationship for the exercise of your virtues, you would move on from their loss relatively quickly without any major damage to your long-term well-being.

We saw that winning the lottery or losing one's legs didn't bring their expected happiness returns. And consistently, changes in well-being, or even depression, seem not to correspond to the external losses or gains in our lives, but to their effects on the virtue we are able to bring to them.

There is a strong correlation between depression and the presence of certain virtue domains. If you are unemployed, your odds of depression jump up.[65] If you don't have a romantic partner, your odds of depression jump up.[66] If you don't have any friends, your odds of depression jump up.[15] In other words, the more virtue domains you are cut off from, the more likely you are to be depressed.

Why do we observe that depression is significantly more common in women than men?[67] One explanation would be that women are systematically held back from bringing their full, innate virtues into the world. Perhaps bias and sexism are more likely to keep women out of virtue domains that would bring well-being. In other words, oppression leads to depression.

Another explanation some would offer is that women feel pressured to enter virtue domains that may not be most rewarding to them, in the name of equality. In other words, the backlash to oppression leads to depression.

If I had to pick one, I lean toward the former. But it's likely a combination. Women likely get more confusing messages from society about who they're supposed to become and which virtue domains they should enter, and this leads them off of their virtue paths in higher percentages.

Why does depression seem to have skyrocketed in young people recently?[68] One of the most prominent explanations is that social media is to blame.[69] If the link between social status, self-esteem, and depression are what they appear to be, it's really no surprise that teenage depression rates have skyrocketed as social status has become mediated through new, questionable avenues. Social media imposes a new system for determining individual worth that scarcely resembles our evolutionary environment.

What about the genetic basis for depression?[70] Any evolutionary adaptation is going to be genetic, and hence there will inevitably be genetic variation within populations. As far as we can tell, everyone has "depression genes" that will be activated in certain circumstances, but everyone's systems are calibrated in slightly different ways, and some people have more or less sensitive systems.

Since depression is facilitated by chemicals, there is always the possibility that physiological issues could activate the system at the wrong time. But given the extreme genetic risk in activating a program as crippling as depression at the wrong time, I'm inclined to think this is a rare exception.

Most of our sociometers work properly. But we must keep in mind that they evolved in the context of our evolutionary environment, not the modern world, and that they operate through statistical probabilities, not perfect knowledge.

In the next few chapters, I will make clear some of the implications for this theory of depression. For now, understand that our mood states can be viewed along a vertical scale. Based on its calculations, the social simulator in your mind will move you up or down along this scale.

When the system likes what it sees, meaning it deems you "approvable," it moves you up on the sliding scale. When it deems you "not approvable," it moves you down.

This scale represents a natural red-light/green-light mechanism, specifically in regard to social contribution. It tells us whether to play on offense or defense. It creates changes in the brain and regulates a whole cocktail of chemicals.

So depression is the bottom end of this sliding scale that was designed to regulate social behavior. But as I have emphasized, this is a book about the opposite of depression. So what is at the top end?

## Key Takeaways:

- Because social standing and approval was so important for our ancestors, we evolved a sociometer capable of triggering mood states. These states cause us to take actions that are more likely to result in positive social outcomes.

- The default mode network's purpose is to induce moods that cause you to act in the best interest of your genes. Self-esteem exists fundamentally to increase or decrease certain chemicals in the brain to bring about adaptive behaviors.

- The tragic condition of clinical depression is not pathology, but an evolutionary adaptation. It is most likely a part of a natural "red light" mechanism to get us to lay low, keep us from damaging our social standing, and promote socially risk-averse behavior.

- Depression is not caused fundamentally by a chemical imbalance, but by identity failure. We get depressed when we, for one reason or another, fail to see evidence of our own virtues in our behavior, and our sociometer authorizes a defensive social strategy.

- Depression occurs when we hit a dead end on the pathways on which our self-esteem has been built. But it represents the bottom end of this sliding scale that was designed to regulate our behavior, and it is also possible for us to approach the top end of that scale.

# 8

# The Synthesis: Virtue Self-Signaling Theory

## The Opposite of Depression

I have now argued that clinical depression lies at one end of a natural well-being scale. We get depressed when our brains conclude we are not behaving admirably in the core domains of our lives. We are failing to signal our own strengths to ourselves, and our brains respond pragmatically to these perceptions.

Chemical changes, like decreased serotonin, initiate a strategy of lying low and restructuring goals. The brain gives the red light and initiates a program that will minimize social damage while we reform our identity and virtue strategies. But don't let the depressing data behind this argument distract you from the positive side of this mechanism.

The top end of that very same mood scale is the state of eudaimonia. As you may recall, the ancient Greeks believed that the highest form of happiness, or the good life, was a state called eudaimonia. But is it really reasonable to say eudaimonia is the opposite of depression?

Well, what core traits define depression in humans? For starters, I would say 1) low mood, 2) low vitality, and 3) low and strong sense of self. You feel bad, you have no motivation, and you are very focused on your personal inadequacies.[1]

So it follows that the opposite state would be one of 1) high mood, 2) high vitality, and 3) high and strong sense of self. And this is exactly how the ancients described eudaimonia.[2]

The third point is essential. The role of the self is often left out of our understanding of both depression and well-being. But it isn't left out of our minds, even when we would like it to be.

Those who are depressed don't just feel bad—they feel bad about themselves.[3] And those who have achieved eudaimonia don't just feel good—they feel good about themselves.

> When you are depressed, you invariably believe that you are worthless. The worse the depression, the more you feel this way. You are not alone. A survey by Dr. Aaron Beck revealed that over 80 percent of depressed patients expressed self-dislike. Furthermore, Dr. Beck found that depressed patients see themselves as deficient in the very qualities they value most highly: intelligence, achievement, popularity, attractiveness, health, and strength.
>
> —David Burns, *Feeling Good*[4]

Negative self-evaluations are a staple of depression. And the ancient Greeks were adamant that eudaimonia was attained through virtue, and virtue alone. We could be happy, they insisted, to the extent that we exercised admirable traits in our actions and decisions.

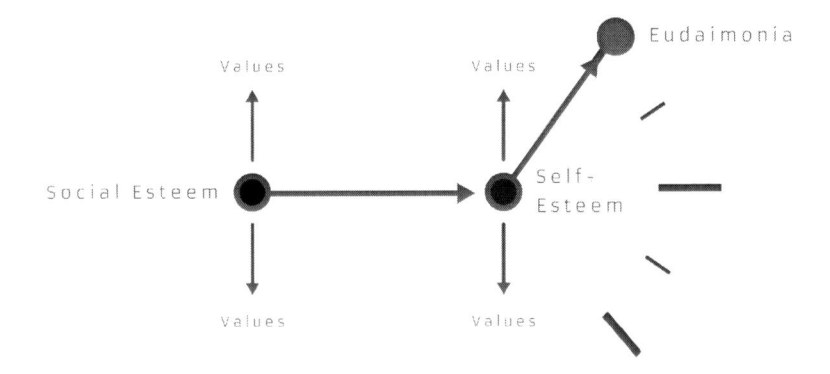

```
                    Values              Values            Eudaimonia
                      ↑                   ↑                  ●
                                                           ╱
                                                         ╱
Social Esteem    ●  ─────────────→   ●     Self-      ─
                                           Esteem
                                                         ╲
                      ↓                   ↓                ╲
                    Values              Values              ╲
```

But the study of virtue didn't die in ancient Greece. It has been revitalized within positive psychology. Martin Seligman has made and tested a hypothesis much like what the ancients proposed: Your personal virtues are at the heart of your happiness.[5]

And Seligman explains the reason why cultivating these traits results so consistently in increased well-being and decreased depression:

> When well-being comes from engaging our strengths and virtues, our lives are imbued with authenticity. Feelings are states, momentary occurrences that need not be recurring features of personality. Traits, in contrast to states, are either negative or positive characteristics that recur across time and different situations, and strengths and virtues are the positive characteristics that bring about good feeling and gratification. Traits are abiding dispositions whose exercise makes momentary feelings more likely.[6]

This distinction captures why the z-axis is the true path to happiness. Though both the y and z axes may operate through chemicals like serotonin, the traits you develop are enduring properties of your mind that will continually and increasingly pay off as you build them. External accomplishments may quickly fade, but your strengths are yours to keep.

The ancient Greeks were ahead of their time. They discovered one of the most profound insights into human nature—something deep in the programming of our brains. They understood that there was some mechanism, some algorithm inside our brains that was measuring our virtue and rewarding or punishing us accordingly.

This mechanism at the heart of both depression and its opposite is integral to understanding the human mind and well-being. Up to this point, it has evaded proper understanding, and, as a result, limited our potential for treatment and growth. And I want to bring it to light.

## The Formula

On the cover of my first book, *Designing the Mind*, there is an illustration of the brain made up of circuit-like "algorithms."

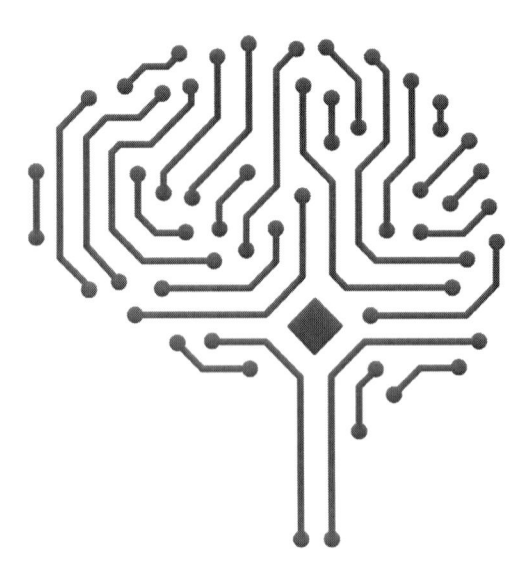

The image represents the many ingrained tendencies, habits, and reactions that make up our habitual state of being: our psychological software. But occasionally, a reader will ask me about the diamond-shaped "chip" that appears in the middle. What does this symbol represent?

That chip represents a mechanism at the heart of human nature—at the center of the human mind. A mechanism that is both highly prevalent in, and largely unique to the human mind. It's a kind of master algorithm. I call it the self-appraisal system.

It's the system that observes our own behavior for signs of virtue and admirability. The system that simulates social status and approval. The system that dictates our mood to regulate our social behavior. It's the sociometer. The default mode network. The ego.

The term "appraisal" captures two different elements of this system. One is the evaluation of worth, in the familiar sense in which one has their home appraised. The other is the related clinical concept of cognitive appraisal, in which we ruminate over situations or ourselves and decide how to interpret them, which determines our emotional response.[7]

The self-appraisal system compares actions with our values to determine how closely they align with them. It determines our own worth based on how closely our own total virtues align with those values. And it provides a chemical catalyst for corresponding behaviors.

We're now in a position to connect all the dots of this theory. Virtues exist because values exist—we evolved to signal our fitness to our tribe and to evaluate others through the lens of our values. We've all been endowed with unique virtues to demonstrate our social value.

Self-esteem is there to monitor and simulate our levels of social approval. Our brains observe our behavior and determine how admirable others are likely to find us. They reflect and ruminate over our strengths and contributions, any time we are not actively engaged in another activity, in order to optimize our behavioral strategies.

Certain neurochemicals like serotonin have the role of regulating our social strategies and rewarding virtue according to the conclusions of this self-appraisal system. Our mood states are there to trigger behaviors and actions that facilitate social, and hence self, esteem and approval.

The varying levels of depression we may experience are there to give us the red light and get us to play social defense when our virtues aren't making their way out. Low mood results in risk-averse social strategies that minimize damage to our social standing.

And the opposite extreme of this mood scale, eudaimonia, exists to give us the green light and get us to play social offense when we are successfully cultivating and exercising our virtues. To make us feel good, energized, and confident so as to put our virtues on display and take advantage of their social benefits.

This system determines our overall well-being. This system is the reason why what I call the third dimension of happiness, the z-axis of virtue, is the true regulator of well-being. Happiness is an evolutionary tool. And to realize maximum well-being and avoid depression, we need to understand and learn to wield this tool effectively.

We are now ready to construct our complete framework. I call it Virtue Self-Signaling Theory. This theory, and its name, incorporates several important elements of the argument I have put forward in this book.

The "Virtue" component evokes the ancient virtue theories that intuitively understood the link between virtue and well-being. "Virtue signaling" refers to the coevolution of our virtues and values as social signals and fitness indicators. "Self-Signaling" captures the important idea that our mood state is determined by the evaluations of the self-appraisal system, and the virtues we signal to ourselves.

Taken together, this synthesis forms a whole that is greater than the sum of its parts. Geoffrey Miller and others have shown that our virtues had their roots in fitness signaling, sexual selection, and social approval.[8] Mark Leary's sociometer theory showed that self-esteem is an internal simulator for social status.[9]

Aaron Beck's work on cognitive therapy showed us that depression and self-esteem were intimately connected, and that the most effective treatments involved putting these virtues into action and learning to see them clearly.[10] And Martin Seligman has demonstrated what the ancient virtue theorists proposed, that the exercise of our strengths is at the heart of happiness.[11]

The final task is to piece them all together. Now here is that formula you've been waiting on:

**$E = nV^s$**

Here is how it translates: Eudaimonia = net Virtue self-signaled. Let's break it down further.

E, or Eudaimonia, is the holy grail of practical philosophy, the ultimate measure of the good life, and the measure of happiness that we prize above all else. nV, or net Virtue, is simply the sum of all your virtue. $^s$, or self-signaled, specifies that your virtues must be successfully signaled to yourself to factor into the equation. Successfully signaling virtues to yourself requires both 1. behaviorally sending the signal of a virtue, and 2. cognitively receiving this signal.

Now, let's return to our three-dimensional centerpiece:

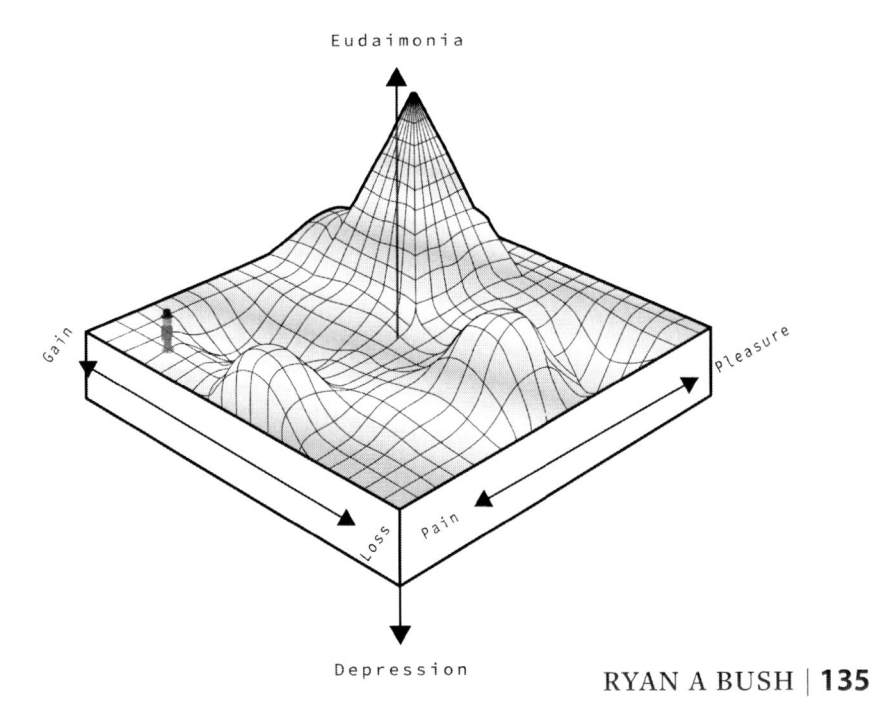

We understand that the z-axis, represented by the vertical topography seen in the mountains and valleys, refers to virtue. But now we can see, like the suffering and ecstasy on the extreme ends of the x-axis, depression and eudaimonia lie at opposite extremes of the z-axis.

When you find yourself at a place in life in which you are neglecting to exert your virtues, when you are failing to receive the signal, or when you cannot find domains through which you can integrate your strengths, you sink toward depression.

When you find yourself at a place in which you have deeply integrated your virtues into your lifestyle—when you are sending and receiving powerful signals of admirability in your daily activities, you climb toward self-admiration and eudaimonia.

The vertical scale you see in this diagram, which runs from the negative selfhood of depression to the positive selfhood of eudaimonia is the z-axis. The place on this scale that your self-appraisal system decides you belong determines the deep satisfaction you will feel in your life.

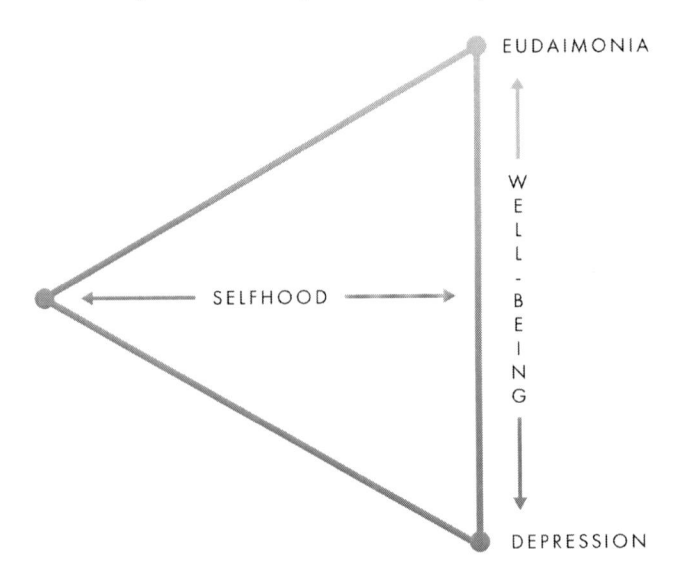

So often we talk about becoming a better person with no clear idea of what that means. Here is what it means: increasing the net virtue you are able to signal.

> Herein is my formulation of the good life: Using your signature strengths every day in the main realms of your life to bring abundant gratification and authentic happiness.
>
> —**Martin Seligman**, *Authentic Happiness*[6]

If the idea of living to "signal" or display your virtues rubs you the wrong way, I can't entirely blame you. Though I think our well-being is wired to respond to the signals we send to ourselves, there are plenty of more compelling ways of thinking about this task in our lives.

Your job is to exercise your virtues. To model them. To share them with the world. It must be your goal to bring your unique strengths to life. And this is what it means to live a great life.

## In Praise of Pride

> We like to speak casually about "sibling rivalry," as though it were some kind of byproduct of growing up, a bit of competitiveness and selfishness of children who have been spoiled, who haven't yet grown into a generous social nature. But it is too all-absorbing and relentless to be an aberration, it expresses the heart of the creature: the desire to stand out, to be the one in creation. When you combine natural narcissism with the basic need for self-esteem, you create a creature who has to feel himself an object of primary value: first in the universe, representing in himself all of life.
>
> —**Ernest Becker**, *The Denial of Death*[12]

The self-appraisal system is the mechanism that's been hiding in plain sight. And the reason it has remained hidden from popular and scientific understanding is that it is seen as somehow distasteful.

We dislike the idea that we would be so self-obsessed, so status-obsessed, that a healthy brain's default activity would center around the contemplation of ourselves and our place in a social hierarchy. Just as we were once in denial that the earth revolves around the sun, today we are in denial that the human mind revolves around the self.

The very notion of self is taboo. We are expected to live our lives without regard for ourselves, despite the fact that the need to be special, to be seen, and to be approved of is at the center of all human motivation. When we do recognize the central place of self-esteem in our innate wiring, we pathologize it and tie it to unhealthy deficiencies.[13]

But counterintuitively, building a strong ego doesn't make you seem more egotistical. It makes you seem less egotistical. The people who seem egotistical have poorly designed egos. Their self-regard is fragile and tied to traits that may not even have a real basis in their behavior.[14]

I was once described by a podcast host as having "enlightened energy," saying I seemed egoless. He was surprised when I pointed out that I was in fact quite "egofull" and that I consider this a good thing. Often the most altruistic, purpose-driven individuals are. They may not want to admit it, even to themselves, but their contributions all flow out of their self-actualization. Their virtue overflows.

Depression is self-dissatisfaction. Eudaimonia is self-satisfaction. Yes, the ultimate metric of human well-being is self-centered. Humans are self-centered. Denial of this fact will get you nowhere—it certainly won't get you to happiness.

This is the fundamental reason why no translation of the word "eudaimonia" is adequate. Happiness, well-being, flourishing... these terms simply do not indicate the self-oriented nature of human beings.

The ancient Greeks knew this. Their conception of eudaimonia fully captures that the good life was the result of being an admirable person, not just having good life circumstances. But do not assume this self-oriented view of personal well-being diminishes the role of love and relationships in our well-being.

We don't just care deeply about our own virtues and how greatly our relationships enable us to bring them out. We care deeply about the cultivation of virtue in our loved ones. In fact, thinking about the type of happiness we want for our children can bring our intuitive understanding of our own happiness into perspective.

In her book on Epicureanism, *Living for Pleasure*, Emily Austin offers a thought experiment, pointing out what we are really saying when we wish future happiness for someone's child.

> We are not simply wishing that their child will feel good however she lives her life, even if she passes her days as a friendless narcissist who sells drugs to children. Wishing someone happiness comes with rich details that include things like healthy relationships, virtuous actions, and meaningful pursuits. This is even more clear when we imagine happiness for our own children.[15]

A book called *Virtue Ethics: A Contemporary Introduction* makes a similar point about well-being:

> Some philosophers claim that the virtues are necessary for happiness, that for someone to live a good or happy life, they have to possess the virtues. There is some intuitive support for this idea. It seems plausible that parents encourage their children to become kind, generous and just, not just for the sake of those around them but also for their own sakes. Being selfish, cruel, or dishonest can make one miserable.[16]

I have presented a theory that the virtues we exercise are inextricably tied to our well-being, on an evolutionary and neurobiological level. But thinking about the life you want for your children—who you want your children to become—can bring the real nature of the good life clearly into view.

We want our children to be happy in a deep sense—the kind of happiness that comes from strong character and genuine, high self-esteem. We want them to have reason to feel good about the people they are, not just to feel good.[17] And this is what we want for ourselves too.

When I argue that happiness is self-centered, I do not mean "selfish," in the traditional sense that contrasts with "altruistic." I mean that the self is at the center of our motivations and concerns. The self is at the center of altruism. Our goals, our drives, and our values begin at the center, and they branch out from there. And when we do good in the world, we feel pride in ourselves.

Nietzsche often talked about what he called the gift-giving virtue, and the idea behind it was that genuine contribution comes from a place of pouring into yourself, to the point that your gifts overflow. Not helping others out of obligation, pity, or self-sacrifice.[18]

His ideal of the "overman" was not the barbaric and egocentric being it is sometimes interpreted to be. Nietzsche argued that a focus on oneself needn't come at the expense of others. Although pity and a contracted kind of selfishness were harmful for everyone, the gift-giving virtue represented a healthy kind of generosity in which "you force all things to and into yourself that they may flow back out of your well as the gifts of your love."[19]

> [The modern] individual focuses too narrowly on his own short lifespan… and wants to pluck the fruit himself from the tree he plants, and so no longer likes to plant those trees that demand a century of constant tending and are intended to provide shade for long successions of generations.
>
> —**Friedrich Nietzsche**, Human, All Too Human[20]

Nietzsche believed that serving one's own health was conducive to altruism, and not something to feel guilty about.[21] When you picture a modern-day Übermensch, don't think Putin—think Parton (as in Dolly Parton). Picture someone striving for the actualization of their own potential, and benefiting the world with their gifts and generosity in the process.

Throughout Abraham Maslow's work, he frequently shows how apparent dichotomies of human nature actually merge together. He saw ways to merge facts with values. Ways to merge the scientific with the spiritual. And ways to merge altruism and egoism. When we fully comprehend the meaning his notes were meant to capture, we can understand how these boundaries dissolve for ourselves.[22]

> An interesting aspect of the B-Values is that they transcend many of the traditional dichotomies, such as selfishness and unselfishness, flesh and spirit, religious and secular. If you are doing the work that you love and are devoted to the value that you hold highest, you are being as selfish as possible, and yet are also being unselfish and altruistic......When I pursue 'selfish' gratifications, I automatically help others, and when I try to be altruistic, I automatically reward and gratify myself also.
>
> —**Abraham Maslow**, *The Farther Reaches of Human Nature*[22]

Maslow referred to a set of higher needs that provide higher pleasure. When we get in touch with our deepest "instinctoid" nature, we get in touch with these higher pleasures and unlock a higher level—you might even say another dimension of happiness.[23]

Happiness and goodness, he argued, were not at odds with one another, but effectively synonymous. And he used the concept of "metamotivation" to communicate how these happier, more developed beings were fueled toward their altruistic missions.[22]

Maslow even goes so far as to suggest that there are metapathologies—psychological disorders that appear to stem from an absence of the Being values he lists. Is this not an ultimate, selfish reason to bring these ideals into our character? That we may face emotional diseases in their absence?[22]

Some people believe they simply lack the selfless altruism needed to overcome their ego and do great things in the world. But Maslow's insights make clear that this is an illusion. The great sages throughout history were not the selfless saints they are often assumed to be. They just had the wisdom and introspective insight needed to see that what was good for the world was also good for them. They were better at being selfish.

I said before that self-esteem is like a fuel gauge. And we all know that you can't drive with an empty tank. To ask a person to do good without regard for themselves is to siphon the fuel from their vehicle and then ask them to drive a thousand miles.

The interconnected nature of self-regard, action, and virtue should make this clear. When we fail to see evidence of our virtues, we suck the very mood and motivation needed for action from our minds. Regard for others is not in conflict with the regard for the self. Altruism flows from self-regard—it is rooted in self-actualization.

## The Accountability Mechanism

Everything from our spiritual prescriptions to our disinterested ethical systems attempts to sweep the self under the rug. They turn the "self" into a dirty word and try to strip it out of our motivations, not realizing that it is foundational to those motivations.

Our entire modern view of ethics has attempted to remove the self from the human being. We believe that humans should all be motivated by a universal and disinterested sense of moral obligation.[24]

> The ordinary (and quite indispensable) terms "should," "needs," "ought," "must"—acquired this special sense by being equated in the relevant contexts with "is obliged," or "is bound," or "is required to," in the sense in which one can be obliged or bound by law, or something can be required by law.
>
> —Elizabeth Anscombe, *Modern Moral Philosophy*[25]

I think the self-appraisal system could have significant implications for ethics. For millennia, philosophers and mystics have searched for a rational reason to be good. An accountability mechanism to align self-interest with human values. A reason to do the "right thing," even when no one is watching.

Three thousand years ago, Zoroaster, also known as Zarathushtra, first proposed the good/evil dichotomy.[26] And ever since then, religions have invented omniscient judges and karmic cycles to lead us to believe we would face supernatural consequences for our actions.[27]

Philosophers like Bentham and Kant tried to convince others, and themselves, that moral demands were imposed by the very structure of logic.[28] And today, otherwise astute thinkers continue to promote contrived metaethical systems in the hopes of creating a more virtuous world.[29]

The self-appraisal system provides the origin story and accountability mechanism for virtue that religions and philosophers have sought after. A coherent and perfectly self-interested reason to exemplify human values, without any mythical forces or fuzzy logic.

A significant body of evidence supports the idea that anti-social actions lower our views of ourselves and our overall well-being.[30] And we know the opposite is true as well. The psychological benefits of altruism are numerous and well-documented.[31]

> When we are altruistic, we may begin to view ourselves as kind and compassionate people. We may also become more aware of our strengths, abilities, and resources (Lyubomirsky, 2007). This new identity can foster increased perceptions of competence and self-efficacy.[32]

Altruistic activities lead us to perceive ourselves as altruistic people. Becoming an altruist isn't just good for the world, or for a momentary mood boost. It's a massive upgrade to your identity.

> A study conducted by Schwartz and Sendor (1999) tracked five women volunteers over a period of three years, all of whom had multiple sclerosis (MS). These volunteers were chosen to act as peer supporters for 67 patients who also had MS. The volunteers were instructed to call each patient once per month, for 15 minutes, and were trained to use active and compassionate listening techniques. After three years of volunteering, the helpers reported increased satisfaction, self-efficacy, self-esteem, self-acceptance, and feelings of mastery. They expressed greater confidence in their ability to manage their own MS and the inevitable ups and downs that came with living with an uncurable disease.[33]

Just as we saw that depression is characterized by a vicious cycle between our actions, self-perceptions, and mood, eudaimonia is characterized by a virtuous cycle of positive and admirable actions, positive self-perceptions, and positive mood.[34]

A telling and relevant paper on the link between well-being and "well-doing" called "The Virtuous Cycle" cites numerous studies supporting the idea that virtuous behavior is linked to positive mood, life satisfaction, and overall well-being.

It turns out that people are happier when they are engaged with activities and goals that carry eudaimonic value rather than sheer hedonistic value (King, 2008). For instance, Steger, Kashdan, and Oishi (2007) found using the daily diary method that engaging in eudaimonic behaviors (e.g., expressing gratitude, volunteering one's time, persevering at a valued goal even in the face of obstacles) was associated with significantly higher subjective well-being than engaging in hedonic behaviors (e.g., getting drunk, having sex with someone one doesn't love, obtaining material goods).

The more participants reported engaging in eudaimonic behaviors, the higher was their life satisfaction, positive affect, and meaning in life. No such relationship was observed for hedonic behaviors. Remarkably, daily eudaimonic behaviors predicted higher life satisfaction and higher meaning in life the following day, whereas daily hedonic behaviors did not.

Further support for the positive impact of doing good on subjective well-being comes from studies examining how the content of one's goals relates to happiness. Having goals that can be described as virtuous, eudaimonic, or self-transcending is consistently linked to higher well-being than pursuing hedonic or egoistical goals.[34]

Furthermore, it cites evidence this link is not accounted for by artificially high self-esteem.[35] The strong correlation between well-being and virtue holds even when these virtues are assessed by knowledgeable others—not just individual self-reports. The paper concludes that "possessing and using character strengths in general is associated with elevated happiness."[34]

The fact that we're all going around trying to impress one another is something most of us refuse to admit to ourselves, let alone to one another.

It seems distasteful, but the only consolation the truth-seekers have had is that science prevails over preference.

But I believe Virtue Self-Signaling Theory can turn the distasteful, tasteful. The ugly reality of signaling is transformed into gold when we consider the role of self-signaling, integrity, and value alignment.

Altruism is supposed to be all about others—it is thought to entail great sacrifice. And yet, if you look closely at the benefits listed above, it doesn't seem so sacrificial. The feeling we suffer when we violate our values is a sense of self-disapproval. The shame of failing to live up to our own expectations.

The reason to act according to your values when no one is watching is that someone is always watching. No one else's opinion could possibly have greater consequences for you than yourself. To violate your own values is to take a step toward self-disapproval and depression. To live in alignment with them is to climb toward eudaimonia.

## Key Takeaways:

- Eudaimonia is the positive extreme of the mood state scale—the opposite of depression. Just as depression is characterized by low mood, low vitality, and low and strong sense of self, eudaimonia is characterized by high mood, high vitality, and high and strong sense of self.

- Eudaimonia exists to bring about socially proactive behavioral strategies and get us to signal our fitness to our tribe. Our brains observe our behavior and determine how admirable others are likely to find us, and trigger the release of appropriate chemicals and behaviors.

- Increasing levels of eudaimonia exist to give us the green light and get us to play social offense when we are successfully cultivating and exercising our virtues. And this system as a whole determines our happiness.

- This theory is called Virtue Self-Signaling Theory, and you can think about it through the lens of this formula: $E=nV^s$. This stands for Eudaimonia = net Virtue self-signaled, meaning that our overall well-being is determined by the net amount of virtue we signal to ourselves.

- The mechanism in our brain monitoring us and regulating our well-being is called the self-appraisal system. This system naturally holds us accountable for our actions by delivering well-being that corresponds to our self-perceived admirability. A self-interested reason to exemplify human values.

# PART 3

# The Application

# 9
# Paths to Enlightenment: The Tale of Transcendence

## Three Approaches to Happiness

We've now laid out the framework of the overview, the function of the self-appraisal system, and the elements of Virtue Self-Signaling Theory. Now it's time to answer the most important question: What do we do with this information?

This is going to be the most concrete, action-oriented part of the book. This being said, it has always been my view that books are best for instilling mindsets, while courses, workbooks, and programs are best for concrete, actionable steps and exercises.

If you find that you need more in-depth guidance than a book can provide, I have developed a program called The Flourishing Function that provides detailed steps to optimizing your self-appraisal system and overcoming depression. But it won't be necessary for everyone—the core ideas in the next few chapters have tremendous power to kickstart positive change, so don't take them lightly.

Before I lay out the conclusion, let's take a look at three popular approaches you may be tempted to try.

## 1. Obey Your Self-Appraisal System

Should we simply accept our fate as approval-seeking automatons?

You could be forgiven for concluding that we should all be working to maximize social approval and praise. After all, this is what our entire sense of self was designed to maximize. It seems to follow that the higher we climb up the social ladder, the higher our self-esteem will rise, and the happier we'll become.

I actually think you could do a lot worse than this strategy. It's probably true that most people who attain high social approval will also approve of themselves. Our values are largely universal, so odds are, if everyone around you admires you, you'll probably generally be on the same page.

This strategy is exactly the one evolution designed you to take. You weren't supposed to be aware of this mechanism in your own mind. You were simply supposed to say: "People don't seem to like me, and that feels bad. I should try to get them to like me."[1]

But there's another important thing to point out about evolution's design: It didn't design you to be happy. Not optimally happy at least. It designed you to make babies. Lots and lots of babies. Good babies, who will be good at making babies when they grow up.[2]

And for you to be an optimal gene-propagator, it's best that you don't get too satisfied. Satisfied, sure—maybe a seven out of ten. But not a ten out of ten.

If you optimize for social approval, your well-being will be completely reliant on other people reacting to you the way you want. And other people seem to have a way of not doing what you want. Even if you manage to attain this coveted peak social status, you could lose it at a moment's notice, either by doing something wrong or entering a new social circle with different values.

Demonstrating virtue for its social rewards can be a perilous game. You also won't always be socially rewarded for virtue, as people often don't show their admiration in straightforward ways through praise and outward signs of approval. They may respond with jealousy, resentment, or even sabotage.[3]

What's more, even if you're sending all the right signals to your current social circles, you won't necessarily be sending all the right signals to yourself. Your values are uniquely yours, and despite the inevitable overlap, the people around you won't care about all the exact same things you do in the same proportions.

If you get others to like you, you may generally approve of yourself. But generally approving of yourself isn't eudaimonia. For this, you'll need to highly approve of yourself.

Don't look for compliments to brighten your day. Work to become someone complimentable to brighten your life. The compliments will follow.

If you live to maximize external approval, you may pass on your genes, but if your actions are at the whim of those in your social circles, you very well may fail to align with the most important values: your own. You might secure social esteem as your sociometer intended, but it would come at the expense of your self-esteem.[4]

## 2. Distort Your Self-Appraisal System

So we don't want to live for the approval of others. We want to live for our own approval. So why not go right to the source? Why not try to hack our self-esteem for maximum self-approval?

I can appreciate the spirit of this approach. Hacking our genetic wiring is at the heart of my philosophy, after all. And our culture has given us plenty of tools for hacking our self-esteem. You can find it in the popular sentiment of self-love and the practice of positive affirmations.

Here, do me a favor and read the phrase: "Accept yourself, just as you are. Love yourself unconditionally." How do you feel? If you're anything like me, you feel comforted and relieved. I'm glad I could do that for you. But I also think you'll find that by this point in the paragraph, that feeling is already fizzling out. I made you feel nice for a few moments, but the effect has already worn off.

Here let me fix that for you: "Accept yourself, just as you are. Love yourself unconditionally." Ahhh much better. Just let that flow through your veins. Up for another hit? "Accept yourself, just as you are. Love yourself unconditionally." Mmmmmm.

If only you could keep this feeling going forever. Maybe you should put sticky notes all over your house or set notifications to go off every ten minutes. Maybe you should just repeat it to yourself in the mirror every day. "I accept myself, just as I am. I love myself unconditionally." There we go.

I know how appealing the idea is. Believe me, I understand how right it seems. But the next time you experience a setback in your life, the next time someone disrespects you, the next time you face failure, this idea won't help you.[5]

When you approve of yourself just for existing, you flatten out the complex and critical landscape of your values. Harmless and comforting as it may seem, when you tell yourself you are perfect just as you are, you don't just say "My flaws don't matter."

You inevitably also say "My strengths don't matter. My skills don't matter. My virtues don't matter." No one's virtues matter. There's no basis for comparison because everything is just fine. Scammers and serial killers—even social media influencers—all worthy of our highest approval. No one needs to change. No one needs to improve. No one needs to grow.

Some of you may be thinking you're simply more enlightened than me. You may be saying, "Yes that's correct! Everyone is good. It is only from our limited human viewpoint that we see serial killers as bad people." You may then play a trick where you replace "bad" with "lost" or "confused."

Ultimately, I agree with you. In the grand scheme of things, there is no transcendent good or bad. It's all subjective human evaluation. The universe cares less about the entire human race than you and I care about the life of a single bacteria on the floor of a Chili's bathroom. You're not edgy, nihilists—wipe that smug frown off your face!

Good and bad are not properties of the universe. They are properties of the human mind. Values are subjective. But why should this mean they are unimportant? They are the most important thing. They are the only important thing. Prove me wrong. Tell me something more important than our values.

If you answered, you probably said something like life, love, awareness, or maybe a broad, spiritual vagary like Source, God, etc. But all you've told me is what you value. You can only refute values through the lens of values. And this is to admit that some things are good, some are better, some are worse. Don't play word games with yourself. Be honest. Honesty is one of my values.

When you accept this, you must also accept that there are some ways for a person to be that are better or worse than others. There are some ways for you to be that are better than others. If you agree with this, you agree that self-approval is conditional.

And this is why unconditional self-admiration and affirmations are hollow attempts to hack the self-appraisal system. This is not a recipe for eudaimonia, but it is a recipe for something: narcissism.[6]

Contrary to popular belief, narcissists aren't people with big egos. Narcissists are people with inaccurate egos. A false positive sense of self.[7]

And apparently, it's not as easy to fool yourself as you might think.[8] Though you may be able to manipulate your explicit, or conscious self-esteem, your implicit, or unconscious self-esteem won't be tricked by these games.[9]

Narcissism can be viewed as an over-calibration of the self-appraisal system. Narcissists are not just those with high self-esteem or "big egos," but those whose sociometer is over-calibrated and inaccurate.[10]

This may be achieved temporarily by shielding yourself from real external data. It may seem tempting, but in the long run, this would not bring a desirable outcome.

Results and external opinions are a valuable source of course-correcting feedback. Designing a robust identity is just like designing a product, starting a business, or writing a book. You must get accurate feedback and brutal honesty as early as you possibly can.[11]

If you convince yourself that what you are creating is gold in the short run, you're eventually going to face a rude awakening. It's better to bear a little pain now and adjust your strategy than to face it all at once and accept that you've got years of backtracking to do.

In the late 20th century, it was widely believed that self-esteem was crucial for academic performance and success and hence that inflating it would increase academic performance.[12] But research has not validated this assumption, and in fact, this artificial inflation of self-esteem has even been found to harm performance and success.[13] In summarizing the research, one psychology researcher said:

> Attempts by pro-esteem advocates to encourage self-pride in students solely by reason of their uniqueness as human beings will fail if feelings of well-being are not accompanied by welldoing. It is only when students engage in personally meaningful endeavors for which they can be justifiably proud that self-confidence grows, and it is this growing self-assurance that in turn triggers further achievement.[14]

Artificial ego inflation is not actually self-acceptance. Self-acceptance doesn't mean let go of your values. It doesn't mean you are perfect. It means accept who you are not, accept that you have flaws, accept that you are not perfect, and that you never will be. Accept that there is lots of room to improve yourself. And most importantly, accept your real, genuine strengths. This is true self-acceptance.

Should you tell yourself you're a boss-ass bitch? Maybe. Are you a boss-ass bitch? If so, you probably don't need a reminder. If you're not a boss-ass bitch but your ideal self is, set your goals and accept that you have some work to do.

Unconditional love is unambiguously positive and necessary for a child's development.[15] Unconditional praise is another story. Children who are praised unconditionally don't learn the meaning of virtue. They don't learn that their praiseworthiness corresponds to their actions.[16]

Children who are praised for working hard do far better than those who are praised for being smart or pretty—traits that are largely fixed and don't correlate to their actions.[17] Highly gifted children often struggle later in life because they are sent the message that their praiseworthiness is unconditionally ingrained in them and isn't based on their virtue decisions.[18]

There is truth to the notion of cultivating love for yourself. You don't just have to go out and cultivate new virtues. You need to get better at seeing the ones you already have. Paying more attention to your strengths allows you to pick up on the virtues you may have become convinced don't exist or don't matter.

I don't want to sound like a heartless jerk who doesn't think you should love or approve of yourself. You should love yourself to death. But you should love yourself for a reason.

You shouldn't repeat mantras about how much you love yourself without any substance behind them. Give yourself a reason to love yourself. Show yourself what's so great about you. Get up and do the things you do best every day. And put in the work to get better at them.

### 3. Disable Your Self-Appraisal System

↓

## The Transcendent Tale—May 2015

When I was in college, I challenged myself to take on mindfulness meditation. I had heard so many raving reviews of the practice and had spent so many years trying to optimize my mind, it was surprising I wasn't already a meditator.

I had tried it several times and noticed no effect, but I understood that it required consistent practice. I committed to meditating every day for a year. And I did; I sat and meditated every day for one year, without missing a single day.

I read books and used apps to ensure I was doing it correctly. It was nothing crazy—fifteen to twenty minutes a day. At first, it was difficult to count even ten breaths without losing focus and having to start over.

But after a few weeks, I had actually gotten pretty good at noticing my thoughts as soon as they arose. And I started noticing some changes.

Usually the experience of meditating was calming but mundane. But occasionally, I would have a particularly interesting experience. Sometimes the boundaries between my skin and the world around me would seem to dissolve, and I would feel intense energy circulating all around me. It would spiral into what I can only describe as a "pleasurable dizziness."

On a daily basis, my concentration seemed to be improved. I say "seemed" because it's difficult to measure subjective changes like this and all too easy to allow the placebo effect to convince you something is working. But it certainly seemed like I could focus on boring lectures for longer without zoning out. I started feeling a buzzing feeling around my temples—not just while meditating, but regularly throughout my days.

But I also noticed changes in my sense of self. It was notably decreased. I had fewer self-referential thoughts. I spent less time looking in the mirror. I was less preoccupied with what others thought about me.

No, I didn't completely transcend my sense of self. Not even close. But it gave me a taste of what it would be like not to have one.

This all seems like an improvement, right? I'm not so sure. Certainly, this decreased self-hood would have been an improvement if I had started as a depressive ruminator. But at the time, I didn't have much experience with depression, and my perception was that I had already mastered my cognitive habits.

The thing is, before I started meditating, most of my self-thoughts were positive. I was generally proud of who I was. Aside from the occasional sting caused by my social faults, I had overwhelmingly positive self-esteem, and thinking about myself usually evoked positive emotions.

After becoming a meditator, this self that I was coming to see as illusory was less present. I experienced less shame, less embarrassment. But also less pride. I had managed to weaken my identity, as these practices often encourage. You could say that I became less vain in a sense, but I wouldn't exactly describe it as positive. I would describe it as neutral.

You might argue that I just didn't meditate enough. I should have done at least an hour a day. I should have gone on a full-immersion retreat. Or maybe I didn't do it correctly. If I had, I would have experienced this dissolution of self as nothing short of blissful!

But even if ego transcendence is as great as spiritual teachers make it out to be, I have a hard time imagining it being better than the real happiness and pride I have experienced. And this state hasn't resulted from weakening my ego.

About a year after my meditation experiment ended, I took on an internship in a small, North Carolina mountain town, which I call home today. After adjusting to my intern responsibilities, I found myself wishing I had other people to enjoy this beautiful place with.

It was a small town, and none of my coworkers were my age. I wanted to make friends, but my social difficulties often prevented me from meeting new people. One Saturday morning, I looked in the mirror and told myself I was going to meet new people today. I was going to go out and have fun.

But first, I was going to do my laundry. I gathered my laundry and promised myself that if I bumped into anyone at the laundromat, I was going to start a conversation, no matter how uncomfortable it made me. As it happened, I was not let off the hook. I immediately noticed a young woman doing coursework at a table while she waited for her laundry to finish. She was approachably attractive—I had no excuse.

I struck up a conversation and endured a few moments of awkwardness before things started to flow. She was friendly and engaged, and I challenged her to a game of ping pong.

My difficulty making friends had always stemmed primarily from the monumental energy it required for me to commit to socializing. It wasn't normally rewarding enough, and it usually didn't take long before I felt exhausted and lost interest.

But this time I had already made a commitment to myself, and I was set on keeping it. We chatted between scores, cracked jokes, and exchanged stories. As it turns out, I could be pretty charming when I really decided to be.

I wasn't about to miss the opportunity to make a friend as she gathered her laundry and headed out. I made sure we exchanged numbers, and I felt proud of myself for the courage and charisma I had shown that day.

We started texting regularly and began coordinating our laundry trips to hang out on the weekends. We became good friends in the process of inventing new variations of games to be played with ping pong balls, exploring abandoned university buildings, and even drinking wine at her rustic, moss-covered cabin.

In case you're expecting a love story, it isn't one—at least not one between me and my new laundry-buddy. We both knew I was heading back to school at the end of the summer and never got romantically attached. We catch up every now and then, but we both found our own partners that we love.

It's really a self-love story. Genuine self-love, not inflated self-love. It was a period in which I felt a genuine appreciation for the person I was—one in which I reaped the benefits of the personal growth I had invested in. It was a time of authentic joy and pride.

I had experienced this kind of self-satisfaction at several points throughout my life, and it has always struck me as the peak experience of being human. It was far more enjoyable than immediate pleasure, more rewarding than status or financial gain. And it was more enjoyable than minimizing my sense of self.

What was notable about this period was the contrast between it and my meditative phase. Having come from a rather self-less state of mind, I couldn't help but notice how much better it felt to have a self. And to be proving to myself what a great self it was.

In this friendship, I had unlocked a domain to bring out my virtues, some that I had forgotten I had. I was able to see the evidence of the social charm I hadn't gotten to see much lately. I was able to appreciate the ambition I had fostered. I was receiving the signals of my laid back sense of humor.

If this is sounding a bit self-indulgent, it should. Indulging myself was exactly what I was doing. And it was a significant improvement over reducing myself.

I was in love with myself—in a sense that I believe is exceedingly healthy. I was thrilled to get to wake up each day to be myself. When I thought about "me," that great illusion of the self, positive thoughts and emotions came to mind. The exact opposite is true of the worst periods of my life.

## Eckhart's Ego

It's never been easier to become a guru. You don't need insight. You don't need originality. You just need to memorize your lines. Repeat after me: You are not who you think you are. You are not your brain. You are not your thoughts.

All the ideas you have about your identity—your gender, your social class, your strengths, your weaknesses, your personality, your favorite color… even your name—these are not actually you. You are what's left when you empty yourself of these concepts. You are the observer of the thoughts. You are pure awareness. You are the universal consciousness which pervades all beings.

All of your negative feelings and behaviors are rooted in the delusion of self. You can come to learn to see through this illusion, to become the mere observer of your thoughts. In fact, you already know how to do this. Enlightenment is already there. You've just forgotten it.

Congratulations, you are now a certified spiritual teacher. You are qualified to teach the same message that everyone else is teaching. It's not just mystics. It's Silicon Valley. It's self-help. Self-transcendence transcends all other advice. It's the untouchable prescription.

It's edgy to criticize Western culture and say the East got it right when you live in the West. "We should accept and love ourselves, unconditionally, exactly as we are. Becoming is a pathology of the modern world. A symptom of consumerist culture that says you will never be enough. Don't become. Simply be."

I know, I know. It feels right, just like I said before. You feel a wave of peace wash over you when you read the words "simply be." Ahhh. The idea of transcending yourself is a relief for anyone who is caught in a spiral of self-doubt. And rest assured, I don't want to take this away from you.

I don't want to stop you from being. In fact, I want to give you more of this relief. More gentle waves of peace. I want to let you experience the joy of being on a daily basis instead of just for about 7 seconds when you read these words in a semi-spiritual self-help book.

Everyone encourages you to question things—dogmas, beliefs, assumptions. But this thing about your ego, don't question this. This is the real deal. What I'm going to do here will be appalling to some. To others, it will be a delightful relief. I'm going to question the narrative. I'm going to kill a million gurus.

We have all heard that the ego is the root of our problems. Having a big ego is a bad thing, and transcending the ego is often regarded in spiritual teachings as the holy grail of happiness.[19]

I technically agree that the ego, or the sense of self, is the source of the most profound suffering humans experience and that eliminating or weakening it would remove much of that suffering. But I don't think you should do it. Let me explain why.

The Buddhist belief called anattā, or nonself, states that the concept of the self is entirely an illusion and that the person you think you are today is a different entity from what you were ten years ago or even ten seconds ago.[20]

You are not a unified ego, but an ongoing and constantly evolving process — an aggregation of uncontrolled perceptions and cognitions. The idea at the very core of Buddhism is that the key to liberation from suffering is to transcend the delusion of self which perpetuates our insatiable craving.[21]

The Buddha was far ahead of his time and asserted truths that would only be confirmed by neuroscience millennia later. The idea that there is a monolithic executive underlying all your actions and decisions has been debunked.[22] Buddhist teacher Walpola Rahula reminds us that "what we call a 'being', or an 'individual', or 'I'... is only a combination of ever-changing physical and mental forces or energies."[23]

Your thoughts, emotions, and actions are all determined by a multitude of bottom-up processes, merely leaving you with the impression that "you" were in control of it all along.[24] And it does make sense that evolution would have built us with this sense of singular autonomy.

> In short, from natural selection's point of view, it's good for you to tell a coherent story about yourself, to depict yourself as a rational, self-aware actor. So whenever your actual motivations aren't accessible to the part of your brain that communicates with the world, it would make sense for that part of your brain to generate stories about your motivation.
>
> —**Robert Wright**, *Why Buddhism Is True*

There is evidence that reflecting less on our personal life narratives can mitigate suffering. A decrease in narrative-self thoughts has been found to decrease negative emotions.[25] It does seem possible, at least theoretically, to get rid of your sense of self and live in a state of perpetual present through years of disciplined meditation. And sure enough, many forms of suffering would likely go along with it.

But the rather bold stance I have taken is that the ego (self-concept, identity, etc.) plays a critical role in human well-being. I happen to think that the illusion of self-identity, though it is responsible for despair, is also responsible for true happiness and flourishing. Let's return to our triangular mood-state diagram.

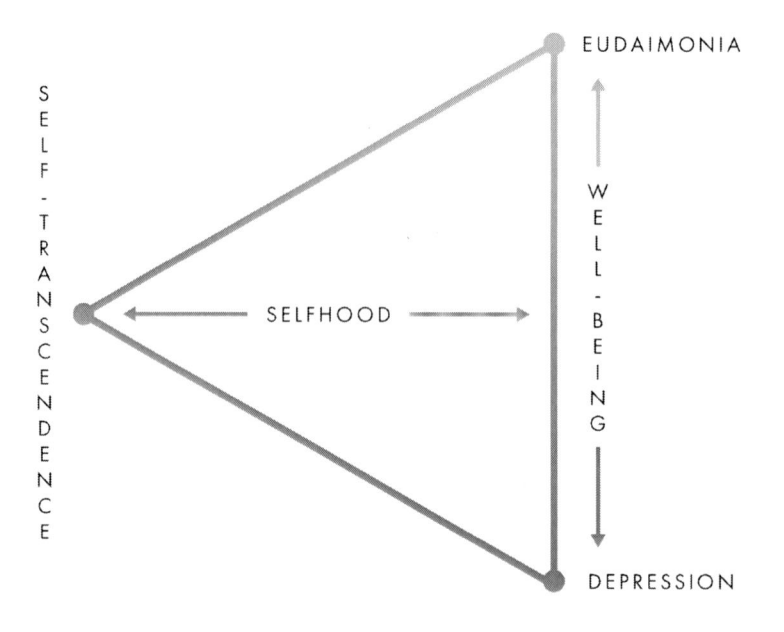

```
S
E
L
F
-
T
R
A
N           EUDAIMONIA
S
C           ↑
E
N           W
D           E
E           L
N           L
C           -
E           B    ← SELFHOOD →
            E
            I
            N
            G
            ↓
            DEPRESSION
```

Here, we see self-transcendence represented as the center-left extreme. Ego transcendence, a massive reduction in functional connectivity of the default mode network, is a state outside of the well-being scale. It isn't positive or negative.

For the purpose of this argument, let's say that overall well-being runs from -1 to 1. We would characterize -1 as severe depression. 1 represents peak eudaimonia. I propose that the state of self-transcendence is effectively 0. It is in fact a cessation of identity-related suffering, and there is no doubt it would feel like absolute bliss for anyone who arrived at it from below.

But this state would also represent the cessation of identity-related joy and flourishing. Psychological well-being is the product of living in alignment with your own values. The self-concept is the engine of well-being. By removing your ego, your sense of self, your identity, you take the batteries out of the happiness/unhappiness machine.

By transcending your ego, if you could achieve such a feat, you would cut yourself off from the deep despair that results from failing to align with your own values. But you would also cut yourself off from the eudaemonia that results from aligning with them.

> The mind is a superb instrument if used rightly. Used wrongly, however, it becomes very destructive. To put it more accurately, it is not so much that you use your mind wrongly — you usually don't use it at all. It uses you. This is the disease. You believe that you are your mind. This is the delusion. The instrument has taken you over.
>
> —**Eckhart Tolle**, *The Power of Now*[26]

At the start of his bestselling spiritual manifesto, *The Power of Now*, new age guru Eckhart Tolle tells the story of his enlightenment. He had struggled with anxiety and suicidal depression his whole life, but he begins his enlightenment story in his late twenties.

He woke up in the middle of the night so full of self-loathing and misery that he decided he could no longer live with himself. This phrase and the seemingly paradoxical nature of not being able to live with oneself launched him into a life-altering experience. He realized the illusory nature of the self in a deep, experiential way. He transcended his ego. He went from -1 to 0.

He then spent the next few years living a free-floating existence without a care in the world, sitting on park benches and listening to birds chirp. He had "no relationships, no job, no home, no socially defined identity."[26] In the process of writing his book, sharing his ideas, and becoming a guru, I imagine Eckhart went through yet another powerful, positive shift.

He had, intentionally or not, constructed a new identity for himself. He was no longer the miserable and unremarkable man he had been before. He was enlightened. He was a guru. He was a bestselling author. His ideas were so valuable that people would travel across the world to hear him speak. He went from 0 to 1.

I should point out that I am quite fond of Tolle's work. His ideas have positively impacted my life, and I highly recommend his books to others. But I don't think it is likely that he lives without a sense of identity today.

I would propose that Tolle un-transcended his ego. He lost it, and then he found it again. I'm sure he experiences some cognitive dissonance as he praises freedom from selfhood while enjoying his own strong, positive sense of self. But it's not enough to take him back to his park bench existence.

This type of enlightenment is for people who are so unhappy with themselves that having no self would be far better than living with their current self. If you are one of these people, it is possible that a journey of ego transcendence could be beneficial for you.

But I want to assure you that nonself and misery are not your only two options. It is possible to construct and affirm that positive identity for which you long.

## The Choice

The source of your problems is not your ego. The solution to your problems is not to eliminate or weaken your sense of self. The argument for letting go and accepting is fatally flawed. All prescription and conscious effort fall apart without the drive to improve.

Your sense of self is your greatest source of strength and satisfaction. Your sense of self is your superpower. Increase it. Strengthen it. Get as much self as you can. Don't transcend it, except temporarily so as to better strengthen it in the long run.

Now I know this is sounding an awful lot like a view that was popular a decade or two ago, that high self-esteem is the key to happiness. Haven't I heard? Self-esteem is out! Self-transcendence is in! Perhaps I need someone to explain this to me, preferably in the form of one of those long, one-star reviews that are always so thoughtful and lucid.

I realize this view is not in fashion at the moment. I know there is a chance you are fond of the view that the ego is the enemy of happiness. If so, please know that it is not my goal to attack you, your beliefs, or even, dare I say, your ego. I don't know for sure that this alternate perspective is correct.

But it deserves to be stated and defended.

Proponents of ego transcendence will urge you to stop trying to become—simply be. But as Heraclitus, Nietzsche, and even the Buddha himself have contended, all being is fundamentally a dynamic process of becoming. At each moment, you are evolving in some direction, whether you like it or not. Why not embrace and take an active role in shaping this great process?

The irony of becoming is that it is exactly what makes the joy of being possible. It is not a matter of whether to be or become. It is the work you have already done to become a person you are proud of that enables you to let go and enjoy your life in the present. The ongoing act of virtue cultivation sustainably delivers the gentle waves of peace that spiritual teachings promise.

Being a self that you love is the best feeling available to you. No, I didn't say loving yourself. I said being a self that you love. Yes, the ego is a real thing with a complex evolutionary origin. And in order to maximize our well-being, we must learn to understand and harness it.

The ego, the sense of self, self-concept, or simply self—these are all interchangeable terms for a particular mechanism that evolution built into human minds many centuries ago. It is, just as the story goes, a central component of the human condition.

And so it stands to reason that practices known for decreasing our self-absorbed ruminations would lower its activity. But I have come to think its functions are absolutely critical for human well-being.

Let's think about this through a quick thought experiment. Imagine it's a freezing cold night and your heater suddenly quits working. But even worse, it starts blowing out freezing cold air (you've got one of those fancy all-in-one-units).

Before long, it's going to be colder inside than it is outside. You don't know anything about HVAC repair, and your internet and cell service are out so you can't Google it or call someone. You have to think quickly.

You realize you have two options. First, you can open things up and attempt to tinker your way to fixing the heating component. This will force you to stand right in front of the freezing air, and there's no guarantee that you'll be able to figure it out.

Second, you can take your trusty baseball bat and start smashing. True, if you destroy the unit, you are guaranteed not to get any warm air, but at least you won't have to deal with the freezing air, and you'll probably make it through the night without turning into a human ice sculpture. What would you do?

This is essentially how I view the conundrum of the ego, and likely the default mode network. It is possible for our sense of self to take on a very negative state, either due to the actual lack of character we are exhibiting, or a distorted mechanism for judging ourselves. And these issues can result in low self-esteem, extremely negative ruminations about ourselves, and depression.

But it is also possible for us to become the kind of person who we so highly approve of, who we so deeply admire, that we get to reap the benefit of extreme eudaimonia. This self-surveilling system in our brains has the power to deliver either fulfillment or misery to us.

And this means we all face a difficult decision. Do we attempt to tinker with our default mode network to try and make it put out the most pleasant heat (happiness), or do we simply smash it to pieces to cut our losses and put an end to the cold air (despair). Do we try to make it so that we approve of what we observe when we think about ourselves? Or do we just try to make the thoughts stop?

Don't get me wrong. I believe there is immense value in metacognitive awareness, practices like mindfulness meditation, and experiences that reveal the illusory nature of self. In fact, I regard them as prerequisite steps for personal growth.

But these practices are useful, not because they help you to permanently transcend your sense of self, but because they give you greater clarity, awareness, and capacity to design a better self. And designing a better self is exactly what we're going to dive into next.

## Key Takeaways:

- If we attempt to obey our self-appraisal systems and live for the approval of others and the elevation of social status, we will put our happiness entirely in the hands of others and fail to align with our own highest values.

- If we attempt to trick our self-appraisal systems through mantras, affirmations, and unconditional self-approval, we will fail, and we will send ourselves the message that our values and strengths don't matter.

- If we attempt to disable our self-appraisal systems and achieve complete self-transcendence, we may succeed in eliminating our sense of self and our identity-related suffering. But it would come at a cost.

- Transcending the ego would also eliminate the possibility of eudaimonia, and the identity-related satisfaction and pride that represent the highest well-being available to us.

- The best approach is to work to become the kind of person of whom you so highly approve, who you so deeply admire, that you get to reap the benefit of extreme eudaimonia. We must use mindfulness, not to transcend ourselves, but to gain the clarity, awareness, and capacity to design a better self.

# 10

# Virtue Vision: Seeing Your Strengths Clearly

## The Triangle

We've now covered the misguided strategies for reaching eudaimonia. We've revealed the flaws with the efforts to obey, distort, and disable the sense of self. So what's the right approach?

The short answer is to engineer your ego for maximum strength and positive self-regard. To not only convince yourself you are, but genuinely become a person of whom you highly approve. To elevate your self-appraisal system beyond its default settings.

Your self-appraisal system can be viewed as a cycle of actions, thoughts, and emotions. You take certain actions, and your self-appraisal system interprets those actions and forms self-beliefs accordingly. These beliefs result in your mood, your mood then influences your actions, and the cycle continues.[1]

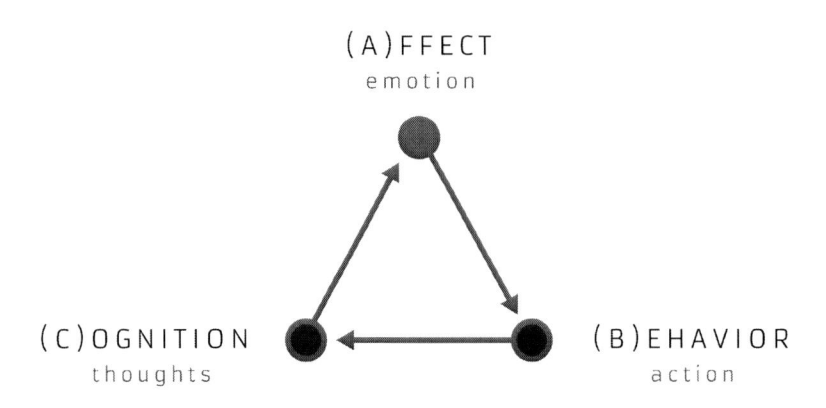

```
        (A)FFECT
         emotion


(C)OGNITION          (B)EHAVIOR
  thoughts              action
```

The clinical terms for emotions, actions, and thoughts are affect, behavior, and cognition, or ABC. Memorize this triangle and the relationships between these mental phenomena. This diagram is sometimes referred to as the CBT triangle because it represents the model used in cognitive behavioral therapy to treat depression.[2]

But the following advice applies equally to those who are thriving and looking to grow more, and those who can hardly find the will to keep going some days. I am not going to distinguish between "depression treatment" and "self-becoming" sections of this process, because there is no distinction to be made.

The process you should follow here is exactly the same for those who are depressed and those who are flourishing. They will simply operate on different scales.

Whether you are at the bottom of the z-axis and currently depressed, around the middle and vaguely dissatisfied, or even near the top and thriving, the great question of your life at this moment is "how can I get higher? How can I elevate my position and get a bit closer to eudaimonia?"

You are in your current position because of the level of net virtue you are signaling to yourself. Some might be quick to jump to an unfortunate conclusion: The reason I'm not happier is that I lack virtue. What a relief—I'm just depressed because I'm a bad person!

I promise this is not the case. You do not lack virtue. You have your own brilliant, unique personal strengths. You have greatness within you. But you may not be able to see it very well.

There are two primary reasons why this might be the case. One reason is that you are not sending the signal of your virtues through your actions, which will be the topic of the next chapter.

But the other reason, which will be the topic of this chapter, is that your brain is not properly receiving the virtue signals that are being sent. You are acting out your virtues on a daily basis, and everyone can see it except for you. We're going to explore a few reasons why this might be the case.

This is the C component of CBT, and of the triangle we mentioned above. When your self-appraisal system fails to properly interpret your virtue signals, it creates a distortion like this. And this affects the entire cycle of mood, action, and belief.[3]

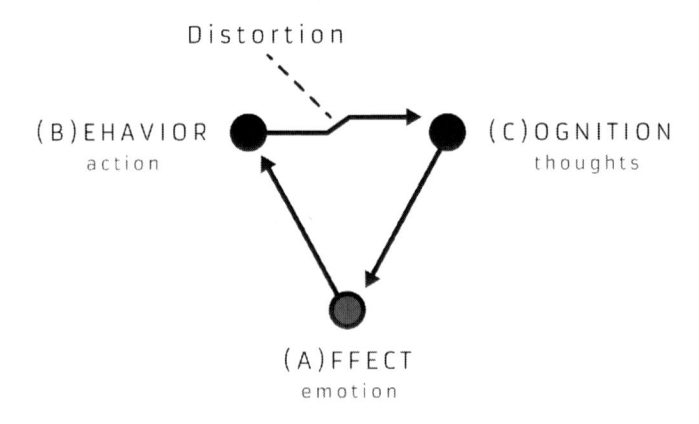

```
                    Distortion

    (B)EHAVIOR    •----------→•    (C)OGNITION
      action                          thoughts


                       •
                    (A)FFECT
                     emotion
```

Depression occurs when you cannot, for one reason or another, see enough evidence of your own virtues. You may not be able to see the evidence because it is not being provided.[4] You may not be seeing this evidence because you are looking through a broken lens.[5] You may not be able to see it because something else—trauma, crisis, or loss—is consuming your view.[6]

Whatever the reason, your mental scanner for personal strengths is drawing a blank, or dangerously close to it. You can become unhappy by becoming convinced that your real virtues aren't present or don't matter.

# Value Introspection

You may recognize this diagram if you've read DTM.[7]

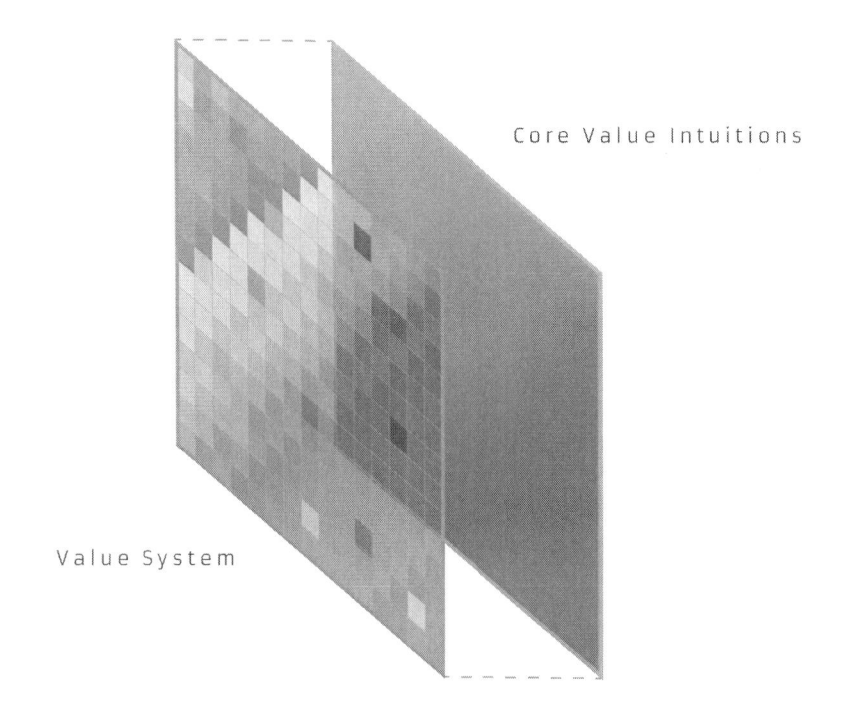

Core Value Intuitions

Value System

The left side represents the conceptual map you build to understand your own values and ideals. The right side represents the actual territory of your personal patterns of approval and disapproval. And this box and the virtue spectrum we've been examining are one and the same.

The colors you see flowing through this gradient are the same ones that fill the landscape of the overview. And this normally hidden continuum of values holds the key to becoming who you are.

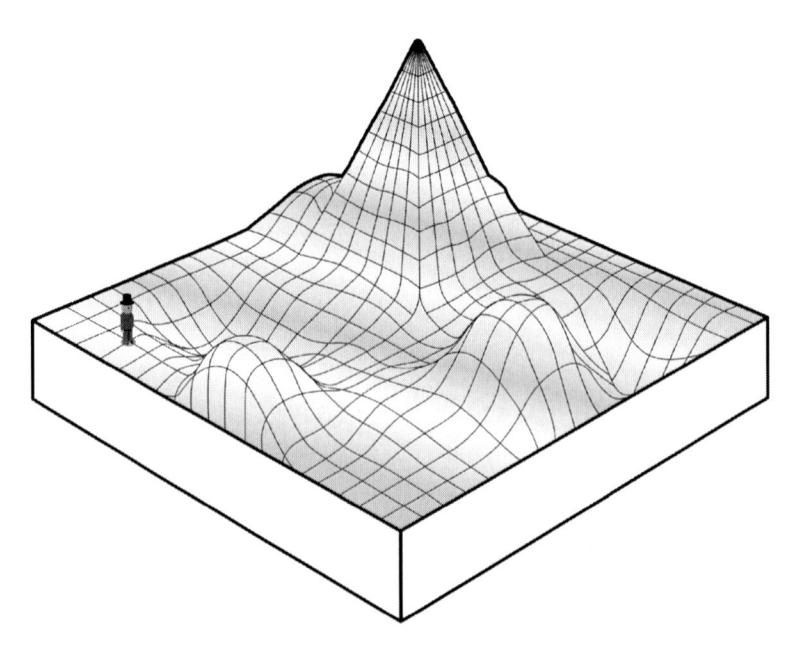

You have within you a unique combination of values and ideals. A map of everything you care about, everything that resonates with you, every "yes" and every "no" to what is admirable in human behavior. This map is inscribed deep within you, largely undiscovered to your conscious mind.

> At the bottom of us, really 'deep down,' there is, of course, something unteachable, some granite of spiritual fatum [personal fate or destiny], of predetermined decision and answer to predetermined selected questions. Whenever a cardinal problem is at stake, there speaks an unchangeable 'this is I.'
>
> —**Friedrich Nietzsche**, *Beyond Good and Evil*[8]

Individual values are like fingerprints—almost identical when viewed from a distance and yet so unique as to serve as an individual identification system when viewed up close. Everyone has a slightly different set, but you'd have to look very closely to see that.

They all pretty much look like fingerprints and not, like, volcanos. But much like attributing the fingerprints on a crime scene to the wrong person, the consequences of incorrectly identifying your own value fingerprints can be dire.

In a certain sense, the landscape of your values is more you than you are. If you had perfect clarity into it, you would know exactly what your ideal self would look like. You would be able to see precisely which actions and decisions your highest self would make in each scenario.

But currently, you don't have such perfect clarity, and you are not a perfect embodiment of this landscape. There are times, both due to ignorance and failures of self-control, when you don't act according to your values.

You sometimes neglect to do the thing you would most highly approve of. You sometimes take the actions you frown upon. You have not integrated all your chaotic and conflicting drives toward coherent ends. You haven't yet become who you are.

It's inevitable that you won't be a perfect embodiment of your values. And this should not evoke guilt, but aspiration. Getting closer, becoming more and more fully whole, is a lifelong path of mastery that has no end.

This path calls for a process that you might call scientific in nature. It requires discovering the highest values within us. It means creating a system for organizing and identifying these chaotic impulses. But it also requires finding ways to bring our virtues out into our lives.

We must be obsessive specialists in the nuances of virtue. Like birdwatchers who see a Black-billed Magpie where most of us just see a "bird," we must learn to see fifty different situational shades of virtue where most just see "compassion." We must discover the territory of our ideals through creation and experimentation. According to Lester Hunt, author of *Nietzsche and the Origin of Virtue*:

> After scientific theories have demolished the old moralities, scientific method can build something new in its place: "then experimentation would be in order that would allow every kind of heroism to find satisfaction—centuries of experimentation that might eclipse all the great projects and sacrifices of history to date."[9]

If we commit to the quest, we can develop the map of our own values in greater and greater resolution. And we can also discover new ways to bring them out. We can get closer to a life, and a mind, that makes increasing virtue actualization possible.

> In contending with one another in the pursuit of excellence—the individuals within it are working to change themselves. They are trying to become more excellent individuals. One cannot predict what form this development will take.

They may acquire greater courage, boldness, ambition, or self-control; or, since creating new ideas about life is one conspicuous form of human excellence, they may develop in unheard-of new directions. The one thing Nietzsche's model does predict is that the inhabitants of such a system will acquire a view of the world that enables them to love life as it is, and if one does that one already is, according to him, a different person and lives a better life.[9]

And how might we evaluate the results of this experimentation? Nietzsche gives an answer. He advocated for "the enhancement of life as a standard of value." How do we feel when we take certain types of behaviors? Are we energized and enlivened? Or do we feel weak and deadened?

> Let the youthful soul look back on life with the question: what have you truly loved up to now, what has elevated your soul, what has mastered it and at the same time delighted it? Place these venerated objects before you in a row, and perhaps they will yield for you, through their nature and their sequence, a law, the fundamental law of your true self.
>
> —**Friedrich Nietzsche**, *Untimely Meditations*[10]

So where can we look for guidance into these values and virtues that are so central to our happiness? The best place to look is in the actions of the people you most admire. Identify the virtues of your friends, family, public figures, and ancient philosophers to try to find traces of inspiration. What do you observe others doing that you admire?

We should 'withdraw to the society of the good and excellent men' and compare our conduct with the ideal standard of the Sage or what we consider praiseworthy in others. When such passions arise in the future, if we're ready to confront our initial impressions with the 'beautiful and noble' examples set by exemplary people, we will weaken and not be 'carried away' by them.

—**Donald Robertson**, *Stoicism and the Art of Happiness*[11]

You need not admire everything about an individual to gather insight from their behaviors. Simply identify individual traits and compile them into a master list to form your ideal. Play with the way it is organized. Restructure and refine your value categories—represented in the left plane of that image—and keep adjusting until it feels right.

We can learn a lot about human virtues by studying those who were split on them. The Greeks praised traits like temperance and justice.[12] Christians praised[14] benevolence and modesty.[13] Buddhists praised compassion and discipline. Nietzsche bashed all of these and praised boldness and creativity.[15]

Each of these philosophies tells us something about the virtue portfolios of their originators, but they all represent different shades within the virtue spectrum. And interestingly enough, the values these philosophers espoused can be seen as reactions to the prevalent values of their cultures. You see, cultures don't create their own values so much as they take the full spectrum of universal values, highlight a small portion of them, and exclude the others.

And sometimes thinkers react to this cultural sliver of virtues with an opposing value system. Aristotle praised the intellectual virtues above all, perhaps because he felt they were neglected by the Homeric values of valor and honor he saw around him.

Perhaps Jesus praised compassion and modesty because he only saw pride and courage being promoted by his culture. And Nietzsche saw creativity and zest were being neglected by the Christian culture he found himself in and reacted by championing them and opposing the values of his time.

When we look at Seligman's list of universal values, we can see that each of these cultures and philosophers had part of the puzzle:

1. (Nietzsche) Creativity: Thinking of new ways to do things[16]
2. (Aristotle) Curiosity: Taking an interest in a wide variety of topics[17]
3. (Nietzsche) Open-mindedness: Examining things from all sides; thinking things through[16]
4. (Aristotle) Love of learning: Mastering new topics, skills, and bodies of research[17]
5. (Stoics) Perspective: Being able to provide wise counsel to others; looking at the world in a way that makes sense[11]
6. (Aristotle) Honesty: Speaking the truth; being authentic and genuine[17]
7. (Stoics) Bravery: Embracing challenges, difficulties, or pain; not shrinking from threat[11]
8. (Nietzsche) Persistence: Finishing things once they are started[16]
9. (Nietzsche) Zest: Approaching all things in life with energy and excitement[16]
10. (Jesus) Kindness: Doing favors and good deeds[13]
11. (Jesus) Love: Valuing close relations with others[13]
12. (Hume) Social intelligence: Being aware of other people's motives and feelings[18]
13. (Stoics) Fairness: Treating all people the same[11]
14. (Nietzsche) Leadership: Organizing group activities and making sure they happen[16]
15. (Aristotle) Teamwork: Working well with others as a group or a team[17]
16. (Jesus) Forgiveness: Forgiving others who have wronged them[13]

17. (Jesus) Modesty: Letting one's successes and accomplishments stand on their own[13]

18. (Hume) Prudence: Avoiding doing things they might regret; making good choices[18]

19. (Stoics) Self-regulation: Being disciplined; controlling one's appetites and emotions[11]

20. (Nietzsche) Appreciation of beauty: Noticing and appreciating beauty and excellence in everything[16]

21. (Jesus) Gratitude: Being thankful for the good things; taking time to express thanks[13]

22. (Jesus) Hope: Expecting the best; working to make it happen; believing good things are possible[13]

23. (Hume) Humor: Making other people smile or laugh; enjoying jokes[18]

24. (Jesus) Religiousness: Having a solid belief about a higher purpose and meaning in life[13]

This is a highly simplified breakdown, but it illustrates an important point. When we study the value system crafted by any one of these philosophers, we find it lacking. But when we mix the virtues of each philosopher together, the full spectrum begins to reveal itself.

Though Nietzsche's value system appears to be incomplete, he did have some powerful insights into the nature of our virtues. He understood the idiosyncratic nature of our values.[19] He did not have the understanding of evolution or genetics that we have today, but his intuitions told him that each person must have their own value-virtue map, no two alike.

> My brother, when you have a virtue, and it is your own virtue,
> you have it in common with no one.
>
> —**Friedrich Nietzsche**[19]

And so we must dig deep into our own minds to discover and map these ideals. We must develop metacognitive awareness. We must examine and organize our own impulses of admiration. We must penetrate the outer crust of our culture's values to find the individual values at their core.

## Your Virtue Portfolio

A little-known and not-so-fun fact is that each increase in birth order is related to an 18% higher suicide risk.[20] That means if you are a second-born, your odds of committing suicide are 18% higher than if you were a firstborn. If you are a third-born, your odds of committing suicide are 18% higher than if you were a second-born... and so on.

What could explain this odd phenomenon? The fact that this is a matter of birth order means we can completely rule out genetics. Maybe it has to do with firstborns receiving more parental care and attention. This is possible, but I think it's only part of the story.

My suspicion is that people born earlier than their siblings have a kind of first-mover advantage when it comes to constructing a strong, positive identity. Self-worth begins with the process of trying to impress your parents and compete with your siblings, and firstborns get first dibs on the strengths and qualities they acquire.[21] It would be very difficult for younger siblings to compete with their more developed and practiced older siblings, so they have to choose from a reduced pool of niches.[22]

Each younger child has a lesser chance of succeeding at this because there are fewer niches that have not yet been taken. And this childhood identity struggle sets the stage for the rest of life (note that we're only dealing with statistical averages here — being the youngest in your family does not seal your destiny of despair).

This could explain why younger siblings tend to be funnier, and why comedians are thought to have lower mental health and an increased risk of depression.[23][24][25] It seems humor may not be a common first choice for one's identity.

The most common correlate of depression is loss.[26] But if you look closer at the data, you find that the nature of this loss is anything but simple and concrete.

Jonathan Rottenberg, author of a book on the evolutionary roots of depression, *The Depths*, offers an analysis of his own depressive episode.

> I fully defined myself by my potential career. My depression probably originated in part out of struggles to develop a dissertation topic and from the ominous signs of a poor academic job market. Once I became significantly depressed, my ability to work and think about history deteriorated. I could no longer do the only thing that I thought I could do well. My original life plan collapsed.
>
> ...To the extent that my depression offered a warning, I think it was about the hazard of putting all one's eggs in a single basket. I stay well in part because I have diversified my portfolio, evolutionarily speaking. With research psychology, yes, I re-created a career. But I also married, had a daughter, and even developed full-blown hobbies like marathon running. And for the past few years I have been writing a book that aims to help others understand depression...[27]

His tale of a collapsing career on which his entire identity had been supported will sound familiar to anyone who has studied depressed patients. Though these episodes are not always accompanied by traditional loss, and in fact are often precipitated by a positive life change, they always involve damage to one thing: identity.[28]

> Becoming the best version of yourself requires you to continuously edit your beliefs, and to upgrade and expand your identity.
>
> —**James Clear**, *Atomic Habits*[29]

As I suggested in Chapter 7, depression may be best viewed as the product of failed identity. It may be that your collection of cherished virtues is no longer working. It may be that you never managed to build a strong collection in the first place. Or it may be that your collection has grown stale and stagnant, and needs to be brought back to life.

You must actively design your identity. You must manage your virtue portfolio. You might lack clarity into your values, so you don't know what is important to you or what kind of person you want to be.

If you don't have a strong virtue portfolio, you have to try things. Lots of things. Don't wait for your virtues to come and find you. Go out and build them.

My virtue portfolio looks something like this:

- Ingenuity: creativity/originality/resourcefulness
- Wisdom: insight/critical thinking/curiosity
- Charm: humor/playfulness/appreciation/zest
- Self-control: diligence/tranquility/integrity/courage
- Vision: purpose/ambition/humanity/tenacity

Though I could list many more, these are my core signature strengths—the virtues on which my identity is largely supported. What are yours?

When you think about yourself one year from now, how do you feel? What emotions fill you when you contemplate this future self? Excitement? Boredom? Nausea?

I propose that this is actually a pretty good test for your current trajectory toward eudaimonia. If you aren't excited about this future self, it would indicate that you have not tapped into a compelling vision for yourself. You have not set inspiring virtue aims for yourself.

Whether you realize it or not, you have a portfolio of personal strengths that you monitor continuously. Sure, we all want to be as good as possible at everything. But there are some virtues that we have learned to invest in heavily.[30]

Maybe it's your kindness and likability. Maybe it's your cleverness and ingenuity. Whatever these precious powers are, they make up your identity—your virtue portfolio.

But like an investment portfolio, the strengths you've invested in may need some work. For one thing, you may not have enough different virtues. You may have placed all your eggs in one basket. This lack of diversification would make your portfolio fragile and vulnerable to collapse.[31]

On the other hand, you may have too many different virtues. Yes, this can be a problem too. It's impossible to be good at everything, simply because you have finite resources. You won't be able to balance the demands of all these competing virtues, and as a result, you won't end up doing well at any of them.

You may have invested in dead ends. Like the stock of a video rental company, the virtues you've selected aren't going anywhere, as they aren't rooted in your actual innate capacities.

Depending on your natural capacities, some virtues will be "low-hanging fruit virtues" and others will be "uphill battle virtues." In other words, you'll find that certain virtues, which Seligman calls "signature strengths," will come more easily to you than others, making your efforts in these areas more fruitful than others.[32] He provides a method for determining your signature strengths:

> When you read about these strengths, you will also find some that are deeply characteristic of you, whereas others are not. I call the former your signature strengths, and one of my purposes is to distinguish these from strengths that

are less a part of you. I do not believe that you should devote overly much effort to correcting your weaknesses. Rather, I believe that the highest success in living and the deepest emotional satisfaction comes from building and using your signature strengths.

Take your list of top strengths, and for each one ask if any of these criteria apply: A sense of ownership and authenticity ("This is the real me"), A feeling of excitement while displaying it, particularly at first, A rapid learning curve as the strength is first practiced, Continuous learning of new ways to enact the strength, A sense of yearning to find ways to use it A feeling of inevitability in using the strength ("Try and stop me"), Invigoration rather than exhaustion while using the strength, The creation and pursuit of personal projects that revolve around it, Joy, zest, enthusiasm, even ecstasy while using it, If one or more of these apply to your top strengths, they are signature strengths.

—Martin Seligman, *Authentic Happiness*

Seligman offers a questionnaire for determining your signature strengths called the VIA Survey of Character Strengths on his website.[33] I highly recommend taking it to get a clearer view of your own core virtues.

When you get the results, save them, write them down, and reformulate them until they feel right. Whatever helps you to keep these traits in your mind.

Ask someone close to you what they think your greatest qualities are. A close friend or significant other, your boss or coworker, or even your mom. Ask them what they see as your greatest character strengths, talents, or skills.

No, actually do this. This will probably make you feel great in the moment, but you also might be surprised by what they say. This will give you your next task.

Ask yourself how you can activate and amplify these virtues. Which situations can you place yourself in which will demand and display these strengths that your closest confidants know you have? Design your life to bring these qualities out on a daily basis.

And of course, simply ask yourself what you believe you have always thrived at. Depending on your current state, it may be hard to determine, as your view may be distorted. Do your best to write down these strengths, even if they don't feel legitimate right now.[34]

## Cognitive Restructuring

The final component to cultivating virtue vision is called cognitive restructuring, the C part of CBT.[35] If you read my previous book, this process was the topic of chapter 5. It's also the main topic of excellent books like *Feeling Good* and *Mind Over Mood*, which I highly recommend. Let's go through the main ideas.

If you frequently experience identity-suffering, it is likely that you have false, negative thoughts or beliefs distorting your view of yourself, causing you to see yourself as a failure when you aren't. You may even experience thought spirals and ruminations that seem to attack you relentlessly throughout the day.[36]

Cognitive restructuring was designed to identify and correct distorted beliefs and bring patients back to reality. The premise of cognitive restructuring is that your self-appraisal system can sometimes develop distorted, inaccurate beliefs about you. Maybe you're in a loving relationship, are at the top of your field, and have great friends. But you still think you're incompetent and unlovable.[37]

Why does this happen? For one thing, our brains aren't infallible. They form their judgments based on unreliable environmental cues and probabilistic reasoning.[38] Your self-appraisal system is working to mitigate social damage, so it might have a tendency to err on the side of assuming the worst.[39]

But I think a major reason has to do with the modern world. The self-appraisal system was built to pick up cues from the environments of our ancestors. These signals probably looked quite different from the ones we receive today.[40]

Our relatively simple and tight-knit tribes have been replaced by weak, remote, and fragmented ties. Our interactions and signs of approval have changed form, and this makes it all too easy for our brains to form false negatives.[41]

How should your brain interpret cues from a performance review, where you truly may only be evaluated based on the proxy virtue of profit. How should your brain make sense of likes on social media platforms?

The answer is that it may not properly interpret this data, and this could lead you to develop a distorted view of yourself.[41] And this means it's time to un-distort it.

The process of cognitive restructuring is relatively simple but certainly not easy. Begin by creating a log, either on a sheet of paper or in an app.

When you find yourself in a bad mood or feeling depressed, start off by writing down the situation that may have triggered this mood. Then take a note of the thoughts that popped into your head around this situation.

Maybe you thought "He thinks I'm a terrible employee" or "I'm going to be alone forever." Maybe you thought "Only an idiot would get a C on an assignment" or "Everyone ignores my ideas." Write down as many of these automatic thoughts as you can.

Next, it's time to evaluate them. For each thought, write down the objective evidence that supports it, and the objective evidence that contradicts it. No matter how true the thought feels, try to determine if it's really true and if you would still think it was true if the same thing happened to someone else.

Formulate more reasonable and balanced perspectives for each of your thoughts. So you might conclude "He probably thinks I'm a valuable employee, because he said so the last time I asked for feedback, and he wouldn't keep me around if I weren't." You might say "It may take me a while to find someone new, but there is no reason to think I won't ever find someone I'm happy with."[42]

See if you can identify the specific cognitive distortion you committed in your original thought. Here are ten of the most common distortions:

### 1. All-or-Nothing Thinking

The tendency to think in extremes like "always" and "never" without considering nuanced degrees between.

"My boyfriend broke up with me; I always ruin my relationships."

### 2. Overgeneralization

The tendency to make broad assumptions based on limited specifics.

"If one person thinks I'm stupid, everyone will."

### 3. Mental Filter

The tendency to focus on small negative details to the exclusion of the big picture.

"My A+ average doesn't matter; I got a C on an assignment."

### 4. Disqualifying the Positive

The tendency to dismiss positive aspects of an experience for irrational reasons.

"If my friend compliments me, she is probably just saying it out of pity."

### 5. Jumping to Conclusions

The tendency to make unfounded, negative assumptions, often in the form of attempted mind reading or fortune telling.

"If my romantic interest doesn't text me today, he must not be interested."

### 6. Catastrophizing

The tendency to magnify or minimize certain details of an experience, painting it as worse or more severe than it is.

"If my wife leaves me, then I will never be able to recover from my misery."

### 7. Emotional Reasoning

The tendency to take one's emotions as evidence of objective truth.

"If I feel offended by someone else's remark, then he must have wronged me."

### 8. Should Statements

The tendency to apply rigid rules to how one "should" or "must" behave.

"My friend criticized my attitude, and that is something that friends should never do."

### 9. Labeling

The tendency to describe oneself in the form of absolute labels.

"If I make a calculation error, it makes me a total idiot."

### 10. Personalization

The tendency to attribute negative outcomes to oneself without evidence.

"If my wife is in a bad mood, then I must have done something to upset her."[43]

I've shared this list before, but it's an invaluable tool for correcting distorted thinking, and I think everyone should memorize it forward and backward. There's another tool that will be essential for some to develop insight into these mental tendencies.

It lies in the practice of mindfulness and the cultivation of metacognitive awareness. As I stated earlier, I am wary of using mindfulness with the aim of transcending our sense of self. But this does not mean that mindfulness has no important place in our psychological health.

We are naturally close to, fused with, and identified with our thoughts. When we have the thought "I'm worthless," we are wired to perceive this thought as the truth. But this isn't the only way to relate to our thoughts.[44]

Learning to distance yourself from your moods and thoughts and identifying them as nothing more than moods and thoughts, though deceptively simple, is a powerful hack to your operating system. You can't develop metacognitive awareness, or cognition about your own cognition, if you are completely fused with your thoughts and moods. For this reason, we must learn to defuse.[45]

> In a state of defusion, you can see a thought for what it is: nothing more or less than a bunch of words or pictures "inside your head." In a state of defusion, you recognize that a thought may or may not be true; is definitely not a command you have to obey or a rule you have to follow; is definitely not a threat to you; is not something happening in the physical world—it's merely words or pictures inside your head... you have a choice as to how much attention you pay it.
>
> —*ACT Made Simple*

So we must learn to "objectify" our thoughts. To turn them into objects or events in the mind. And the first component of this process is to develop genuine curiosity into our mental events. We must accept our thoughts and emotions, no matter how problematic they may seem.[46]

When you notice difficult emotions arising in your mind, don't add fuel to the fire by criticizing yourself for having these feelings. Instead, ask questions like "when did that feeling arise?", "how long did it last?", and "which situations, thoughts, or bodily reactions came along with it?"[45]

This attitude of accepting curiosity will help you develop a new relationship with your mental experiences and stories. It will encourage you to pay more attention to your inner world. It will counter your tendency to get sucked into your thoughts and moods. And it will bring you into the present experience and out of the fog of rumination.[45]

The insight found in the most recent wave of CBT is that these restructuring processes are far less effective if patients haven't learned to develop a different relationship with their thoughts. Acceptance and Commitment Therapy (ACT), Metacognitive Therapy (MCT), and Mindfulness-Based Cognitive Therapy (MBCT) all teach that defusion is a necessary step for eliminating and preventing rumination and depression from recurring.[44]

Once you start mindfully observing and logging your mental tendencies, you should start getting better and better at identifying and rooting out flawed self-beliefs. Before long, your brain will start sorting these thoughts out in the background so that they stop being triggered altogether.

This practice of restructuring your distorted beliefs will go a long way in improving your well-being and self-esteem. In fact, cognitive therapy frames depression entirely as a cognitive disorder that results from mistaken self-perceptions. Negative emotions and mood disorders, it argues, occur when we develop cognitive distortions—negative and inaccurate beliefs, generally about ourselves.[47]

David Burns says:

> Our research reveals the unexpected: Depression is not an emotional disorder at all! The sudden change in the way you feel is of no more causal relevance than a runny nose is when you have a cold. Every bad feeling you have is the result of your distorted negative thinking. Illogical pessimistic attitudes play the central role in the development and continuation of all your symptoms. Intense negative thinking always accompanies a depressive episode, or any painful emotion for that matter.[43]

And this perspective makes perfect sense within a particular context. Yes, mood disorders like depression are mediated by your self-beliefs, and this makes them a powerful leverage point for altering them. But I've developed an appreciation for the broader context.

The assumptions of cognitive therapy are correct only when the self-appraisal system is under-calibrated. It does not account for scenarios in which it is over-calibrated, and self-beliefs are distorted in the overly-positive direction, such as narcissism.

More importantly, it fails to account for the properly calibrated self-appraisal system. In other words, what if you really are terrible at the trombone? What if there is no contrary evidence that you're bad at your job? How do you counter the belief that you don't have a life when you really haven't left your house in months?

Cognitive therapy is effective for depression when it manages to see the error in your self-esteem's judgments. Negative self-thoughts can be inaccurate, but they can also be entirely accurate, and cognitive restructuring won't help in this case.

In the next chapter, we're going to explore a practice that I believe is even more crucial for well-being than cognitive restructuring. The most important method for overcoming depression and pursuing your highest ideals.

## Key Takeaways:

- Your aim is to engineer your self-appraisal system for maximum strength and positive self-regard. To not only convince yourself you are, but genuinely become a person of whom you highly approve.

- The self-appraisal system can be viewed as a cycle of actions, thoughts, and emotions. You take certain actions, and your self-appraisal system interprets those actions and forms self-beliefs accordingly. These beliefs result in your mood, your mood then influences your actions, and the cycle continues.

- We may become depressed if we are not sending the signal of our virtues through our actions. But we also may become depressed if our brains fail to properly receive and interpret the virtue signals that are being sent.

- Particularly in the modern world, it is easy for our self-appraisal systems to become distorted and cause us to develop false, negative beliefs about ourselves and our virtues. To correct these issues, we need to engage in practices to get in touch with our own values and virtues.

- We can also practice cognitive restructuring to identify and correct the false beliefs and ruminations characteristic of depression. We must examine and log our thoughts, identify the distortions in them, and replace them with alternative, balanced beliefs.

# 11

# Virtue Activation: Bringing Your Strengths to Life

## Going Straight to the Source

We've established that mood is determined by a cycle of actions, thoughts, and emotions. And we've looked at how we can use our thoughts as leverage points for improving our self-esteem and mood.

In this chapter, we're going to cover how we can use our actions as leverage points for change. But before we do, I want to deal with an important point.

Why can't our affect, or emotion be a point of change too? Aren't there ways to improve mood directly? If you want to be happier, or less depressed, why not just raise your neurotransmitter levels directly? They make drugs for this, after all.

Antidepressant drugs have become a controversial topic, with some touting them as the solution to depression and others vehemently opposing them. Their efficacy has been hotly debated, with some analyses suggesting their effects are little more than placebos, making them clinically insignificant.[1]

One of the most popular types of antidepressant is the SSRI, or selective serotonin reuptake inhibitor. To keep it simple, these operate by increasing the amount of serotonin present in the brain. If low serotonin is a big part of depression and why it feels so bad, it makes sense that increasing it would improve mood.

But if the self-appraisal system was built to deliver these chemicals under certain conditions, increasing them out of these contexts could have confusing and problematic results.

Let's imagine you have been dealing with low self-esteem and mild depression recently. So you go to a psychiatrist who quickly prescribes you an SSRI, the most common type of antidepressant drug.[2] Over the course of weeks, the antidepressant increases your serotonin levels.

Your mood feels lighter, your motivation improves, and your confidence increases. Now you're feeling like going out, socializing, and sharing your strengths and skills with the world. Problem solved, right?

Though it may be hard to hear, the reason for your low self-esteem and depression was that there was a problem. Your self-appraisal system determined you weren't approvable enough in certain domains, so calling attention to yourself could hurt more than it helps.

Now that you've boosted your serotonin levels and increased your confidence, you're going out and displaying yourself against your brain's better judgment. And if this causes people to disapprove of you and triggers your own self-disapproval, guess what's going to happen?

Your brain will say, "hmmm that's weird, serotonin levels are higher than they should be. We need to lower those ASAP." As this happens, the SSRIs will lose their effectiveness—an extremely common phenomenon in psychiatric treatment.[3] You may be prescribed a higher dose, which will improve things for a little while until your brain adjusts the levels back to baseline once again.

If you haven't done the work on your virtues, taking these chemicals will amount to treating a symptom. The dynamic systems in your brain will respond to abnormal chemicals by normalizing them. They will correct the error of high serotonin you created by taking the antidepressant, yielding them ineffective.

Then, when you decide to stop taking the drug, your serotonin levels will plummet until your brain catches on and says, "wait a minute, I could have sworn there was more serotonin here a minute ago." You will experience withdrawal symptoms until your brain adapts and normalizes the chemicals to what it sees as appropriate levels.[4]

When these medications first hit the market, they came with a compelling message that was being marketed both to physicians and direct to consumers. Depression was caused by a chemical imbalance, and antidepressants were the proven tool for restoring that balance.[5]

Unfortunately, even the most optimistic studies of the most effective antidepressant medications in existence have found that they are almost no better than a placebo, or sugar pill.[6]

And though the vast majority of prescriptions are made for mild or moderate depression, studies show that the effects of antidepressants are nonexistent for these cases, only showing any kind of reliable effect in severe depression.[7]

Therapeutic interventions, like mindfulness-based therapy and cognitive behavioral therapy, have been found by many studies to work better than antidepressants.[8] Furthermore, it is well-understood that the effects of these therapeutic treatments like CBT last longer than those of medications, whose effects often wear off in a matter of months.[9] And behavioral activation, the next approach we're going to cover, has been found by some studies to have a 56% recovery rate among severely depressed patients, compared with only 23% on SSRIs.[10]

The side effects of most antidepressants are particularly common and alarming. These drugs often result in an overall numbing of affect, and sometimes a long-term inability to feel pleasure or joy. They are linked to weight gain, insomnia, and sexual dysfunction. Most disturbingly of all, suicidal thoughts and actions are twice as likely among young people who are taking antidepressants as they are in those who are taking a placebo.[6]

To give another example, a drug called ketamine is a relatively new antidepressant with more promising and faster-acting results than others like SSRIs.[11] It has some nasty side-effects, so it is generally only used for those who have tried other antidepressants with no improvement.[12]

Ketamine is considered a "dissociative" and is used recreationally to induce hallucinogenic effects and a reduced sense of self. At high doses, it causes users to dissociate from themselves and sometimes feel like detached observers outside their body.[12]

So it's not too surprising that ketamine is associated with decreased connectivity in the default mode network.[13] It seems that ketamine may work by weakening the sense of self and quieting the self-critical ruminations we see in depression.[14]

We see a similar effect in mindfulness meditation. Experienced meditators appear to have reduced activity and connectivity in their default mode networks.[15] But like we said earlier, a weakened sense of self is not the ideal mental state.

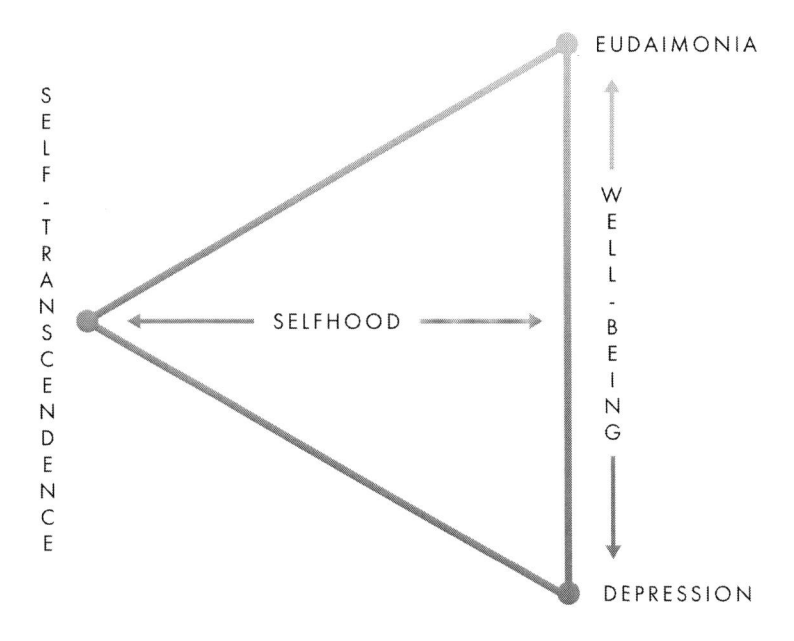

I'm not saying that antidepressant drugs, or even SSRIs should have no place in depression treatment. It is possible that even a crude instrument for changing the brain could make enough of a difference to serve as a springboard for personal change.

Maybe temporarily fixing one tenth of the problem will buy you enough time and strength to take action and improve your virtue strategies. Maybe they could give you enough of a leg up to escape the gravity of depression. But it's best to view them for what they are. Turning to drugs isn't breaking out the big guns—it's throwing a hail Mary.

If you believe that antidepressants have created significant and enduring positive changes for you, you should appreciate the fact that you are one of the lucky few. And if you are currently taking antidepressant medications, you should never stop taking them without consulting a professional.[16]

But the knee-jerk method through which antidepressant drugs are prescribed today causes and prolongs more problems than it solves. I would strongly encourage those who are facing early or mild depression to prioritize the methods I lay out before turning to pharmaceuticals.

## Behavioral Activation

> How can a man come to know himself? Never by thinking, but by doing. Try to do your duty and you will know at once what you are worth.
>
> —**Johann Wolfgang von Goethe**, *Maxims and Reflections*[17]

We get depressed when our brains "learn," rightly or wrongly, that we are not virtuous—not lovable, not competent, not valuable. As we explored in the previous chapter, it is possible to correct these beliefs by reasoning with them.

But when it comes to psychological change, reason is a relatively weak tool. There is one way to accelerate the unlearning process immensely: Prove it.

Consciously direct your aims toward becoming the kind of person you genuinely admire. Signal your personal virtues to yourself, to the highest degree possible, every single day.

For many, this effort will already represent a chief aim in life. But without making it your explicit goal, without adopting a model to help you understand it, this aim can get lost in a sea of desires and motives.

During my depressive period, I was well aware that many of the views of myself I had succumbed to were irrational. I had studied more than enough cognitive therapy to know how to question and counter these assumptions.

And yes, I'm sure that without my psychological toolkit, I would have fared far worse and fully believed the negative views that were being thrust upon me. But just knowing they weren't right wasn't enough to fight them off. I wasn't proving them wrong.

Behavioral activation, the B part of CBT, is needed when your sociometer is working properly.[18] Your brain isn't getting the signals of your personal virtues because you aren't sending them. Your lifestyle isn't bringing them out.

Behavioral activation involves simply scheduling rewarding activities each day, increasing activity, motivation, mastery, and personal value alignment, in baby steps until you are back to healthy functioning. And it works.[19]

A number of studies have found that behavioral activation outperforms antidepressant medication by a significant margin.[20] And it has even been found by some to outperform cognitive therapy, the gold standard of therapeutic interventions.[21] Despite seeming simple, the practice is staggeringly effective.

If you find yourself feeling depressed, or just vaguely dissatisfied with yourself, your behaviors and lifestyle may not be matching up with your values. You consider yourself a musician, but you let work keep you from playing regularly. You identify as a kind, altruistic person, but you haven't engaged in any acts of kindness or charity recently.

You must demonstrate to yourself, through your actions, that you do have the virtues your self-appraisal system has cast doubt on. Provide the jury inside your brain with indisputable proof that you are creative, kind, or courageous. Self-signal your virtues.

Notice I said to demonstrate through your actions—not through your results. A healthy identity is centered around ongoing processes rather than results. Your identity is based on the activities you engage in, the time and energy you dedicate to them, and the gradual progress you make along the way.

You should pride yourself on being a writer if you get up and write every day, can see improvement over time, and believe you are doing the best you are currently capable of. Are you aligning, or in the process of aligning with your values as a writer?

Results like winning awards or selling millions of copies are on the y-axis. Results and feedback can help you get a better view of your strengths and weaknesses. But they don't matter in-and-of themselves, and this is clear when we look at the many highly successful but depressed individuals.

The simplest version of this advice is this: Do things. It sounds silly, but this is the exact opposite of what depression makes you feel like doing. You feel like laying around in bed all day. The exact opposite of what is going to improve that depressed feeling.[22]

One of the most effective exercises for depressed patients is the daily activity schedule. Depending on what you are currently doing most days, create a daily schedule that you find slightly challenging.[23]

For those lowest on the z-axis, this might mean simply getting out of bed each day. For those a bit higher up, it might mean showering, brushing your teeth, and washing the dishes. These may seem basic, but even these minimal activities allow some of your virtues to find expression.

Write down your activity schedule for each day in advance, along with how rewarding you think it will be to complete these activities on a scale from one to ten. This rating is important because it allows you to show yourself that these activities often allow for more pleasure and mastery than you expect them to.[24]

In my quest to understand happiness, I once noted that "life is good as long as you keep moving." There is a lot of truth in the idea that we have to keep progressing to remain content, but it isn't quite right to say happiness boils down to our activity level. Just staying busy is not the essence of what moves you toward greater health.

Success in behavioral activation isn't measured in busyness. It's measured in pride. So do something that makes you feel the tiniest bit proud of yourself. Simply making sure you are doing something each day and don't remain idle is a start.

Almost any action is better than no action at all. It's hard to come up with a behavior that demonstrates no virtue at all. Even behaviors that demonstrate a vice generally also demonstrate virtues. But idleness is the absence of any behavior.

A satisfying life consists in setting and pursuing goals that relate to your values and virtues. You don't just need to do lots of things, but to move toward doing things that increasingly utilize your personal capabilities and align with your values.[24]

Sometimes we get attached to these goals themselves, but the real purpose of the goals is to give us the opportunity to signal as much virtue to ourselves as possible. This is how we must measure the value of our activities.

Once we get past the basics of hygiene and maintenance, we can branch into activities that exercise virtue at greater scales. Going on a walk, reading a book, exercising, or talking to a friend can bring out more virtue than just cleaning your house. As you progress through this hierarchy, the tasks you schedule each day should increase in autonomy, mastery, and alignment with your personal values.[22]

It's essential that you take baby steps in creating your activity schedule. You must find the sweet spot between too easy and too difficult, and this is entirely relative to your current level of ability.

As you get better at completing these activities, you can increase the difficulty and complexity. But setting goals that are too difficult too early will increase the risk that you'll fail and walk away with the wrong takeaways. You must be forgiving if you are unable to complete your schedule, no matter how easy you think it should be, and try again the next day.[23]

For someone who is severely depressed, this process is far easier said than done. But one of the reasons it is so difficult is that there are a million things you feel like you should be doing differently, and this can be paralyzing. That's why it's important that you set your sights on your activity schedule, and allow yourself to feel accomplished just for completing these specific tasks.

One of the biggest mistakes people make is waiting until they feel like doing these activities. Those who don't understand their self-appraisal system fail to grasp why they should engage in activities if they don't feel motivated to do them.[22]

If you have been staying home and lounging around for weeks, your self-appraisal system is desperate to find some semblance of virtue in your behavior. Depriving it of virtue is like depriving your lungs of oxygen.

You are going to remain miserable if you sit around waiting to feel like doing something. Those happy people you see going on hikes and reading books all the time aren't necessarily doing these things because they feel like it. They do it because they have learned it makes them feel good about themselves afterward. As you complete the activities on your schedule, make a point of writing down, on a scale from one to ten, how rewarding that activity ended up being.

Maybe you really didn't feel like going on a walk. Maybe when you first started walking, you thought "this isn't even fun—why didn't I just stay home?" But don't give these thoughts any weight, and instead pay careful attention to how you feel about yourself after doing it.

The idea that leisure activity doesn't need to be structured—that you should only spend your free time on things you feel like doing—is one of the great fallacies shared by chronically unhappy people. When choosing how to spend your time, don't ask whether you feel like it or even how enjoyable you think it will be in the moment. Your ultimate consideration should be "How will this activity make me feel about myself after I've done it?"

You might think you are different. You might think you just don't enjoy activities like this. Or you might think you will only enjoy them if you have someone else to do them with. But rest assured, you are not different—you just may not be as observant into your own mental processes.

No matter how pointless it seems, build a schedule and stick to it—preferably one that gets you out of your house. Do these activities, and notice how much better you feel about yourself at the end of the day when you do compared to when you don't.

Don't wait for motivation. If you've scheduled an activity for the day, just do it, and let the feeling of motivation come later if it wants.

Depression is generally an excellent guide on what not to do. To escape its gravity, you must do the opposite of what your depressed instincts tell you to do. If they tell you to stay in bed, use every ounce of will to get out of bed. If they tell you not to call your friend, force yourself to call your friend. No matter how easy you feel this activity schedule should be, you have to give yourself credit and take pride in the accomplishment when you successfully complete a scheduled activity.

As you climb the ladder of well-being, you will find that different types of actions, and different ways of looking at them, will be most helpful. Scheduling individual actions may become less necessary, and examining and changing the broader domains and strategies may yield greater growth.

# The Hierarchy of Becoming

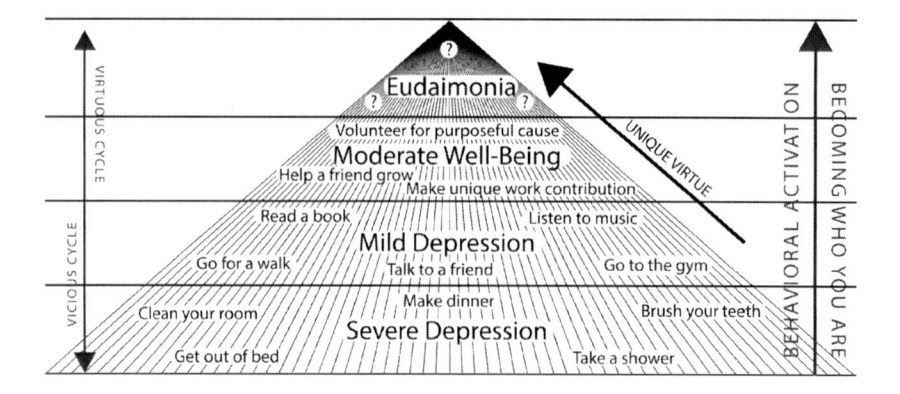

```
                          Eudaimonia
                    Volunteer for purposeful cause
                    Moderate Well-Being
                Help a friend grow
                            Make unique work contribution
        Read a book                      Listen to music
                    Mild Depression
        Go for a walk    Talk to a friend    Go to the gym
                        Make dinner
    Clean your room                         Brush your teeth
                    Severe Depression
        Get out of bed                  Take a shower
```

(Left axis: VIRTUOUS CYCLE / VICIOUS CYCLE; Right axis: BEHAVIORAL ACTIVATION / BECOMING WHO YOU ARE; Arrow labeled UNIQUE VIRTUE)

This image is meant to show a hierarchy of becoming—an upward path directly away from clinical depression and toward health and eudaimonia. The activities listed in each section are examples of prescriptive behaviors to schedule and take each day to elevate you to the next level.

You can think of this hierarchy as the mountains of the overview from a side angle. This is what it looks like to ascend the mountains of well-being, broken down by specific tasks. They are intended to signal more and more of your virtue to yourself, gradually and organically increasing your self-esteem and elevating your mental state along with it.

Behavioral activation is one of the most effective treatments within the most effective therapeutic methodology for depression, CBT. As simple as it seems, practicing the daily activity schedule has proven to gradually lift depression. But the process doesn't end with recovery.

The upward arrow on the right shows "behavioral activation" on one side and "becoming who you are" on the other side to indicate that these are fundamentally the same process. We call it "treatment" when the individual is clinically depressed. We call it something like "self-actualization" when they are healthy and thriving. But I believe it is a single, undifferentiated process of self-becoming.

While activities like getting out of bed and brushing your teeth are essentially common to everyone, and hence don't require much individual virtue, the higher activities get harder to define because they increasingly vary from one person to the next. The diagonal arrow shows that more "virtue convergence," or bringing together of one's unique character strengths, is necessary the higher you go.

Virtue convergence requires a concurrent process of introspection and experimentation—simultaneously learning more about your virtues/values and trying out strategies to integrate them with one another and into your lifestyle. Then you learn more and apply these new observations, in a process not too unlike the scientific method.

Virtue convergence is the process by which we integrate multiple virtues together and bring them out in a consistent and unified way. If you have a great gift and a strong value for public speaking, you must find a way to integrate this virtue into your actual day-to-day behaviors. Otherwise, that virtue will go unsignaled to yourself and remain dormant. You will have no recent evidence of this virtue, and hence it will be as if it didn't exist.

To actually take part in this becoming, your virtues must be integrated into the whole of yourself. The "New Years resolution" style of bringing out a virtue will not work.[25] You can't simply decide to be a kinder person from now on. As Nietzsche argued, building virtue into your character is a sort of integration of the many parts of the self.[26]

You'll see that the arrows on the left show the vicious and virtuous feedback loops at play. The reason depression has such gravity is that it's a vicious cycle.[27]

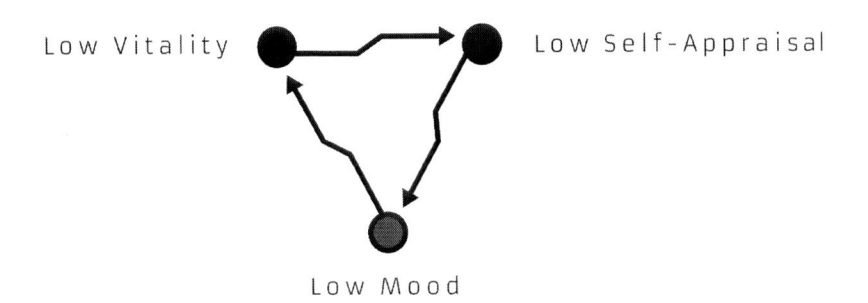

Low Vitality    Low Self-Appraisal

Low Mood

Feeling bad causes you to decrease your activity, which gives you less evidence of your own strengths, which in turn causes you to feel worse and decrease your activity even more. This is why getting out is so difficult, and why those dealing with severe depression often struggle to get out of bed each day.

But for those who can push past this struggle, there is a virtuous cycle to be tapped into on the higher end.[28] As we have explored, efforts to bring our your strengths, little by little, can gradually bring about a positive spiral of behavior, perceptions, and moods, that can elevate your happiness and character in tandem.

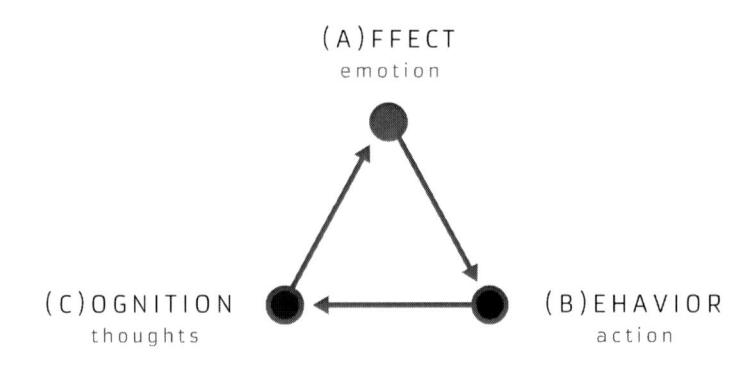

(A)FFECT
emotion

(C)OGNITION
thoughts

(B)EHAVIOR
action

## Domain Design

At a certain point in your journey of becoming, you will find that moving higher will require you to find new ways to exercise your virtues. To develop your virtue domains. You build your relationships to be a vessel for interpersonal virtues. You build your career to be a vessel for leadership and creativity.

Developing virtue domains can allow you to coordinate and consolidate multiple virtues in one place. Your virtues can work together synergistically instead of competing for your time.

Seligman provides the following exercise to boost your happiness by putting them to use in your life:

I want you to create a designated time in your schedule when you will exercise one or more of your signature strengths in a new way either at work or at home or in leisure—just make sure that you create a clearly defined opportunity to use it. For example:

If your signature strength is creativity, you may choose to set aside two hours one evening to begin working on a screenplay.

- If you identify hope/optimism as a strength, you might write a column for the local newspaper in which you express hope about the future of the space program.

- If you claim self-control as a strength, you might choose to work out at the gym rather than watch TV one evening.

- If your strength is an appreciation of beauty and excellence, you might take a longer, more beautiful route to and from work, even though it adds twenty minutes more to your commute.

—**Martin Seligman**, *Flourish*[7]

There is compelling data to back this practice up. Seligman found that prompting people to identify and use their signature strengths in a new way is an effective intervention for flourishing.[7]

It increased happiness and decreased depression for 6 months.[29] And these findings have been replicated many times. To list a few:

The use of one's top strengths leads to a decreased likelihood of depression and stress and an increase in satisfaction in law students.[30]

The signature strengths intervention was found to have a positive impact on happiness, depression, and life satisfaction.[31]

A randomly controlled study of a multi-step, single-session intervention focusing on signature strengths showed significant increases in well-being and decreases in depression and anxiety in the long-run while stress levels decreased in the short-run.[32]

A group of students randomly assigned to an 8-week, online strengths intervention showed significant gains in well-being, compared to a control group.[33]

Character strengths like courage, future-mindedness, optimism, interpersonal skills, work ethic, hope, and perseverance have been found to correlate with lower levels of mental illness, suicide, violence, and substance abuse.[7]

One study found that activities centered around "doing good" like expressing gratitude, volunteering, persevering at a goal in the face of obstacles was associated with much greater subjective well-being than activities centered around "feeling good" like getting drunk, having casual sex, or obtaining material goods.[34]

Another study found that virtue-based goals were consistently linked to higher well-being than hedonic or material goals.[35]

Seligman found that the strengths of love, gratitude, hope, curiosity, zest, and wisdom were most strongly linked to life satisfaction. They were followed by lower but still significant correlations between satisfaction and strengths like persistence, self-regulation, spirituality, forgiveness, social intelligence, humor, leadership, bravery, citizenship, integrity, kindness, fairness, prudence, love of learning, judgment, appreciation of beauty, creativity, and modesty/humility.[35]

At the one-month, three-month, and six-month follow-ups, participants asked to exercise their personal strengths in a novel way were happier and less depressed compared to controls.[36]

Another study found that students participating in a "Strengths Gym" program for harnessing personal strengths had higher life satisfaction than those who did not participate.[37]

When you open up new avenues, or virtue domains, to express your strengths through, it gets easier to converge upon them. And increasing virtuous activity makes you happier, more energized, and more motivated, which enables more ambitious pursuits.

It's also possible that existing domains may be depriving your virtues of expression. If you don't feel that your job provides your virtues with an outlet, leaving may be the best thing you can do.

If your degree program or career feels like an exhausting dead end, dropping out or changing careers may be the only way forward. If you're in a relationship with someone who doesn't value your virtues, leaving may be the most promising path toward eudaimonia.

You may be surprised by how quickly your well-being improves when you make a change like this. Unhealthy domains can suck up all of your resources and take away your ability to exercise your signature strengths.

Navigating this landscape is not easy, and unfortunately, there are no foolproof rules for when you should enter a new virtue domain or exit an old one. You have to allow your knowledge of your strengths and skills to guide you.

Typical depression treatment tells patients to practice behavioral activation for a few weeks, or until the depression lifts.[38] But this highlights the problem with this medical model of depression.

The practice of integrating your strengths into your character is a never-ending process. This process is what elevates and maintains your well-being—what keeps you from slipping into the valleys of virtue.

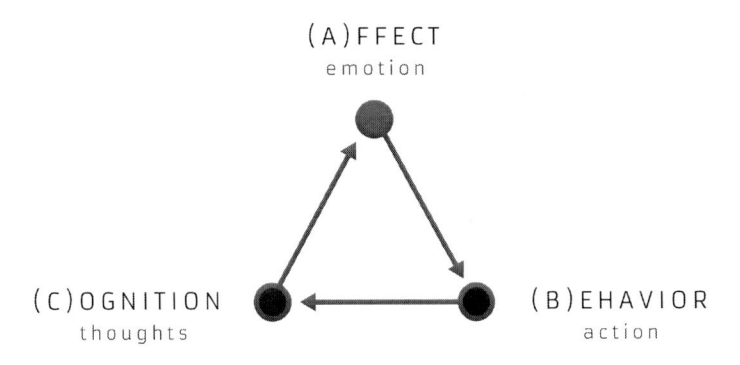

(A)FFECT
emotion

(C)OGNITION
thoughts

(B)EHAVIOR
action

Sometimes we get so caught up in our goals that we forget to appreciate it when we achieve them. We move on to the next goal without experiencing pride or gratitude for the virtues we've shown.

If this describes you, start journaling whenever you exercise a virtue, demonstrate a strength, or accomplish a goal that means something to you. Remember to pause and take pride in it.

Pride is essentially the feeling of your virtue portfolio going up in value. So if you want to build a strong identity, don't forget to acknowledge what makes you great.[39] Bask in yourself. And don't feel bad about it.

Your job in life is to maximize your virtue. This is the most healthy, energizing, life-affirming, and truly altruistic thing you can do. Don't ever let anyone convince you that you should feel guilty for working toward excellence.

And in the process of trying to be great, work to make the world around you great as well. Treat every person you encounter like you are trying to serve them in the cultivation of their character. Ask yourself, not how you can help make someone else's life easier, but how you can help them cultivate the latent virtues within them.

# Key Takeaways:

- Anti-depressant medications have abysmally low success rates. And the reason they are not the most promising treatment for depression is that they typically treat the neurochemical symptoms of the condition instead of its root cause.

- As long as your identity is in disrepair and you are not seeing evidence for your virtues, you will remain in the vicious cycle of depression. This is why the most promising and effective treatment for depression is behavioral activation.

- To use this tool, simply create a daily activity schedule, designed to slightly increase the amount of virtue you bring out through your daily behaviors. Focus on actions that create a sense of pleasure, mastery, and virtue-utilization, and take these actions even if you don't feel like it.

- Virtue convergence is the process of integrating increasing amounts of virtue into your lifestyle, merging your greatest strengths together through your personal endeavors. Gradually work to embody your ideal self through your habits and behaviors.

- Try to identify new ways to exercise your signature strengths and cultivate domains that bring them out. Your job in life is to maximize your net virtue, and this is the most healthy, energizing, life-affirming, and truly altruistic way you can live your life. Your self-appraisal system can be viewed as a cycle of actions, thoughts, and emotions. You take certain actions, and your self-appraisal system interprets those actions and forms self-beliefs accordingly. These beliefs result in your mood, your mood then influences your actions, and the cycle continues.[1]

# 12

# The Path of Self-Becoming: You Shall Become The Person You Are

## Sight of the Summit—January 2021

The year of 2021 was a time of identity restructuring for me. As I wrapped up the book and lockdowns began to lighten, I slowly started moving back into the virtue domains in which I could thrive.

I started making friends and working to rebuild the social skills that had slowly atrophied through the pandemic and my writing process. I started reading, creating music, and going on spontaneous adventures with my partner again. And I started pushing out of my comfort zone, going on podcasts to talk about my new book.

I also started working with an early-stage startup that was building some ambitious technology. It allowed me to replace my part-time job with another part-time gig—one that better utilized my skills and valued my work far more. I knew I needed to use this opportunity to prove my own beliefs wrong and straighten out the story of my identity, so I gave it everything I had.

This role helped to reveal just how distorted my view of my own capacities had become. Where I had struggled to fill the needs of the previous company I worked with, my work was clearly bringing value and creativity every single week at this one. I took on a co-founding role as Chief Design Officer as my work became more integral to the operations of the business.

And some interesting things happened with that first book I was so convinced had failed. It kind of took off. Consistent optimization work led to more and more monthly sales. It ended up selling over 50,000 copies in the first year, which is virtually unheard of for a self-published book.

And gradually, the thousands of kind messages I received from readers reminded me that my book was no trivial obsession, but had a deep and genuine impact on many readers. Though not for everyone, it was clear that the book had radically changed perspectives, minds, and lives for the better.

Designing the Mind has proven to be the ultimate vessel for the actualization of my virtues—the convergence of nearly everything I'm good at and fascinated with. Whether I'm writing books, having philosophical debates with readers, or going on podcast interviews, I have nearly endless opportunities to exercise, self-signal, and share my unique character strengths.

I had always thought of myself as a leader. But in the testing ground of real-life, corporate leadership, I had no choice but to question this competency I had grown attached to. But I've now acknowledged that corporate leadership is far from the only kind. It turns out I was a cult leader all along!

Shortly after publishing the book, I built an online community and mental training platform called Mindform (no, it's not an actual cult—unless you're into that kind of thing). Through this community, my leadership skills are continually demanded and exercised. My regular articles are an opportunity to share my practical insights and help others master their minds. Our weekly member events allow me to exercise many of the virtues I had always prided myself on, but never had an outlet for before. And my daily decisions guide the quality and direction of the community.

A few years ago, my virtues as a thinker and writer had few paths to expression. I knew I had a set of virtues, unique to me and largely unactualized, but I didn't have a clear path to bringing them out.

But by publishing DTM, engaging with my readers and trying to help them grow, going on podcasts, launching Mindform, and continuing my writing, I have been able to give life to many of these virtues in a way that is synergistic rather than competitive. A single mission guides all of these endeavors, and it brings integration to many of my seemingly disparate strengths.

Today I couldn't suppress these traits if I tried. They are too deep a part of my motivational system now, too connected to my lifestyle, too tightly programmed into my mental software. Of course, my journey to greater virtue actualization is far from complete. There are many social virtues, like personability and warmth, that I haven't managed to integrate into my character very well yet.

The events of 2020 altered my self-esteem because I was cut off from most virtue domains and failing in the others. I gradually returned to my happy self in 2021 because my book opened new virtue domains, and I refocused of being better in the others while maintaining greater balance in my projects.

As I approached the end of my depressive period, my self-esteem remained unstable for several months. I would start to feel like a competent, likable person, only to feel this sense throttle in response to minor failure. This instability makes sense in light of the identity shift going on, but at the time I couldn't help but frame it as my brain trying to shake my confidence.

I would start to patch my personal enlightenment-story back together—to forget about the last year and tell myself that I was happy the whole time. And then life would say "Oh, you think you've got it figured out?" Here's some more. And then there would be that feeling again.

But there was a bright side to the unusual events of the pandemic, for some of us at least. The rapid shift in lifestyle, and relatively rapid shift back, gave me an unusual opportunity to observe the evolution of my mental state. I went from very much not depressed, to depressed for months, to very much not depressed, all in the span of a year.

It allowed me to rule out many possible theories on what depression is and how it is caused. To observe the correlations in my own life and guide my search. No, it's not some kind of random chemical imbalance detached from my life and thinking. No, it's not just a response to concrete loss.

Yes, I realize my experiences are anecdotal. But personal experience can provide a depth of insight that is hard to attain through lifeless data and studies, even when they ultimately tell the same story. The research was already there, but I think I needed to live it to learn how it all came together.

Ultimately, I have this period, and this persistent reminder of my vulnerability, to thank for the theory I present in this book. It's only because I couldn't forget about my broken identity that I was forced to integrate it into a more accurate worldview.

I started examining what had happened to me through the lens of the evolutionary and neuropsychological findings I had spent so much time studying. And then it clicked.

As for Tory, I haven't talked to her since leaving my job. She ended up leaving the company not long after I did due to stress and frustration. Despite her brilliance, there was a kind of desperation behind her ferocity that I could never fully pin down.

I suspect she came into this job from a position of failure that left her with a broken identity. Though I know she didn't intend to play a role in the breakdown of mine, I think she may have seen me as a threat to her reconstruction efforts.

This is all speculation, as I don't know what story led her path to converge with mine, or where it has taken her since. All I know is that I saw only a small glimpse into her personal virtue struggle. I hope it leads her to eudaimonia.

I no longer feel ashamed of my neurodivergence, and have even come to take pride in being autistic. It took time to integrate it into my identity, but has slowly become a part of me to the point that I wouldn't change it if I could.

At this point, my social limitations make up the small percentage of my life that doesn't feel ideal. The rest is made up of constant excitement and joy and love. I have work that is so rewarding and immersive that even using the word "work" to describe it seems disgraceful, and my mind is in a state of tranquil flow most of the time.

I'm in the happiest relationship I could ask for. You know in movies when they show people in a family or relationship having so much fun or bonding so much that you just know something bad is about to happen? That's what our life together is like. Only so far (knock on wood), that cinematic tragedy hasn't come.

I know this may feel like a happy ending. But of course it isn't really an ending. I have a feeling that "happy ending syndrome" is one of the most common issues that leads some to slip into the valleys of virtue.

People become complacent and take their stable job and healthy marriage as signs that they deserve to stop trying. That their job is done, and they can now ride off into the sunset and live happily ever after. That they no longer have to become—they can now just be.

I now know from experience what I have long suspected. As a human being, my job will never be done. I will never graduate from the great school of becoming. I will never retire from the full-time job of virtue convergence. And I don't want to.

My virtue trek began with that crucial realization in middle school that I had a lot of work to do to become a person I truly admired. I slowly climbed my way toward the summits of eudaimonia from there. I lost my footing and slipped down to the base in 2020. And fortunately, I have quickly found my way to my highest point yet since then. Today, my focus remains on reaching the highest peak of self-becoming possible.

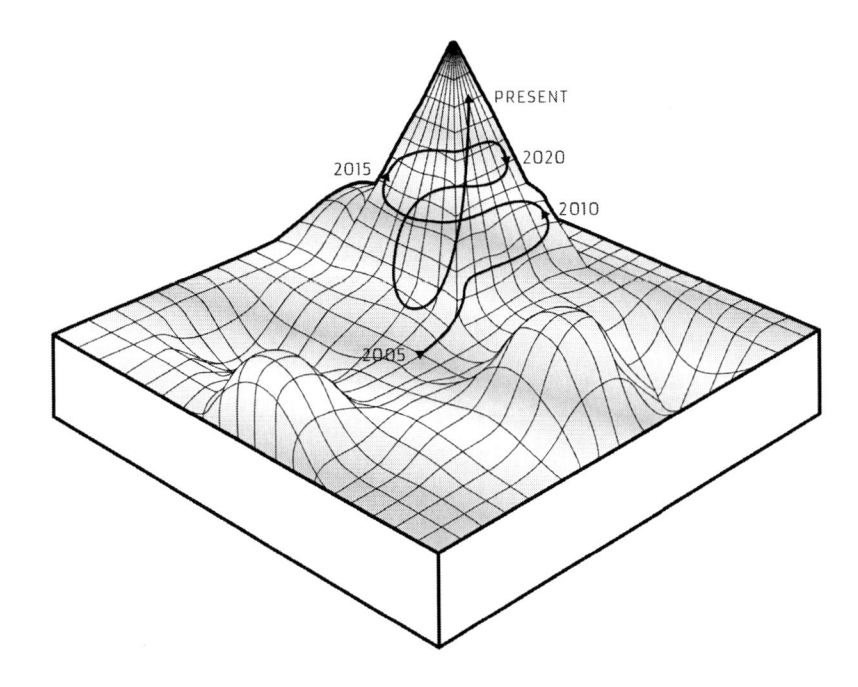

## The Obstacle

Once the pandemic restrictions began to clear in 2022, my partner and I took a trip to Europe and Asia. We visited the site of the porch where the Stoics first shared their teachings in Greece. We meditated inside a 9th-century Hindu and Buddhist temple in Indonesia. And we hiked in the Swiss Alps where Nietzsche formulated his ideas.

As I write this section, we have just finished hiking the Cinque Terre trail in Italy. It is possible to travel to each of the towns in Cinque Terre by train, making the trek seemingly unnecessary. And there is something about mountains and the act of hiking that gets me thinking.

Why am I doing this? Why am I walking up difficult terrain just for the sake of doing it? Why do I feel good after I've done it, even though it feels bad at the time?

I grew up playing video games, and I would often look up cheat codes to give my characters superpowers like invincibility and flying. It was always incredibly fun, for about fifteen minutes. After that, I got bored. The thrill of unlimited power wore off, and the challenge that made the game fun was gone.

Observing this phenomenon, I became disillusioned with these cheat codes, but also with many other ostensible rewards in life. I decided, for example, that I was never going to play the lottery. And it wasn't just because I didn't like the idea of throwing money away to statistically negligible odds. It was because I didn't want to win. I didn't want to ruin the game of life with cheat codes.

Perhaps this preference is a luxury for those comfortable enough to have a choice on how to build wealth. But to me, the way I'm currently making my living, though less extravagant than a mega lottery, is far more rewarding. And it's rewarding specifically because its obstacles have required my unique virtues to overcome.

In Nietzsche's allegorical work, *Thus Spoke Zarathustra*, a hunchback approaches the protagonist and asks if he is able to cure his deformed back. Zarathustra refuses and replies "If one takes the hump from the hunchback, one takes his spirit too—thus teach the people." It may seem cruel to refuse to cure a disability if he was able, but in this case, the decision comes from a place of genuine compassion.[1]

Nietzsche wasn't actually critical of the idea of helping others—he actually referred to the "gift-giving virtue" as the highest of all virtues. He was critical of the popular notion of compassion, calling it a "religion of snug cosiness."[2]

He thought simply removing obstacles from someone's life was a lazy way of helping them. It did more, he thought, to help the helper feel superior than actually benefit the person struggling. And it failed to take a unified account of genuine happiness. It only helped them change their position in the x or y axes.

Nietzsche thought that if you truly wanted to help someone, or help yourself, your efforts must aid in the cultivation of character. You must help them get higher in the z-axis.

Nietzsche scholar Peter Kail says:

> To feel compassion for another involves perceiving someone as suffering in some manner. But determining whether someone is genuinely suffering is not always an easy matter... The person showing compassion "knows nothing of the whole inner sequence and inter-connection," determining the "misfortune" that is the object of compassion. Instead, compassion is superficial and "strips" from the person what is truly personal to him or her.
>
> This brings us back to the hunchback. His identity is partly determined by his physical condition, which not only constitutes a resistance to overcome—hence allowing the exercise of the will to power—but also shapes his character. His character is the product of the "whole inner sequence and inter-connection," of which his hunchback is a decisive part. Thus, if "one takes the hump from the hunchback, one takes his spirit too."[3]

Stoic thinker Marcus Aurelius famously said "The impediment to action advances action. What stands in the way becomes the way."[4] And Ryan Holiday captured this phrase in his book "*The Obstacle Is the Way*," which he emblemized with an image of a winding path going up a mountain.[5] Does this emblem remind you of anything?

*Eudaimonia*

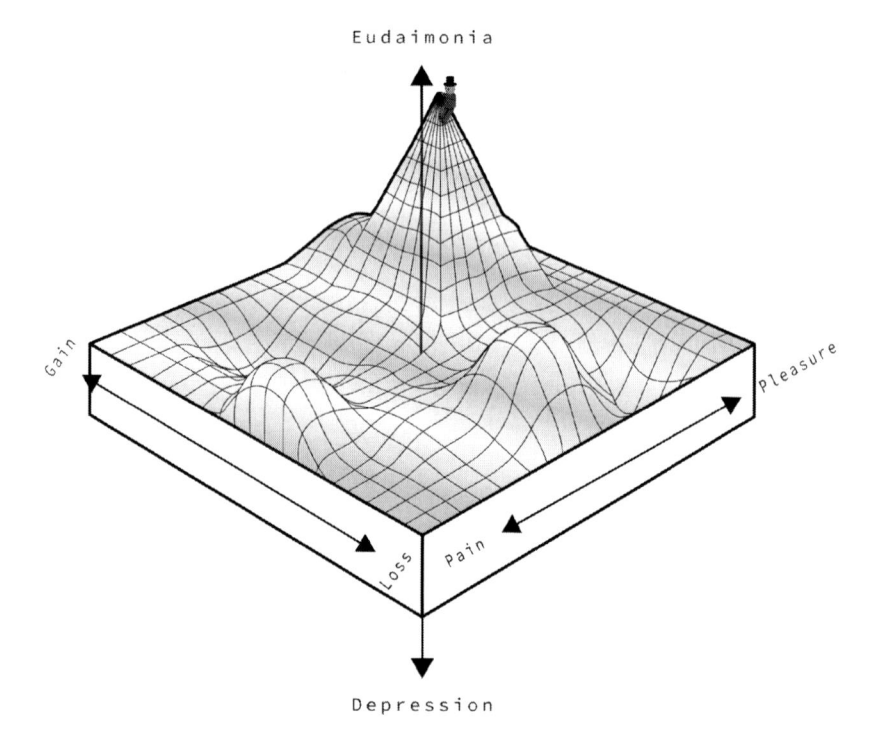

*Gain* · *Pleasure* · *Loss* · *Pain*

*Depression*

This image takes on deeper meaning when we consider that the impediments to our goals can often be seen as the mountains that shape our virtues. The challenges we choose for ourselves provide opportunities to increase or exhibit our personal strengths as we overcome their resistance.

You see, you don't just climb your mountain of virtue. You build it. You sculpt it. If you simply cured the hunchback, you would take away the platform to higher eudaimonia that he had spent his life sculpting. Overcoming obstacles is an inherent task of developing virtue. You can't reach the peaks of eudaimonia without something to stand on.

And the defining struggle of my life that I've shared here is no exception. Being autistic has undoubtedly pushed me to cultivate greater character than if I had been dealt no challenges at all. It's what pushed me to develop my resourcefulness and creativity. It's what pushed me to build persistence and grit. And it's what has made it so rewarding when I've made social progress and managed to build close and fulfilling relationships.

If I had been born neurotypical, it might have been more comfortable. But comfort simply cannot compare to character.

> It can ruin your life only if it ruins your character. Otherwise it cannot harm you—inside or out.
>
> —Marcus Aurelius, *Meditations*

Though he was critical of the Stoics, Nietzsche had more in common with them than he thought. He sided with them in his rejection of hedonism and elevation of virtue. He agreed that it was greatness of the soul that constituted the good life, not pleasure, comfort, or external success.[6] They even echoed the same principles through the same metaphors at times:

> Examine the lives of the best and most fruitful people and peoples and ask yourselves whether a tree that is supposed to grow to a proud height can dispense with bad weather and storms; whether misfortune and external resistance, some kinds of hatred, jealousy, stubbornness, mistrust, hardness, avarice, and violence do not belong among the favorable conditions without which any great growth even of virtue is scarcely possible.
>
> —Friedrich Nietzsche, The *Gay Science*[7]

Why, then, do you wonder that good men are shaken in order that they may grow strong? No tree becomes rooted and sturdy unless many a wind assails it. For by its very tossing it tightens its grip and plants its roots more securely; the fragile trees are those that have grown in a sunny valley. It is,

> therefore, to the advantage even of good men, to the end that they may be unafraid, to live constantly amidst alarms and to bear with patience the happenings which are ills to him only who ill supports them.
>
> —**Seneca**, *On Providence*[8]

The character-cultivating power of hardship is exactly why the Stoics were known to wish bad luck and betrayal on one another.[9] It's why Nietzsche said "To those human beings who are of any concern to me I wish suffering, desolation, sickness, ill-treatment, indignities."[10]

And it's why Martin Seligman and the research he cites on post-traumatic growth suggest that individuals who have experienced difficult and painful events in their lives end up with stronger character, more intense strengths, and higher well-being than those who haven't.[11] Our character, like our muscles, can only be strengthened by being exercised.[12]

> A loss scarcely remains a loss for an hour: in some way or other a gift from heaven has always fallen into our lap at the same moment—a new form of strength, for example: be it but a new opportunity for the exercise of strength!
>
> —**Friedrich Nietzsche**, *The Gay Science*[7]

I remember when I was in the throes of writing DTM. After months of planning, consolidating notes, and outlining, I now had to actually do the work.

It was harder than I had anticipated. I somehow thought the process would be relatively smooth given all the notes I already had in place. But here I was struggling to put words on a page that didn't make me cringe.

I talked to my partner about this challenge, almost questioning whether

I was capable of doing the task I had been planning for years. I can clearly remember how she replied: "I think you knew writing a book wouldn't be easy. And if you're like me, you probably wouldn't want it to be."

It was exactly what I needed to hear, and she was exactly the person to hear it from. She had thru-hiked the Appalachian Trail just a couple of years prior. She hiked two thousand miles, even though her car was working just fine.

Hiking a long-distance trail like this is the epitome of a project one takes on purely for the challenge. If you had wanted to do something easy, you just wouldn't do it at all. And it served as a perfect reminder that obstacles are the reason we take on these endeavors.

I did know writing the book wouldn't be easy. But I think I had convinced myself that I wanted it to be. When she said that, it became obvious that I didn't want it to be easy. It wouldn't be an accomplishment if it were easy. It wouldn't require much virtue—wouldn't bring me much pride to complete it if it were.

Our little hike across Cinque Terre was nothing compared to her two-thousand mile trek, but it still demonstrated the rewarding nature of challenges. If someone had offered us a free train pass in our hike across the coastal villages, they might have thought they were doing us a favor by taking away the need to walk twelve miles. But we would not have taken them up on this gesture—we were hiking it because we wanted to hike it. And we found ourselves feeling bad for those who had gone with the train pass.

We got the opportunity to do something difficult—to exert and develop our strengths and push through the challenges and pain. And we got an incredible view while doing it. The coastal towns are beautiful, but the mountain trails between them are even more beautiful and multiplied our appreciation for them.

There is a rich connection in our minds and culture between the cultivation of virtue and the ascent of mountains. It's all too perfect that the ancient Greek term for virtue, areté, is defined today as "a sharp-crested ridge in rugged mountains." And I think it is no accident that Nietzsche makes this comment about tourists climbing mountains.

> Tourists — they climb the mountain like beasts, stupid and sweating; it seems that no one bothered to tell them that there are beautiful vistas along the way.
>
> —**Friedrich Nietzsche**, *Human, All Too Human*[13]

One of my core goals in this book is to break the illusion that your challenges are mere obstacles in the way of your goals. To get you to stop approaching life like a tourist climbing incredible mountains, frustrated by the fact that it isn't easy.

No matter what challenge you are facing, the act of overcoming it is the entire point of life—it's where true happiness lies. It's the act of cultivating virtue—the only true good in life. The act of becoming who you are.

How have the challenges of your life defined your character? Who would you be today without these mountains? And which heights will you ascend next?

## Advice for Self-Becoming

In my previous book, I coined the term "psychitecture" and laid out a framework for this practice. How do these ideas fit into the ones in this book?

Psychitecture is the process of designing your own mind—of optimizing the internal patterns of your own beliefs, emotions, and behaviors.[14] With the framework of the overview, we can fit this practice into a broader perspective.

The structural components of *Designing the Mind*, cognitive, emotional, and behavioral self-mastery, are not just regular virtues. They are meta-virtues that make it possible for an individual to see and act out their virtues.

These traits of wisdom, equanimity, and self-control are not likely to get you social approval because they probably were not selected for in the same way others were. But the mastery of your own cognition, emotions, and behavior is what makes it possible for you to climb to higher peaks of virtue without getting in your own way. This has led some to refer to self-mastery as "the master virtue."[15]

When you develop these traits, people will admire you for the virtues they see without knowing that the cultivation of self-mastery is what makes them possible to such a high degree. And psychitecture is an endeavor that can help you cultivate self-mastery and refine your internal software so that you can go out and become who you are.

Whether you are altering your automatic thoughts, your map of your values, or your own character, you are redesigning yourself—changing your mind so that you can begin to align with your values as closely as possible. If you haven't taken on your own psychitectural journey, I invite you to join us.

We must remember that our happiness mechanism was not built for our own sake. It was not meant to be gamed for maximum well-being. It was meant to maximize social status and genetic outcomes. For this reason, we are not wired to be conscious of it directly. In fact, we probably evolved not to understand this mechanism very well.

Some studies show that we systematically underestimate the role that virtue plays in our happiness—almost like evolution didn't "want" us to figure it out. One study called "The Virtue Blind Spot" concludes that we predict less satisfaction from virtuous behaviors than we actually reap and that "affective forecasting errors drive people away from the exercise of virtue."[16]

Your genes want you preoccupied with accumulating resources, attracting mates, and maximizing social status—not the internal indicator that actually regulates your happiness. That's why placing virtue above all else and living for your values is an act of rebellion.[17]

To take part in it, you must cultivate metacognitive awareness, use reason to strategically coordinate your virtues, and change the habitual patterns of your character. We must overcome our external bias and focus on internal optimization. We must be psychological software optimizers first and circumstance optimizers second. We must be psychitects.

It can be incredibly difficult at times to act in alignment with our values, and you may need a way of reminding yourself of its importance. After reading a pre-release version of this book, one Mindform member actually said he had turned the acronym for the book, BWYA, into a kind of mantra that he pronounced "Booyah."

Thinking "BWYA" was a prompt for him to recall the principles in the book and act in a way he would admire instead of giving in to anxiety or inertia. He described this simple practice as an "amazingly effective" tool, and I would like to offer it to readers who want to ensure they exercise their virtues. When you don't feel like you can bring yourself to take the actions you admire, just say BWYA.

I want to offer a bit of simple advice, which I have put together thinking specifically about the people in my life, the readers I have connected with over the last few years, and myself. If you ever need a reminder of some of the core practical insights of this book without getting into all the intellectual arguments and studies, feel free to return to this section.

You have within you a guide to what kind of life you should be living. You may have learned to ignore it, in the name of fitting in, being practical, or simply getting through your life. But it's there, telling you where to go next.

And you can access it by asking yourself a few questions. What do you admire in others? What are you good at? What have others complimented you on? What has made you feel proud? What makes you like yourself? What makes you feel alive? How can you align your life with your answers to these questions?

Spend time with yourself. If you don't know the answer to how you should live, a decision to make, a habit to form or break, you've got some introspective work to do. It is considered normal to use the endless supply of information and entertainment available today to distract you from your own inner voice and the sometimes troubling, self-critical thoughts it produces. You must listen to it and resist the urge to escape.

Popular culture is hotly engaged in debates over how others should live their lives. Should you get married? Should you do drugs? Should you move out of your parents' house? Should men be more masculine or less? Should women pursue careers or raise children?

Let me assure you that all of these questions are irrelevant distractions. In every case, this general advice about how different groups should live would be improved greatly by simply urging individuals to inquire into their own nature—their own self-approval—and educating them on how this can be done.

It doesn't matter what anyone says someone of your background, your gender, your ethnicity, or your neurotype is supposed to do. You already have a compass, inscribed in your DNA—a blueprint for your own self-approval. You need only get in touch with this sense to know how you should live your life.

Happiness and unhappiness aren't determined simply by the balance of chemicals in your brain. If you aren't happy, your brain isn't broken and in need of repair. It is telling you that your actions need to change. You have to listen.

Depression is a vicious cycle in which idle behaviors lead to negative self-evaluations, which lead to negative emotions, which lead to idle behaviors. You must break the cycle by taking action that causes you to admire yourself. Little by little, increase the amount of admirable behavior in your lifestyle.

Do not numb yourself to the pain of self-disapproval, self-loathing, or shame. Do not try to drown out the self-critical thoughts or feelings. Learn from them. Make changes to the root problem and not just its symptoms. Improve your actions, your virtues, and the domains you bring them out through.

Don't believe everything you think. Toxic work environments, unhealthy relationships, and technological echo chambers can lead us to adopt distorted views of ourselves. Be skeptical of the negative self-beliefs you develop, and practice cognitive restructuring to sort out the truth about your strengths.

You have to take the actions that you admire in others—that make you admire yourself. Even if you don't feel like it. The modern world, the demands of work, and of course, the internet all make it tempting and easy to forget that you must become who you are.

But your neurochemicals don't care what you feel like doing. Your self-appraisal system doesn't care how much fun Candy Crush is. If you don't insist on living in alignment with your ideals and taking actions that make you proud of who you are, you won't approve of yourself and won't be happy.

You may not feel as if you have permission to truly pursue the actions and domains of your ideals. It may seem silly. But not only can you build your life around these things, you must. You will be unhappy as long as you are simply getting by and not tapping into your deepest passions and ideals.

The point of living is not to figure out what others want you to do. It isn't to craft a life that looks like the "right answer" to the people around you. Stop worrying about how your life looks on paper, or on your social media accounts. Craft your character, not your image. Figure out what kind of person you truly admire, and then go work to become that person. Though it is not easy by any means, it really is that simple.

Do not allow the state of the world, or your perception of it, to bring you down with it. There are many deep, unsustainable issues in our world that have major implications for individual well-being. To deny that is delusional. But blaming, dwelling on, and reacting emotionally to these problems will get you absolutely nowhere.

Do not make excuses for not making yourself happier. Do not blame your genes, your parents, or your neurotype. Not because you're wrong, but because you don't have control over these things and don't have time to dwell on them.

Insist on living a great life, even if the world seems to be crumbling around you. There is truly no point in mourning the state of the world when you only have a few brief moments to experience it. If you want to improve the world, let your path to personal excellence lead you to action.

Acknowledge the problems and inequities that have contributed to where you are now. See if you can use your gifts to do anything about them. And take full responsibility for your choices, attitudes, and flourishing going forward.

Beware of complacency, and do not mistake the life of idle comfort for the end-goal of human existence. Situations of comfortable mediocrity are more dangerous for your long-term well-being than acutely negative ones, because these are the situations that will never force you to improve.

The good life is hard. It's active. It involves pushing yourself to your limits each day. No, mindless work done for profit alone is not a rewarding part of the good life. But when it applies your greatest strengths and contributes to others, hard work can be one of the best things in life.

No one is going to make you become who you are. Your culture, your friends, and your boss are not going to remind you to become who you are. In fact, many others have it in their best interests that you remain a limited version of yourself. You are the only one who can become who you are.

If a job, a community, or a relationship consistently causes you to feel that your virtues are dead, stagnant, or worthless, your path to eudaimonia will likely demand that you leave. If you find yourself in a comfortable position that is holding you back from your potential, but you don't feel you have a strong enough push to leave, let me be that push for you. Leave. Don't walk—run.

Right now is the right time to make a change that will bring you closer to your ideals. The many reasons you have as to why it isn't possible to become who you are right now—not enough time, not enough money, physical, mental, social limitations... these are stories you tell yourself to try to get off the hook for your growth.

I'm not saying that you don't lack money—I'm saying you are overlooking creative funding opportunities. I'm not saying you don't have tendencies or weaknesses that might prevent a particular path—I'm saying there are ways to work around, alter, or even turn those weaknesses into strengths that you haven't allowed yourself to consider yet.

Here is the question you must ask yourself: Are you pursuing greatness? Yes, greatness! When we criticize those with delusions of grandeur, we forget that it's the delusion, not the grandeur, that warrants reproach.

On the other hand, if you currently find yourself grinding away at your work in an attempt to achieve your highest potential, consider that there may be other ways of exercising your virtues. I respect the drive to make the most of your life. But you may achieve greater net virtue by striving for balance.

If you look in the mirror and see only a worker—someone without loving connection, humor, or peace, you probably will not have full admiration for yourself. You have been cut off from important virtue domains, lowering your overall virtue in the pursuit of productivity. Your full potential lies in love just as much as or more than leadership.

Happiness does not come from achievements, wealth, or success. It doesn't come from any outcome in your life. It comes from the actions you see yourself taking. The positive traits that these actions demonstrate. The virtues you exercise on a daily basis.

Navigating your way in life is like a game of hot and cold—do I like myself more or less? How about when I do this? This is the nature of this great experiment—take a step and listen for the message.

Continually ask yourself if your actions make you admire yourself more or less than before. Ask yourself how much your greatest strengths were used in the last day, the last week, and the last year. Make whatever changes are necessary to increase the virtue in your actions and the pride you feel in yourself. And yes, try your hardest. Your virtue trek will be full of treacherous cliffs and dead ends, but you have to find the path upward.

Do not waste precious time on this planet doing anything other than striving toward your highest potential—in your relationships and communities, in your work, and in your daily habits and behaviors—your character. Don't waste a minute of your life being less than you can be. Get out of your house, away from your desk, and experience the world. Embody yourself and your life fully, as much of the time as you can.

You must ascend the peaks of virtue and embody your highest ideals. Your self-esteem needs it. Your relationships need it. The world needs it. Remember the overview. Remember this framework. And remember how easy it is to forget.

# The Task of a Sculptor

Now we return to that mysterious phrase of Nietzsche's, "become who you are." Few have even attempted to explain what it might mean. But I'd like to venture to do just that.

The process of optimizing our minds is fundamentally an act of bringing our actual selves closer to the template of our ideals. Of bringing greater and greater expression to the virtues that lay dormant in us. It is simultaneously an act of discovery and creation—it is a synthesis of existing components into a unified whole.

The you who must do the "becoming" is you in your current form. The you that you must become is the you of your ideals—the preponderance of all your latent virtues.

You are your innate virtues. By becoming who you are, you are bringing those latent virtues to life and signaling them to yourself.

> Let the growing soul look at life with the question: "What have you truly loved? What has drawn you upward, mastered and blessed you?" Set up the things that you have honoured in front of you. Maybe they will reveal, in their being and their order, a law which is fundamental of your own self. Compare these objects. Consider how one of them completes and broadens and transcends and explains another: how they form a ladder which all the time you have been climbing to find your true self. For your true self does not lie deeply hidden within you. It is an infinite height above you — at least, above what you commonly take to be yourself.
>
> —Friedrich Nietzsche, *Schopenhauer as Educator*[18]

We live in a "be yourself" culture, in which people are generally told to accept and express themselves exactly as they are. This is a huge improvement over cultures that tell individuals that there is something deeply, irredeemably wrong with them. But self-acceptance does not go far enough.

As I have argued, we are continually signaling our own virtues to ourselves. Constantly monitoring our own behaviors for admirable and reprehensible traits. It evolved as a social mechanism, but it has control over something far more important than our social status: our happiness.

We climb up in the z-axis, the true dimension of happiness, only when we increase the amount of virtue in our actions. The highest form of well-being is the product of integrating our signature strengths into our behaviors and lives. The lowest levels of depression occur when we can't see the signal of our virtues.

Our well-being fluctuates according to the inner virtues we are able to bring out and actualize. It is not enough to simply have virtues, latent in our capacities. We must use them. We must create them. We must carve the paths to their actualization out of the hard stone of our psyche.

Renaissance sculptor Michelangelo was known for claiming that he deserved little credit for his beautiful works. They were already there inside the rock, he merely cut them out.

> Every block of stone has a statue inside it and it is the task of the sculptor to discover it. I saw the angel in the marble and carved until I set him free.
>
> —Michelangelo[19]

This is more than a clever way of thinking about art. The final product already existed somewhere inside Michelangelo's ideals. In some part of his mind, he knew what the final product should look like.

But it took decades to cultivate the ability to see and give expression to it. It took trial and error, practice, and failure to reach the point of being able to give form to the figure.

And in a similar and very real sense, the "you" which you must become is already there. It's already inscribed in your values, embedded in your genes.

Nietzsche argued that the heights for which we have aimed—that which we have admired—reflect who we are in the truest sense. He urged us to continually strive toward greater heights, courageously taking step after step in our great ascent.[6]

Maslow's notion of self-becoming closely mirrored Nietzsche's, and he wrote about the concept with great clarity and passion. He was focused, not only on helping individuals achieve unusual levels of health, but also to become, more and more fully, who they were.[20]

> We already have a start, we already have capacities, talents, directions, missions, callings, and then the job is, if we are to take this model seriously, to help them to be more perfectly what they already are, to be more full, more actualizing, more realizing in fact what they are in potentiality.
>
> —**Abraham Maslow**, *The Farther Reaches of Human Nature*[21]

With breathtaking vision, Maslow echoes Nietzsche's sentiments of self-becoming, claiming that the gradual embodiment of one's values was the fundamental task of psychological health. And to betray or ignore those inner ideals was to plant the seeds of pathology in our minds.

Although Maslow listed many different symptoms that result from the neglect of our virtues, such as alienation, hopelessness, and despair, every single "metapathology" he proposes is eerily symptomatic of clinical depression.[21]

What Maslow so elegantly illustrates is that psychological health and self-becoming are not two different achievements, but one and the same. He recognized what few fully grasp today: Becoming happier and becoming a better person are not two different things. Of course they aren't! What could possibly make you happier than you being better?

> Do you want to find out what you ought to be? Then find out who you are! 'Become what thou art!'
>
> —**Abraham Maslow**, *The Farther Reaches of Human Nature*

The act of becoming who you are is the act of carving out your ideal self—of experimenting and discovering ways to bring form to the formless. The act of bringing greater and greater refinements to the crude shapes of character that exist now. Of sculpting the mountain that will require your greatest strengths to climb.

> It is a myth to believe that we will find our authentic self after we have left behind or forgotten one thing or another... To make ourselves, to shape a form from various elements – that is the task! The task of a sculptor! Of a productive human being!
>
> —**Friedrich Nietzsche**[22]

Throughout this book, I have provided models and methods for navigating our lives and seeking eudaimonia. I have offered a theory explaining the functions of our minds and well-being. And I've shared the story of my own path to self-becoming in the hopes of demonstrating this powerful way of looking at life.

But it's your ascent of self-becoming that matters now. It's time to stop reading and start climbing. What's your next step?

> What does your conscience say? – 'You shall become the person you are'.
>
> —**Friedrich Nietzsche**[7]

# Resources

While I have tried to provide every mindset, framework, and exercise that I could fit into a book, I have often opined that books are not enough for catalyzing real growth. Psychological change requires application, accountability, and action. Here are a few tools I recommend:

For starters, readers can join a community of psychitects, get **The Book of Self Mastery**, and download the **Psychitect's Toolkit**, a free, 50-page guide on psychitecture, which includes 64 recommendations for incredible books to read next.

**Just go to designingthemind.org/becoming** to get your free books and subscribe to The Psychitect for a weekly dose of codified wisdom.

If you are struggling with severe mental illness, please **find a therapist** and book an appointment: psychologytoday.com/us

If you want to develop a greater understanding of your virtues, the **VIA Survey of Character Strengths** (or the Brief Strengths Test for a shorter version) is a great place to start: authentichappiness.sas.upenn.edu/testcenter

To learn more about the process of cognitive restructuring, visit **Mind Over Mood**: mindovermood.com

To learn more about the process of **behavioral activation**, this is a very helpful document: medicine.umich.edu/sites/default/files/content/downloads/Behavioral-Activation-for-Depression.pdf

To learn more about practicing mindfulness, I recommend Sam Harris's app, **Waking Up**: wakingup.com

If you want to cultivate greater self-knowledge, I developed a tool called **Mindsight: Introspection Cards**: designingthemind.org/cards

If you are interested in a comprehensive program based on the principles in this book, I created **The Flourishing Function: Anti-Depression Program** just for you: designingthemind.org/flourishing-function-program

If you want to join a community of psychological self-optimizers and get access to all DTM programs and resources, apply to join **Mindform: Psychitecture Collective and Training Platform**: mindform.io

Lastly, if this book has been valuable to you and you would like a way to contribute, **please consider writing a quick and honest review.**

# Acknowledgments

I have more people to thank for the development of this book and theory than I will even attempt to mention here. I've been inspired by countless thinkers, from Socrates to Seligman, some of whom I've been fortunate enough to engage in real discussion with, and others who have only been a guiding voice in my head.

To my sister, Caroline, thank you for inspiring my ideas on the good life. May your many virtues guide your life and find full expression.

To my partner, Katlyn, thank you for being my comic relief, my adventure buddy, and my inspiration for pursuing what is difficult.

To my parents, thank you for your feedback, kind words, and lifelong support of my passions.

To my Mindform members who have read and helped me refine this book, I am deeply grateful for your support and friendship. Thank you to Ryan L, Kyle Douglas, Julian Eger-Benninger, Vincent Lally, Shawn Criscito, Michael Jennings, Mark Peppin, Pilar Mejia, Antonio A, Edward Smith, Giò Schoenmaker, Vinh Tran, Alison R., Kat Marie, Lynn Davison, Lucas Golding, Michael Jennings, Matthias Nauwelaers, Eric Jobidon, Natalia Rogovin, Stephen Sager, Michael Dickerson, Keith Walker, Johnston Jiaa, Lynn Jinishian, Matt Hangen, Paul LaFontaine, Luis Walderdorff, Rachel Leyrer, Tim Van-Blon, Michelle Lindquist, Kelli Binnings, Greg Suignard, Fred Brown, Nina L, John Wariner, Zach Baker, and Mufakhrul Shah.

To my friends, mentors, and beta readers, this book is orders of magnitude better because of your thoughtful guidance, feedback, and ideas. Thank you to Eric Weiner, Nir Eyal, Donald Robertson, Jonathan Rottenberg, Peter Andrei, Thibaut Meurisse, Jonas Salzgeber, Will Hart, James Cussen, Matt O'Neill, Saeah Wood, Sertaç Mustafaoğlu, Ben Rogers, Steve Parker, Niranjan Kamath, Felipe Olchenski, Srikanth Vijay, Mark Mulvey, Sabin Șerban, and quite a few podcast hosts who read and discussed the book with me.

And as always, Hootie, thanks for being Hootie.

# Notes

## Chapter 1

1. Busseri, Michael. 2022. "A Review of the Tripartite Structure of Subjective Well-Being: Implications for Conceptualization, Operationalization, Analysis, and Synthesis—PubMed." PubMed. December 3. https://pubmed.ncbi.nlm.nih.gov/21131431/.

2. Lyubomirsky, Sonja. 2007. "The How of Happiness." Penguin.

3. Vaillant, George. 2012. "Triumphs of Experience." Harvard University Press.

4. Hinsliff, Gaby. 2017. "There's a Formula for Happiness, but Will It Make Our World a Better Place? | Gaby Hinsliff." The Guardian. April 15. http://www.theguardian.com/commentisfree/2017/apr/15/formula-happiness-reality-expectations.

5. Snyder, C. 2001. "Handbook of Positive Psychology." Oxford University Press.

6. Breuning, Loretta. 2015. "Habits of a Happy Brain." Simon and Schuster.

7. Gilbert, Daniel. Stumbling on Happiness. Vintage Canada, 2009.

8. Gilbert, Timothy. Affective Forecasting: Knowing What to Want on JSTOR. https://www.jstor.org/stable/20183006. Accessed 5 Nov. 2023.

9. Gilbert, Dan. "The Surprising Science of Happiness." TED Talks, https://www.ted.com/talks/dan_gilbert_the_surprising_science_of_happiness. Accessed 5 Nov. 2023.

10. Tang, Tony Z., et al. Sudden Gains in Recovering from Depression: Are They Also Found in Psychotherapies Other than Cognitive-Behavioral Therapy?https://psycnet.apa.org/record/2002-02267-020. Accessed 5 Nov. 2023.

11. Frankl, Viktor. Man's Search for Meaning. Beacon Press, 1992.

12. Bloom, Paul. The Sweet Spot. HarperCollins, 2021.

13. Bloom, Paul, and Sam Harris. Making Sense with Sam Harris: #266 — The Limits of Pleasure. #266.

14. "University Years Confirmed as the Best Time of Our Lives | Leeds Beckett University." Leeds Beckett University Logo, https://www.leedsbeckett.ac.uk/news/0815-university-years-confirmed-as-the-best-time-of-our-lives/. Accessed 5 Nov. 2023.

15. Steger, Michael F., et al. "Being Good by Doing Good: Daily Eudaimonic Activity and Well-Being." APA Psychnet, https://psycnet.apa.org/record/2008-03005-004. Accessed 5 Nov. 2023.

16. Lindqvist, Erik. "Long-Run Effects of Lottery Wealth on Psychological Well-Being." OUP Academic, 1 Nov. 2020, https://academic.oup.com/restud/article/87/6/2703/5734654.

17. Buss, D. "The Evolution of Happiness—PubMed." PubMed, 1 Jan. 2000, https://pubmed.ncbi.nlm.nih.gov/11392858/.

# Chapter 2

1. Peterson, Christopher, and Martin Seligman. Character Strengths and Virtues. Oxford University Press, 2004.

2. Aristotle. Nichomachean Ethics. Translated by W. D. Ross. Oxford: Clarendon, 1926, Internet Classics Archive, n.d. http://classics.mit.edu/Aristotle/nicomachaen.2.ii.html.

3. Solomon, Robert. Living with Nietzsche. Oxford University Press, 2003, p. Chapter 6: Nietzsche's Virtues: What Would He Make of Us?

4. Seligman, Martin. Flourish. Simon and Schuster, 2012.

# Chapter 3

1. Ancient Ethical Theory (Stanford Encyclopedia of Philosophy). https://plato.stanford.edu/entries/ethics-ancient/. Accessed 5 Nov. 2023.

2. Epictetus. Discourses of Epictetus. Forgotten Books, 2015.

3. Aurelius, Marcus. The Meditations of Marcus Aurelius. 1887.

4. Epictetus. Enchiridion. Courier Corporation, 2004.

5. Stoicism (Stanford Encyclopedia of Philosophy). https://plato.stanford.edu/entries/stoicism/. Accessed 5 Nov. 2023.

6. Liddell, Henry. Liddell and Scott's Greek-English Lexicon, Abridged. Simon Wallenburg Press, 2007.

7. Hooker, Richard. Areté. 15 Sept. 1996, https://web.archive.org/web/20110104052613/http://www.wsu.edu:8080/~dee/GLOSSARY/ARETE.HTM.

8. Ronnick, Michele. Cicero's "Paradoxa Stoicorum." Peter Lang Gmbh, Internationaler Verlag Der Wissenschaften, 1991.

9. Stephens, William O. "Stoic Ethics." Internet Encyclopedia of Philosophy, https://iep.utm.edu/stoiceth. Accessed 5.11.23.

10. Deonna, Julien. In Defense of Shame. Oxford University Press, 2012, p. Chapter 3: Shame, Values, and the Self.

11. Algoe, Sara, and Jonathan Haidt. "Witnessing Excellence in Action: The 'Other-Praising' Emotions of Elevation, Gratitude, and Admiration." Taylor & Francis, 4 Mar. 2009, https://www.tandfonline.com/doi/abs/10.1080/17439760802650519.

12. Alicke, Mark D., and Constantine Sedikides. "Self-Enhancement and Self-Protection: What They Are and What They Do." Taylor and Francis Online Homepage, https://www.tandfonline.com/action/cookieAbsent. Accessed 5 Nov. 2023.

13. Virtue Ethics (Stanford Encyclopedia of Philosophy). https://plato.stanford.edu/entries/ethics-virtue/. Accessed 5 Nov. 2023.

14. Robertson, Donald. Stoicism and the Art of Happiness. Teach Yourself, 2018.

15. Plato's Shorter Ethical Works (Stanford Encyclopedia of Philosophy). https://plato.stanford.edu/entries/plato-ethics-shorter/. Accessed 5 Nov. 2023.

16. Prior, William. Virtue and Knowledge. Routledge, 2016.

17. "The Aristotelian Virtues." Philosophy, https://philosophy.tamucc.edu/notes/aristotelian-virtues. Accessed 5 Nov. 2023.

18. Aristotle's Ethics (Stanford Encyclopedia of Philosophy). https://

plato.stanford.edu/entries/aristotle-ethics/. Accessed 5 Nov. 2023.

19. Swanton, Christine. The Virtue Ethics of Hume and Nietzsche. John Wiley & Sons, 2015.

20. Hunt, Lester. Nietzsche and the Origin of Virtue. Routledge, 2005.

21. Nietzsche, Friedrich. Schopenhauer as Educator. Regnery Publishing, 1965.

22. Nietzsche, Friedrich. The Gay Science. Vintage, 1974.

23. Matthew A. , McIntosh. "A History of Virtue as a Philosophy since the Ancient World." Brewminate: A Bold Blend of News and Ideas, 3 May 2019, https://brewminate.com/a-history-of-virtue-as-a-philosophy-since-the-ancient-world/.

24. Becker, Kelly. The Cambridge History of Philosophy, 1945-2015. Cambridge University Press, 2019.

25. Anscombe, G. Modern Moral Philosophy on JSTOR. https://www.jstor.org/stable/3749051. Accessed 5 Nov. 2023.

26. Nietzsche, Friedrich. Nietzsche: Daybreak. Cambridge University Press, 1997.

27. Sakellariouv, Alexandra. "Virtue Ethics and Its Potential as the Leading Moral Theory." Discussions, http://www.inquiriesjournal.com/articles/1385/virtue-ethics-and-moral-theory. Accessed 5 Nov. 2023.

28. Virtue Ethics (Stanford Encyclopedia of Philosophy). https://plato.stanford.edu/entries/ethics-virtue/. Accessed 5 Nov. 2023.

29. MacIntyre, Alasdair. After Virtue. A&C Black, 2013.

30. Foot, Philippa. Natural Goodness. Clarendon Press, 2003.

31. Van Zyl, Liezl. Virtue Ethics. Routledge, 2018.

32. Maslow, Abraham. The Farther Reaches of Human Nature. Penguin Books, 1993.

33. Maslow, Abraham. Toward a Psychology of Being. John Wiley & Sons, 1998.

34. Seligman, Martin. Flourish. Simon and Schuster, 2012.

35. Peterson, Christopher, and Martin Seligman. Character Strengths and Virtues. Oxford University Press, 2004.

# Chapter 4

1. "Imagining the Tenth Dimension (Annotated)." YouTube, 19 June 2008, https://www.youtube.com/watch?v=XjsgoXvnStY.

2. I also owe this visual metaphor in part to Jonathan Haidt for a similar but distinct framework he presents in The Happiness Hypothesis. Haidt, Jonathan. The Happiness Hypothesis. Basic Books (AZ), 2006.

3. Nozick, Robert. Anarchy, State, and Utopia. Basic Books, 2013.

4. Hindriks, Frank. "Nozick's Experience Machine: An Empirical Study." Taylor & Francis, 1 Dec. 2017, https://www.tandfonline.com/doi/abs/10.1080/09515089.2017.1406600.

5. Woolley, Kaitlin, and Ayelet Fishbach. "Motivating Personal Growth by Seeking Discomfort." Sage Journals. Psychological Science, https://journals.sagepub.com/doi/10.1177/09567976211044685. Accessed 5.11.23.

6. McMillen, J. Better for It: How People Benefit from Adversity on JSTOR. https://www.jstor.org/stable/23718765. Accessed 5 Nov. 2023.

7. Nietzsche, Friedrich. Beyond Good & Evil. Vintage, 1966, p. CHAPTER VII (OUR VIRTUES).

8. Killingsworth, Matthew A., et al. "Income and Emotional Well-Being: A Conflict Resolved." Proceedings of the National Academy of Sciences, https://doi.org/10.1073/pnas.2208661120.

9. Berger, Michele W. "Does More Money Correlate with Greater Happiness?" Penn Today, https://penntoday.upenn.edu/news/does-more-money-correlate-greater-happiness-Penn-Princeton-research. Accessed 5.11.23.

10. "Retirement Depression: How to Regain Purpose After Retiring." Psych Central, https://psychcentral.com/depression/retirement-depression. Accessed 5 Nov. 2023.

11. Miquel, Carlota de, et al. "The Mental Health of Employees with Job Loss and Income Loss during the COVID-19 Pandemic: The Mediating Role of Perceived Financial Stress." National Library of Medicine, https://www.ncbi.nlm.nih.gov/pmc/articles/PMC8950467/. Accessed 5.11.23.

12. Andrews, Melissa. "Losing My Job Was the Best Thing That Could

Ever Have Happened." Possibility Change, 5 Mar. 2015, https://possibility-change.com/losing-my-job.

13. Parkes, Colin Murray. "Bereavement in Adult Life." National Library of Medicine, https://www.ncbi.nlm.nih.gov/pmc/articles/PMC1112778/. Accessed 5.11.23.

14. Guarnaccia, Peter J., and Jacqueline Lowe Worobey. "The Impact of Marital Status and Employment Status on Depressive Affect for Hispanic Americans." Journal of Community Psychology, https://onlinelibrary.wiley.com/doi/10.1002/1520-6629(199104)19:2%3C136::AID-JCOP2290190205%3E3.0.CO;2-6. Accessed 5.11.23.

15. Ilardi, Stephen. The Depression Cure. Da Capo Lifelong Books, 2009.

16. Boiman-Meshita, Maayan, and Hadassah Littman-Ovadia. "Is It Me or You? An Actor-Partner Examination of the Relationship between Partners' Character Strengths and Marital Quality." Journal of Happiness Studies, https://link.springer.com/article/10.1007/s10902-021-00394-1.

17. Ngai, Steven. "Parental Bonding and Character Strengths among Chinese Adolescents in Hong Kong." Taylor & Francis, 11 Feb. 2015, https://www.tandfonline.com/doi/abs/10.1080/02673843.2015.1007879.

18. Rahula, Walpola. What the Buddha Taught. Open Road + Grove/Atlantic, 2007.

19. Robertson, Donald. Stoicism and the Art of Happiness. Teach Yourself, 2018.

20. Epictetus. Enchiridion. Courier Corporation, 2004.

21. Irvine, William. A Guide to the Good Life. OUP USA, 2009.

22. Watts, Alan. Tao. Pantheon, 1977.

23. Nietzsche, Friedrich. Thus Spoke Zarathustra. BoD – Books on Demand, 2015.

24. Maslow, Abraham. Toward a Psychology of Being. John Wiley & Sons, 1998.

25. Maslow, Abraham. The Farther Reaches of Human Nature. Penguin Books, 1993.

26. Maslow, A. Motivation And Personality. Prabhat Prakashan, 1981.

# Chapter 5

1. Carse, James. Finite and Infinite Games. Simon and Schuster, 2011.
2. "Virtue Signaling." Dictionary.Com, https://www.dictionary.com/browse/virtue-signaling.
3. Darwin, Charles. Letter to Asa Gray, April 3, 1860, The Life and Letters of Charles Darwin,
4. El-Showk, Sedeer. "An Introduction to Sexual Selection." Scitable by Nature Education, https://www.nature.com/scitable/blog/accumulating-glitches/an_introduction_to_sexual_selection. Accessed 5.12.23.
5. Zahavi, Amotz. "Mate Selection-A Selection for a Handicap." NASA/ADS, 1 Jan. 1975, https://ui.adsabs.harvard.edu/abs/1975JThBi..53..205Z/abstract.
6. "The Evolution of Sexual Preference." National Library of Medicine—The Eugenics Review, https://www.ncbi.nlm.nih.gov/pmc/articles/PMC2987134/. Accessed 5.12.23.
7. Wharton, Jane. "The Making of a Man: Inside a Bull Jumping Ceremony with Ethiopia's Ha." Express.Co.Uk, 22 Feb. 2015, https://www.express.co.uk/news/world/559757/Hamer-tribe-bull-jumping-ceremony-Omo-Valley-Ethiopia.
8. Miller, Geoffrey. The Mating Mind. Anchor, 2011.
9. Miller, G. "Mental Traits as Fitness Indicators. Expanding Evolutionary Psychology's Adaptationism—PubMed." PubMed, 1 Apr. 2000, https://pubmed.ncbi.nlm.nih.gov/10818621/.
10. McAndrew, Francis T. "Costly Signaling Theory." Encyclopedia of Evolutionary Psychological Science, https://link.springer.com/referenceworkentry/10.1007/978-3-319-16999-6_3483-1. Accessed 5.12.23.
11. Brugha, Traolach. "Epidemiology of Autism in Adults across Age Groups and Ability Levels | The British Journal of Psychiatry | Cambridge Core." Cambridge Core, 2 Jan. 2018, https://www.cambridge.org/core/journals/the-british-journal-of-psychiatry/article/epidemiology-of-autism-in-adults-across-age-groups-and-ability-levels/D4F48E07D1002DE6F75A67

FF9A4FFCF7.

12. Miller, Brittany. "Who Are Elon Musk's Kids? His 10 Children's Names, Ages and Mothers." Page Six, https://pagesix.com/article/elon-musk-children/. Accessed 5.12.23.

13. "20 Famous People with Autism Spectrum Disorder (ASD)." Behavioral Innovations, https://behavioral-innovations.com/blog/20-famous-people-with-autism-spectrum-disorder-asd/. Accessed 5.12.23.

14. Clarke, T. K. "Common Polygenic Risk for Autism Spectrum Disorder (ASD) Is Associated with Cognitive Ability in the General Population—PubMed." PubMed, 10 Mar. 2023, https://pubmed.ncbi.nlm.nih.gov/25754080/.

15. Association, American. Diagnostic and Statistical Manual of Mental Disorders. 2022.

16. "How to Talk about Autism." Undefined, 20 July 2306, https://www.autism.org.uk/what-we-do/help-and-support/how-to-talk-about-autism.

17. Silberman, Steve. Neurotribes. Penguin, 2016.

18. Chasson , Gregory, and Sara R. Jarosiewicz . "Social Competence Impairments in Autism Spectrum Disorders." Comprehensive Guide to Autism, https://link.springer.com/referenceworkentry/10.1007/978-1-4614-4788-7_60. Accessed 5.12.23.

19. Baron-Cohen, Simon. "Autism: The Empathizing–Systemizing (E-S) Theory." Annals of the New York Academy of Sciences, https://nyaspubs.onlinelibrary.wiley.com/doi/10.1111/j.1749-6632.2009.04467.x.

20. "Obsessions and Repetitive Behaviour—a Guide for All Audiences." Undefined, 20 July 2306, https://www.autism.org.uk/advice-and-guidance/topics/behaviour/obsessions/all-audiences.

21. Burch, Kelly. Surprising Benefits of Having ADHD. https://www.verywellhealth.com/benefits-of-adhd-strengths-and-superpowers-5210520. Accessed 5.12.23.

22. Abraham, Anna. "Creative Thinking in Adolescents with Attention Deficit Hyperactivity Disorder (ADHD)." Taylor & Francis, 3 Feb. 2007, https://www.tandfonline.com/doi/abs/10.1080/09297040500320691.

23. Swanepoel, Annie. "How Evolutionary Thinking Can Help Us to Understand ADHD | BJPsych Advances | Cambridge Core." Cambridge Core, 2 Jan. 2018, https://www.cambridge.org/core/journals/bjpsych-advances/article/how-evolutionary-thinking-can-help-us-to-understand-adhd/A4BBE292EB44B2230294367A4ACB3F88.

24. Dunbar, R. I. M. "Neocortex Size as a Constraint on Group Size in Primates." Journal of Human Evolution, https://www.sciencedirect.com/science/article/abs/pii/004724849290081J?via%3Dihub. Accessed 5.12.23.

25. Hedrick, Philip W. "Balancing Selection." Current Biology, https://www.cell.com/current-biology/fulltext/S0960-9822(07)00813-5. Accessed 5.12.23.

26. Genn, Andrea L., et al. "Evolutionary Theory and Psychopathy." Aggression and Violent Behavior, https://citeseerx.ist.psu.edu/viewdoc/download?doi=10.1.1.1065.3767&rep=rep1&type=pdf. Accessed 5 Dec. 2023.

27. Sinervo, Barry, and Curtis M. Lively. "The Rock–Paper–Scissors Game and the Evolution of Alternative Male Strategies." APA PsycNet, https://psycnet.apa.org/record/1996-03101-003. Accessed 5 Dec. 2023.

28. Olendorf, Robert. "Frequency-Dependent Survival in Natural Guppy Populations—PubMed." PubMed, 1 Jan. 2006, https://pubmed.ncbi.nlm.nih.gov/16738659/.

# Chapter 6

1. Muskan, Arora et al. "CORRELATION BETWEEN PROSOCIAL BEHAVIOUR AND SELF-ESTEEM AMONG YOUNG ADULTS." IJCRT, https://www.ijcrt.org/papers/IJCRT1802889.pdf. Accessed 5.15.23.

2. Baumeister, Roy. Evil. Macmillan, 1999.

3. Kuster, Farah. "Rumination Mediates the Prospective Effect of Low Self-Esteem on Depression: A Five-Wave Longitudinal Study—PubMed." PubMed, 6 Mar. 2023, https://pubmed.ncbi.nlm.nih.gov/22394574/.

4. Gray, Rossarin, et al. "Happiness among Thai People: Living a Virtuous Life, Spirituality and Self-Esteem." Virtual Health Library, https://pesquisa.bvsalud.org/portal/resource/pt/sea-130941?lang=en. Accessed 5.15.23.

5. Smith, Eliot. Social Psychology. Psychology Press, 2014.

6. Sedikides, Constantine. The Self. Psychology Press, 2011.

7. "The Causes and Consequences of a Need for Self-Esteem: A Terror Management Theory." Public Self and Private Self, https://link.springer.com/chapter/10.1007/978-1-4613-9564-5_10. Accessed 5.15.23.

8. Bem, D. "Self-Perception: An Alternative Interpretation of Cognitive Dissonance Phenomena—PubMed." PubMed, 1 May 1967, https://pubmed.ncbi.nlm.nih.gov/5342882/.

9. Bem, Daryl. "Self-Perception Theory." Advances in Experimental Social Psychology, https://www.researchgate.net/publication/277682193_Self-Perception_Theory. Accessed 5.15.23.

10. McMurrich, Stephanie L., and Sheri L. Johnson. "Dispositional Rumination in Individuals with a Depression History." National Library of Medicine, https://www.ncbi.nlm.nih.gov/pmc/articles/PMC2814435/. Accessed 5.15.23.

11. Fuchs, Eberhard, and Gabriele Flügge. "Adult Neuroplasticity: More Than 40 Years of Research." National Library of Medicine, https://www.ncbi.nlm.nih.gov/pmc/articles/PMC4026979/. Accessed 5.15.23.

12. Leary, Mark R., and Deborah L. Downs. "Interpersonal Functions of the Self-Esteem Motive." Efficacy, Agency, and Self-Esteem, https://link.springer.com/chapter/10.1007/978-1-4899-1280-0_7. Accessed 5.15.23.

13. Kirkpatrick, L. A., & Ellis, B. J. (2004). An Evolutionary-Psychological Approach to Self-esteem: Multiple Domains and Multiple Functions. In M. B. Brewer & M. Hewstone (Eds.), Self and social identity (pp. 52–77). Blackwell Publishing.

14. Baumeister, Roy F., and Davina A. Robson. "Belongingness and the Modern Schoolchild: On Loneliness, Socioemotional Health, Self-Esteem, Evolutionary Mismatch, Online Sociality, and the Numbness of Rejection." Australian Journal of Psychology, https://www.tandfonline.com/doi/full/10.1080/00049530.2021.1877573.

15. Leary, Mark R., et al. "Self-Esteem as an Interpersonal Monitor: The Sociometer Hypothesis." APA PsycNet, https://psycnet.apa.org/doiLanding?-

doi=10.1037%2F0022-3514.68.3.518. Accessed 18 May 2023.

16. Kraus, Michael. "The Undervalued Self: Social Class and Self-Evaluation." Frontiers, 12 Sept. 2014, https://www.frontiersin.org/articles/10.3389/fpsyg.2014.01404/full.

17. J. Lee, Anthony, et al. A Multivariate Approach to Human Mate Preferences. https://www.sciencedirect.com/science/article/abs/pii/S109051381400004X. Accessed 5.18.23.

18. Flegr, Jaroslav, et al. "What People Prefer and What They Think They Prefer in Short—and Long-Term Partners." Evolution and Human Behavior, https://www.sciencedirect.com/science/article/abs/pii/S1090513818300242. Accessed 5.18.23.

19. Kaplan, Hillard S., et al. "The Evolutionary and Ecological Roots of Human Social Organization." Philos Trans R Soc Lond B Biol Sci, https://www.ncbi.nlm.nih.gov/pmc/articles/PMC2781874/. Accessed 5.18.23.

20. Nowak, Martin A., and Karl Sigmund. "Evolution of Indirect Reciprocity." Nature, https://www.nature.com/articles/nature04131. Accessed 5.18.23.

21. Raichle, Marcus E., et al. "A Default Mode of Brain Function." National Library of Medicine, https://www.ncbi.nlm.nih.gov/pmc/articles/PMC14647/. Accessed 5.18.23.

22. Minoshima, S. "Metabolic Reduction in the Posterior Cingulate Cortex in Very Early Alzheimer's Disease—PubMed." PubMed, 1 July 1997, https://pubmed.ncbi.nlm.nih.gov/9225689/.

23. Binder, J. "Conceptual Processing during the Conscious Resting State. A Functional MRI Study—PubMed." PubMed, 1 Jan. 1999, https://pubmed.ncbi.nlm.nih.gov/9950716/.

24. Andrews-Hanna, Jessica R., et al. "Evidence for the Default Network's Role in Spontaneous Cognition." Journal of Neurophysiology, https://www.ncbi.nlm.nih.gov/pmc/articles/PMC2904225/. Accessed 5.18.23.

25. Dastjerdi, M., Foster, B. L., Nasrullah, S., Rauschecker, A. M., Dougherty, R. F., Townsend, J. D., Chang, C., Greicius, M. D., Menon, V., Kennedy, D. P., & Parvizi, J. (2011). Differential electrophysiological response during

rest, self-referential, and non-self-referential tasks in human posteromedial cortex. Proceedings of the National Academy of Sciences of the United States of America, 108(7), 3023-3028. https://doi.org/10.1073/pnas.1017098108

26. Spreng R. N. (2012). The fallacy of a "task-negative" network. Frontiers in psychology, 3, 145. https://doi.org/10.3389/fpsyg.2012.00145

27. Spreng, R. N., Mar, R. A., & Kim, A. S. (2009). The common neural basis of autobiographical memory, prospection, navigation, theory of mind, and the default mode: a quantitative meta-analysis. Journal of cognitive neuroscience, 21(3), 489–510. https://doi.org/10.1162/jocn.2008.21029

28. Davey, Christopher G., et al. "Mapping the Self in the Brain's Default Mode Network." NeuroImage, https://www.sciencedirect.com/science/article/pii/S1053811916001294.

29. Lieberman, Matthew. "Social Cognitive Neuroscience: A Review of Core Processes—PubMed." PubMed, 1 Jan. 2007, https://pubmed.ncbi.nlm.nih.gov/17002553/.

30. Ochsner, Kevin. "Reflecting upon Feelings: An FMRI Study of Neural Systems Supporting the Attribution of Emotion to Self and Other—PubMed." PubMed, 1 Dec. 2004, https://pubmed.ncbi.nlm.nih.gov/15701226/.

31. Svoboda, Eva. "The Functional Neuroanatomy of Autobiographical Memory: A Meta-Analysis—PubMed." PubMed, 27 June 2023, https://pubmed.ncbi.nlm.nih.gov/16806314/.

32. Andrews-Hanna J. R. (2012). The brain's default network and its adaptive role in internal mentation. The Neuroscientist : a review journal bringing neurobiology, neurology and psychiatry, 18(3), 251–270. https://doi.org/10.1177/1073858411403316

33. Pan, Weigang. "Neural Basis of Trait Self-Esteem Revealed by the Amplitude of Low-Frequency Fluctuations and Resting State Functional Connectivity." OUP Academic, 1 Mar. 2016, https://academic.oup.com/scan/article/11/3/367/2375062.

34. Garrison, K. A., Zeffiro, T. A., Scheinost, D., Constable, R. T., & Brewer, J. A. (2015). Meditation leads to reduced default mode network activity beyond an active task. Cognitive, affective & behavioral neuroscience,

15(3), 712–720. https://doi.org/10.3758/s13415-015-0358-3

35. Gattuso, J. J., Perkins, D., Ruffell, S., Lawrence, A. J., Hoyer, D., Jacobson, L. H., Timmermann, C., Castle, D., Rossell, S. L., Downey, L. A., Pagni, B. A., Galvão-Coelho, N. L., Nutt, D., & Sarris, J. (2023). Default Mode Network Modulation by Psychedelics: A Systematic Review. The international journal of neuropsychopharmacology, 26(3), 155–188. https://doi.org/10.1093/ijnp/pyac074

36. "Psychedelics and Meditation | 16 | A Neurophilosophical Perspective |." Taylor & Francis, https://www.taylorfrancis.com/chapters/edit/10.4324/9781003127253-16/psychedelics-meditation-chris-letheby. Accessed 18 May 2023.

37. Simony, E., Honey, C. J., Chen, J., Lositsky, O., Yeshurun, Y., Wiesel, A., & Hasson, U. (2016). Dynamic reconfiguration of the default mode network during narrative comprehension. Nature communications, 7, 12141. https://doi.org/10.1038/ncomms12141

38. Kaplan, J. T., Gimbel, S. I., & Harris, S. (2016). Neural correlates of maintaining one's political beliefs in the face of counterevidence. Scientific reports, 6, 39589. https://doi.org/10.1038/srep39589

39. Li, Wanqing. "The Default Mode Network and Social Understanding of Others: What Do Brain Connectivity Studies Tell Us." Frontiers, 1 June 2013, https://www.frontiersin.org/articles/10.3389/fnhum.2014.00074/full.

40. Costandi, Moheb. Neuroplasticity. MIT Press, 2016.

41. Rose, Jason P., and Erin Vogel . "Self-Esteem and Social Status." Encyclopedia of Personality and Individual Differences, https://link.springer.com/referenceworkentry/10.1007/978-3-319-24612-3_1172. Accessed 5.18.23.

42. Fleming, J. S., & Courtney, B. E. (1984). The dimensionality of self-esteem: II. Hierarchical facet model for revised measurement scales. Journal of Personality and Social Psychology, 46(2), 404–421. https://doi.org/10.1037/0022-3514.46.2.404

43. Focquaert, Farah, et al. "An Evolutionary Cognitive Neuroscience Perspective on Human Self-Awareness and Theory of Mind." Philosophical Psychology, https://www.tandfonline.com/doi/abs/10.1080/09515080701875156?-

journalCode=cphp20. Accessed 5.18.23.

44. Tracy, Jessica, and Richard Robins. "Appraisal Antecedents of Shame and Guilt: Support for a Theoretical Model." Personality and Social Psychology Bulletin, https://www.researchgate.net/publication/6826552_Appraisal_Antecedents_of_Shame_and_Guilt_Support_for_a_Theoretical_Model. Accessed 5.18.23.

# Chapter 7

1. Murray, Christopher. The Global Burden of Disease. Harvard School of Public Health, Frangois-Xavier Bagnoud Cen, 1996.

2. The epidemiology of major depressive disorder: results from the National Comorbidity Survey Replication (NCS-R), Kessler, Berglund, et al., 1997, https://pubmed.ncbi.nlm.nih.gov/12813115/

3. Prevalence of and risk factors for lifetime suicide attempts in the National Comorbidity Survey, 1.7; Kessler, Walters, et al., 1998b, https://pubmed.ncbi.nlm.nih.gov/10401507/

4. Post-Welfare Employment and Psychological Well-Being, S. Danziger, Carlson, et al., 2001", https://www.semanticscholar.org/paper/Post-Welfare-Employment-and-Psychological-Danziger-Carlson/280a0b4d-34f90594cc0282243ddeaef67e1d5aa5

5. Handbook of Depression, Ian H. Gotlib Constance L. Hammen

6. Dattani, Saloni. "What Is the Lifetime Risk of Depression?" Our World in Data, https://ourworldindata.org/depression-lifetime-risk. Accessed 5.18.23.

7. Prevalence of Heart Disease --—United States, 2005. 16 Feb. 2007, https://www.cdc.gov/mmwr/preview/mmwrhtml/mm5606a2.htm.

8. Kessler, R. "Sex and Depression in the National Comorbidity Survey. I: Lifetime Prevalence, Chronicity and Recurrence—PubMed." PubMed, 1 Nov. 1993, https://pubmed.ncbi.nlm.nih.gov/8300981/.

9. "Obesity and Disease Tied to Dramatic Dietary Changes." ScienceDaily, 21 Oct. 2020, https://www.sciencedaily.com/releases/2020/10/201021163945.htm.

10. Andrews, Paul W., and J. Anderson Thomson Jr. "Depression's Evolutionary Roots." Scientific American, https://www.scientificamerican.com/article/depressions-evolutionary/. Accessed 5.18.23.

11. "Depression." National Institute of Mental Health, https://www.nimh.nih.gov/health/publications/depression#:~:text=Depression%20(also%20called%20major%20depressive,income%2C%20culture%2C%20or%20education. Accessed 5.18.23.

12. Mazure, C. M. (1998). Life stressors as risk factors in depression. Clinical Psychology: Science and Practice, 5(3), 291–313. https://doi.org/10.1111/j.1468-2850.1998.tb00151.x

13. O'Connor, Richard. Undoing Depression. Little, Brown Spark, 2021.

14. Henriques, Gregg. "Depression: Disease or Behavioral Shutdown Mechanism?" JOURNAL OF SCIENCE AND HEALTH POLICY, https://www.researchgate.net/publication/245869482_Depression_Disease_or_behavioral_shutdown_mechanism. Accessed 5.18.23.

15. Andrews, Paul W., and J. Anderson Thomson, Jr. "The Bright Side of Being Blue: Depression as an Adaptation for Analyzing Complex Problems." National Library of Medicine, https://www.ncbi.nlm.nih.gov/pmc/articles/PMC2734449/. Accessed 5.18.23.

16. Watson, Paul J., and Paul W. Andrews. "Toward a Revised Evolutionary Adaptationist Analysis of Depression: The Social Navigation Hypothesis." Journal of Affective Disorders, https://www.sciencedirect.com/science/article/abs/pii/S0165032701004591?via%3Dihub. Accessed 5.18.23.

17. Teo, A. R., Nelson, S., Strange, W., Kubo, H., Katsuki, R., Kurahara, K., Kanba, S., & Kato, T. A. (2020). Social withdrawal in major depressive disorder: a case-control study of hikikomori in japan. Journal of affective disorders, 274, 1142–1146. https://doi.org/10.1016/j.jad.2020.06.011

18. Cooley, E. "Discrimination of Facial Expressions of Emotion by Depressed Subjects—PubMed." PubMed, 1 Nov. 1989, https://pubmed.ncbi.nlm.nih.gov/2620808/.

19. Gao, Shuling, et al. "Associations between Self-Disgust, Depression, and Anxiety: A Three-Level Meta-Analytic Review." Acta Psychologica,

https://www.sciencedirect.com/science/article/pii/S0001691822001731. Accessed 5.18.23.

20. Zahn, R., Lythe, K. E., Gethin, J. A., Green, S., Deakin, J. F., Young, A. H., & Moll, J. (2015). The role of self-blame and worthlessness in the psychopathology of major depressive disorder. Journal of affective disorders, 186, 337–341. https://doi.org/10.1016/j.jad.2015.08.001

21. Cheng, H., & Furnham, A. (2004). Perceived parental rearing style, self-esteem and self-criticism as predictors of happiness. Journal of Happiness Studies: An Interdisciplinary Forum on Subjective Well-Being, 5(1), 1–21. https://doi.org/10.1023/B:JOHS.0000021704.35267.05

22. Diener, E., & Diener, M. (1995). Cross-cultural correlates of life satisfaction and self-esteem. Journal of personality and social psychology, 68(4), 653–663. https://doi.org/10.1037//0022-3514.68.4.653

23. Orth, U., Robins, R. W., Trzesniewski, K. H., Maes, J., & Schmitt, M. (2009). Low self-esteem is a risk factor for depressive symptoms from young adulthood to old age. Journal of abnormal psychology, 118(3), 472–478. https://doi.org/10.1037/a0015922

24. Roberts, J. E., & Monroe, S. M. (1992). Vulnerable self-esteem and depressive symptoms: prospective findings comparing three alternative conceptualizations. Journal of personality and social psychology, 62(5), 804–812. https://doi.org/10.1037//0022-3514.62.5.804

25. "Self-Esteem And Depression." MentalHelp.Net, 25 Mar. 2019, https://www.mentalhelp.net/depression/and-self-esteem/.

26. Sowislo, J. F., & Orth, U. (2013). Does low self-esteem predict depression and anxiety? A meta-analysis of longitudinal studies. Psychological Bulletin, 139(1), 213–240. https://doi.org/10.1037/a0028931

27. Pedersen, Lene. The SAGE Handbook of Cultural Anthropology. SAGE, 2021.

28. Söderberg, Patrik, and Douglas P. Fry. "Anthropological Aspects of Ostracism." Ostracism, Exclusion, and Rejection, https://hhs.uncg.edu/pcs/wp-content/uploads/sites/7/2019/11/2017-Soderberg-Fry-Anthropological-Aspects-of-Ostracism-ch.17.pdf. Accessed 5.18.23.

29. Mole, Beth. "Humans' Murder Rates Explained by Primate Ancestors, Controversial Study Says." Ars Technica, 30 Sept. 2016, https://arstechnica.com/science/2016/09/controversial-study-pins-humans-murderous-ways-on-our-primate-ancestors/.

30. Hess, Nicole H., and Edward H. Hagen. "The Impact of Gossip, Reputation, and Context on Resource Transfers among Aka Hunter-Gatherers, Ngandu Horticulturalists, and MTurkers." Evolution and Human Behavior, https://www.sciencedirect.com/science/article/abs/pii/S1090513823000260. Accessed 5.18.23.

31. Dawkins, Richard. The Selfish Gene. Oxford University Press, 2016.

32. Duerler, Patricia, et al. "A Neurobiological Perspective on Social Influence: Serotonin and Social Adaptation." Journal of Neurochemistry, https://onlinelibrary.wiley.com/doi/full/10.1111/jnc.15607. Accessed 5.18.23.

33. Elmer, Timon, and Christoph Stadtfeld . "Depressive Symptoms Are Associated with Social Isolation in Face-to-Face Interaction Networks." Scientific Reports, https://www.nature.com/articles/s41598-020-58297-9. Accessed 5.18.23.

34. Nesse, Randolph. Good Reasons for Bad Feelings. Penguin, 2019.

35. Prieto-Fidalgo, Ángel, et al. "Reliability of an Interpretation Bias Task of Ambiguous Faces and Its Relationship with Social Anxiety, Depression, and Looming Maladaptive Style." International Journal of Cognitive Therapy, https://link.springer.com/article/10.1007/s41811-022-00154-w. Accessed 5.18.23.

36. Blaine, Bruce, and Jennifer Crocker . "Self-Esteem and Self-Serving Biases in Reactions to Positive and Negative Events: An Integrative Review." Self-Esteem: The Puzzle of Low Self-Regard, https://link.springer.com/chapter/10.1007/978-1-4684-8956-9_4. Accessed 5.18.23.

37. Bandura, A. "Self-Efficacy: Toward a Unifying Theory of Behavioral Change—PubMed." PubMed, 1 Mar. 1977, https://pubmed.ncbi.nlm.nih.gov/847061/.

38. Gotlib , Ian H. "Perception and Recall of Interpersonal Feedback: Negative Bias in Depression." Cognitive Therapy and Research, https://link.

springer.com/article/10.1007/BF01187168. Accessed 5.18.23.

39. Thase, M. E. (2009). Neurobiological aspects of depression. In I. H. Gotlib & C. L. Hammen (Eds.), Handbook of depression (pp. 187–217). The Guilford Press.

40. Moret, Chantel, and Mike Briley. "The Importance of Norepinephrine in Depression." Neuropsychiatric Disease and Treatment, https://www.tandfonline.com/doi/full/10.2147/NDT.S19619. Accessed 5.18.23.

41. Kapur, Shitij, and J. John Mann. "Role of the Dopaminergic System in Depression ." Biological Psychiatry, https://www.sciencedirect.com/science/article/abs/pii/0006322392901370. Accessed 5.18.23.

42. Cuellar, Amy K., et al. "Distinctions between Bipolar and Unipolar Depression." National Library of Medicine, https://www.ncbi.nlm.nih.gov/pmc/articles/PMC2850601/. Accessed 5.18.23.

43. Lacasse, J. R., & Leo, J. (2005). Serotonin and depression: a disconnect between the advertisements and the scientific literature. PLoS medicine, 2(12), e392. https://doi.org/10.1371/journal.pmed.0020392

44. Hari, Johann. Lost Connections. Bloomsbury Publishing, 2019.

45. Kirsch, Irving. "Initial Severity and Antidepressant Benefits: A Meta-Analysis of Data Submitted to the Food and Drug Administration—PubMed." PubMed, 1 Feb. 2008, https://pubmed.ncbi.nlm.nih.gov/18303940/.

46. Olivier, Berend, et al. "Serotonergic Modulation of Social Interactions in Isolated Male Mice." Psychopharmacology, https://link.springer.com/article/10.1007/BF00442239. Accessed 5.18.23.

47. Krakowski M. (2003). Violence and serotonin: influence of impulse control, affect regulation, and social functioning. The Journal of neuropsychiatry and clinical neurosciences, 15(3), 294-305. https://doi.org/10.1176/jnp.15.3.294

48. Kiser, D., Steemers, B., Branchi, I., & Homberg, J. R. (2012). The reciprocal interaction between serotonin and social behaviour. Neuroscience and biobehavioral reviews, 36(2), 786-798. https://doi.org/10.1016/j.neubiorev.2011.12.009

49. BREUNING, Loretta. Status Games Why We Play and H. Rowman &

Littlefield Publishers, 2021.

50. Raleigh MJ, McGuire MT, Brammer GL, Yuwiler A. Social and Environmental Influences on Blood Serotonin Concentrations in Monkeys. Arch Gen Psychiatry. 1984;41(4):405–410. doi:10.1001/archpsyc.1984.01790150095013

51. Miller, Geoffrey. The Mating Mind. Anchor, 2011.

52. Kravitz, Edward. A. "Hormonal Control of Behavior: Amines and the Biasing of Behavioral Output in Lobsters." Science, https://www.science.org/doi/10.1126/science.2902685. Accessed 5.18.23.

53. Sheline, Y. I., Barch, D. M., Price, J. L., Rundle, M. M., Vaishnavi, S. N., Snyder, A. Z., Mintun, M. A., Wang, S., Coalson, R. S., & Raichle, M. E. (2009). The default mode network and self-referential processes in depression. Proceedings of the National Academy of Sciences of the United States of America, 106(6), 1942–1947. https://doi.org/10.1073/pnas.0812686106

54. Grimm, Research Simone, et al. "Reduced Negative BOLD Responses in the Default-Mode Network and Increased Self-Focus in Depression." The World Journal of Biological Psychiatry, https://www.tandfonline.com/doi/abs/10.3109/15622975.2010.545145. Accessed 5.18.23.

55. Helmbold, K., Zvyagintsev, M., Dahmen, B., Biskup, C. S., Bubenzer-Busch, S., Gaber, T. J., Klasen, M., Eisert, A., Konrad, K., Habel, U., Herpertz-Dahlmann, B., & Zepf, F. D. (2016). Serotonergic modulation of resting state default mode network connectivity in healthy women. Amino acids, 48(4), 1109–1120. https://doi.org/10.1007/s00726-015-2137-4

56. Challis, C., & Berton, O. (2015). Top-Down Control of Serotonin Systems by the Prefrontal Cortex: A Path toward Restored Socioemotional Function in Depression. ACS chemical neuroscience, 6(7), 1040–1054. https://doi.org/10.1021/acschemneuro.5b00007

57. Hamani, C., Diwan, M., Macedo, C. E., Brandão, M. L., Shumake, J., Gonzalez-Lima, F., Raymond, R., Lozano, A. M., Fletcher, P. J., & Nobrega, J. N. (2010). Antidepressant-like effects of medial prefrontal cortex deep brain stimulation in rats. Biological psychiatry, 67(2), 117–124. https://doi.org/10.1016/j.biopsych.2009.08.025

58. Hamani, C., Diwan, M., Macedo, C. E., Brandão, M. L., Shumake, J.,

Gonzalez-Lima, F., Raymond, R., Lozano, A. M., Fletcher, P. J., & Nobrega, J. N. (2010). Antidepressant-like effects of medial prefrontal cortex deep brain stimulation in rats. Biological psychiatry, 67(2), 117–124. https://doi.org/10.1016/j.biopsych.2009.08.025

59. Insel , Thomas R. "Faulty Circuits." Scientific American, https://www.scientificamerican.com/article/faulty-circuits/. Accessed 5.18.23.

60. Hamani , Clement, et al. "The Subcallosal Cingulate Gyrus in the Context of Major Depression." Biological Psychiatry, https://www.biologicalpsychiatryjournal.com/article/S0006-3223(10)01003-6/fulltext. Accessed 5.18.23.

61. Seligman, Martin. Authentic Happiness. Hachette UK, 2011.

62. Monroe, S. M., Slavich, G. M., & Georgiades, K. (2014). The social environment and depression: The roles of life stress. In I. H. Gotlib & C. L. Hammen (Eds.), Handbook of depression (pp. 296–314). The Guilford Press.

63. Wiblin, Robert. "Randomised Experiment: If You're Genuinely Unsure Whether to Quit Your Job or Break up, Then You Probably Should." 80,000 Hours, https://80000hours.org/2018/08/randomised-experiment-if-youre-really-unsure-whether-to-quit-your-job-or-break-up-you-really-probably-should/. Accessed 5.18.23.

64. Breuning, Loretta. Habits of a Happy Brain. Simon and Schuster, 2015.

65. Underemployment and Depression: Longitudinal Relationships, David Dooley, Joann Prause and Kathleen A. Ham-Rowbottom, https://www.jstor.org/stable/2676295

66. The impact of marital status and employment status on depressive affect for Hispani ,Americans Peter J. Guarnaccia, Jacqueline Lowe Worobey, https://onlinelibrary.wiley.com/doi/abs/10.1002/1520-6629(199104)19:2<136::AID-JCOP2290190205>3.0.CO;2-6

67. "Depressive Disorder (Depression)." World Health Organization, 31 Mar. 2023, https://www.who.int/news-room/fact-sheets/detail/depression.

68. Wilson, S., & Dumornay, N. M. (2022). Rising Rates of Adolescent Depression in the United States: Challenges and Opportunities in the 2020s. The

Journal of adolescent health : official publication of the Society for Adolescent Medicine, 70(3), 354–355. https://doi.org/10.1016/j.jadohealth.2021.12.003

69. Neighmond, Patti. "A Rise In Depression Among Teens And Young Adults Could Be Linked To Social Media Use." NPR, 14 Mar. 2019, https://www.npr.org/sections/health-shots/2019/03/14/703170892/a-rise-in-depression-among-teens-and-young-adults-could-be-linked-to-social-medi.

70. Kendall, K. M., Van Assche, E., Andlauer, T. F. M., Choi, K. W., Luykx, J. J., Schulte, E. C., & Lu, Y. (2021). The genetic basis of major depression. Psychological medicine, 51(13), 2217–2230. https://doi.org/10.1017/S0033291721000441.

# Chapter 8

1. O'Connor, Richard. Undoing Depression. Little, Brown Spark, 2021.

2. Robertson, Donald. Stoicism and the Art of Happiness. Teach Yourself, 2018.

3. Gao, Shuling, et al. "Associations between Self-Disgust, Depression, and Anxiety: A Three-Level Meta-Analytic Review." Acta Psychologica, https://www.sciencedirect.com/science/article/pii/S0001691822001731. Accessed 5.18.23.

4. Burns, David. Feeling Good. Harper Collins, 1999.

5. Seligman, Martin. Flourish. Simon and Schuster, 2012.

6. Seligman, Martin. Authentic Happiness. Hachette UK, 2011.

7. Lazarus, Richard. Stress, Appraisal, and Coping. Springer Publishing Company, 1984.

8. Miller, Geoffrey. The Mating Mind. Anchor, 2011.

9. Leary, Mark R., et al. "Self-Esteem as an Interpersonal Monitor: The Sociometer Hypothesis." APA PsycNet, https://psycnet.apa.org/doiLanding?doi=10.1037%2F0022-3514.68.3.518. Accessed 18 May 2023.

10. BECK AT. Thinking and Depression: II. Theory and Therapy. Arch Gen Psychiatry. 1964;10(6):561–571. doi:10.1001/archpsyc.1964.01720240015003

11. Seligman, M. E. P., Steen, T. A., Park, N., & Peterson, C. (2005). Positive Psychology Progress: Empirical Validation of Interventions. American

Psychologist, 60(5), 410–421. https://doi.org/10.1037/0003-066X.60.5.410

12. Becker, Ernest. The Denial of Death. Simon and Schuster, 2007.

13. Kaufman, Scott Barry. "The Taboo of Selfishness." Scott Barry Kaufman, https://scottbarrykaufman.com/the-taboo-of-selfishness/. Accessed 5.19.23.

14. Gregg, Aiden P. "Narcissistic Fragility: Rethinking Its Links to Explicit and Implicit Self-Esteem." Self and Identity, https://www.tandfonline.com/doi/abs/10.1080/15298860902815451. Accessed 5.19.23.

15. Austin, Emily. Living for Pleasure. Oxford University Press, 2022.

16. van Zyl, Liezl. Virtue Ethics. Routledge, 2018.

17. Hursthouse, Rosalind. On Virtue Ethics. OUP Oxford, 1999.

18. White, Richard. "Nietzsche on Generosity and the Gift-Giving Virtue." British Journal for the History of Philosophy , https://www.tandfonline.com/doi/abs/10.1080/09608788.2015.1088820?journalCode=rbjh20. Accessed 5.19.23.

19. Nietzche, Freidrich. Thus Spake Zarathustra. BookRix, 2019.

20. Nietzsche, Friedrich. Human, All Too Human. Penguin UK, 1994.

21. Hunt, Lester. Nietzsche and the Origin of Virtue. Routledge, 2005.

22. Maslow, Abraham. The Farther Reaches of Human Nature. Penguin Books, 1993.

23. Maslow, Abraham. Toward a Psychology of Being. John Wiley & Sons, 1998.

24. Matthew A. , McIntosh. "A History of Virtue as a Philosophy since the Ancient World." Brewminate: A Bold Blend of News and Ideas, 3 May 2019, https://brewminate.com/a-history-of-virtue-as-a-philosophy-since-the-ancient-world/.

25. Anscombe, G. Modern Moral Philosophy on JSTOR. https://www.jstor.org/stable/3749051. Accessed 5 Nov. 2023.

26. "Zoroastrianism." Al Islam, https://www.alislam.org/library/books/revelation/part_2_section_5.html. Accessed 19 May 2023.

27. Smith, Huston. The World's Religions, Revised and Updated. Harper Collins, 2009.

28. Kantian Ethics and Utilitarianism. https://risweb.st-andrews.ac.uk/portal/en/researchoutput/kantian-ethics-and-utilitarianism(b42b6192-7f4a-4690-b4d3-2b7bde2319cb).html. Accessed 19 May 2023.

29. Harris, Sam, and Jordan B. Peterson. Making Sense with Sam Harris. #62 What is True?-A Conversation with Jordan B. Peterson, https://www.samharris.org/podcasts/making-sense-episodes/what-is-true. Accessed 5.19.23.

30. Author Kellett, Sarah. "Do Pro-Social and Anti-Social Attitudes Determine an Individual's Happiness and Social Support?" Edinburgh Research Archive Logo, 1 June 2008, https://era.ed.ac.uk/handle/1842/2868.

31. Post S. G. (2005). Altuism, happiness, and health: it's good to be good. International journal of behavioral medicine, 12(2), 66–77. https://doi.org/10.1207/s15327558ijbm1202_4

32. Irani, Anna S. "Positive Altruism: Helping That Benefits Both the Recipient and Giver." University of Pennsylvania Scholarly Commons, https://repository.upenn.edu/cgi/viewcontent.cgi?article=1153&context=mapp_capstone. Accessed 5.19.23.

33. Midlarsky, Elizabeth. "Helping as Coping." Research Gate, https://www.researchgate.net/publication/234039973_Helping_as_coping.

34. Kesebir, P., & Diener, E. (2014). A virtuous cycle: The relationship between happiness and virtue. In N. Snow & F. Trivigno (Eds.), The philosophy and psychology of character and happiness. (pp. 287-306). New York: Routledge.

35. Proyer, R.T., Ruch, W. & Buschor, C. Testing Strengths-Based Interventions: A Preliminary Study on the Effectiveness of a Program Targeting Curiosity, Gratitude, Hope, Humor, and Zest for Enhancing Life Satisfaction. J Happiness Stud 14, 275–292 (2013). https://doi.org/10.1007/s10902-012-9331-9.

## Chapter 9

1. Gilbert, Paul. "Evolution, Social Roles, and the Differences in Shame and Guilt." Social Research: An International Quarterly, vol. 70 no. 4, 2003, p. 1205-1230. Project MUSE, doi:10.1353/sor.2003.0013.

2. Buss, David. Evolutionary Psychology. Psychology Press, 2015.

3. van de Ven, N. (2016) Envy and Its Consequences: Why It Is Useful to Distinguish between Benign and Malicious Envy. Social and Personality Psychology Compass, 10: 337–349. doi: 10.1111/spc3.12253.

4. Mahadevan, Nikhila. "How Does Social Status Relate to Self-Esteem and Emotion? An Integrative Test of Hierometer Theory and Social Rank Theory—PubMed." PubMed, 15 Sept. 2023, https://pubmed.ncbi.nlm.nih.gov/36107697/.

5. Wood, J. V., Elaine Perunovic, W. Q., & Lee, J. W. (2009). Positive Self-Statements: Power for Some, Peril for Others. Psychological Science, 20(7), 860–866. https://doi.org/10.1111/j.1467-9280.2009.02370.x

6. Thomaes, Sander. "What Makes Narcissists Bloom? A Framework for Research on the Etiology and Development of Narcissism | Development and Psychopathology | Cambridge Core." Cambridge Core, 14 Oct. 2009, https://www.cambridge.org/core/journals/development-and-psychopathology/article/abs/what-makes-narcissists-bloom-a-framework-for-research-on-the-etiology-and-development-of-narcissism/F8377C25E2C-5F2A4B7A49AF67539E959.

7. "Narcissistic Personality Disorder—Symptoms and Causes." Mayo Clinic, 6 Apr. 2023, https://www.mayoclinic.org/diseases-conditions/narcissistic-personality-disorder/symptoms-causes/syc-20366662.

8. Geukes, Katharina, et al. "Puffed-Up But Shaky Selves: State Self-Esteem Level and Variability in Narcissists." Journal of Personality and Social Psychology, https://www.researchgate.net/publication/304135726_Puffed-Up_But_Shaky_Selves_State_Self-Esteem_Level_and_Variability_in_Narcissists. Accessed 5.25.23.

9. Zeigler-Hill V. (2006). Discrepancies between implicit and explicit self-esteem: implications for narcissism and self-esteem instability. Journal of personality, 74(1), 119–144. https://doi.org/10.1111/j.1467-6494.2005.00371.x

10. Howes, S. S., Kausel, E. E., Jackson, A. T., & Reb, J. (2020). When and Why Narcissists Exhibit Greater Hindsight Bias and Less Perceived Learning. Journal of Management, 46(8), 1498–1528. https://doi.

org/10.1177/0149206320929421

11. Liu, Maike, et al. "Understanding and Motivating Student Feedback Seeking: Insights from a Lean Startup Based Entrepreneurship Program." The International Journal of Management Education, https://www.sciencedirect.com/science/article/pii/S1472811722001525#sec4. Accessed 5.25.23.

12. Singal, Jesse. "How the Self-Esteem Craze Took Over America." The Cut, 30 May 2017, https://www.thecut.com/2017/05/self-esteem-grit-do-they-really-help.html.

13. Baumeister, R. F., et al. "EXPLODING THE SELF-ESTEEM MYTH ." Scientific American Mind, https://web.archive.org/web/20150402090441/http://www.castonline.ilstu.edu/walsh/Research%20Methods/Baumeister_2005%20-%20self%20esteem.pdf. Accessed 25 May 2023.

14. Owens, Timothy. Extending Self-Esteem Theory and Research. Cambridge University Press, 2006.

15. Rocha Lopes, D., van Putten, K., & Moormann, P. P. (2015). The Impact of Parental Styles on the Development of Psychological Complaints. Europe's journal of psychology, 11(1), 155–168. https://doi.org/10.5964/ejop.v11i1.836

16. Brummelman , Eddie, et al. "Origins of Narcissism in Children." PSYCHOLOGICAL AND COGNITIVE SCIENCES, https://www.pnas.org/doi/10.1073/pnas.1420870112. Accessed 5.25.23.

17. Blackwell, Lisa S., et al. "Implicit Theories of Intelligence Predict Achievement Across an Adolescent Transition: A Longitudinal Study and an Intervention." Society for Research in Child Development, https://srcd.onlinelibrary.wiley.com/doi/abs/10.1111/j.1467-8624.2007.00995.x. Accessed 5.25.23.

18. Grant, Heidi. "The Trouble With Bright Kids." Harvard Business Review, 21 Nov. 2011, https://hbr.org/2011/11/the-trouble-with-bright-kids.

19. McLeod, Melvin. "No Self, No Suffering – Lions Roar." Lions Roar, 28 July 2022, https://www.lionsroar.com/no-self-no-suffering/.

20. "Anatta | Buddhism." Encyclopedia Britannica, https://www.britannica.com/topic/anatta. Accessed 25 May 2023.

21. Chah, Ajahn. "The Key to Liberation." Wisdom Library, https://www.wisdomlib.org/buddhism/essay/the-key-to-liberation. Accessed 5.25.23.

22. Hood, Bruce. The Self Illusion. Oxford University Press, 2012.

23. Rahula, Walpola. What the Buddha Taught. Open Road + Grove/Atlantic, 2007.

24. Wright, Robert. Why Buddhism Is True. Simon and Schuster, 2017.

25. Dor-Ziderman, Yair. "Mindfulness-Induced Selflessness: A MEG Neurophenomenological Study." Frontiers, 17 Apr. 2013, https://www.frontiersin.org/articles/10.3389/fnhum.2013.00582/full.

26. Tolle, Eckhart. The Power of Now. New World Library, 2010.

# Chapter 10

1. "1.2 Affect, Behavior, and Cognition." BCcampus, 25 May 2023, https://opentextbc.ca/socialpsychology/chapter/affect-behavior-and-cognition/.

2. "The Cognitive Triangle: What It Is and How It Works." Hudson Therapy Group, https://hudsontherapygroup.com/blog/cognitive-triangle. Accessed 5.25.23.

3. Beck, Aaron. Cognitive Therapy and the Emotional Disorders. Penguin, 1979.

4. Huang, Yuchai, et al. "Sedentary Behaviors and Risk of Depression: A Meta-Analysis of Prospective Studies." Translational Psychiatry—Nature, https://www.nature.com/articles/s41398-020-0715-z. Accessed 5.25.23.

5. Blake, Emily, et al. "The Relationship between Depression Severity and Cognitive Errors." The American Journal of Psychotherapy, https://psychotherapy.psychiatryonline.org/doi/10.1176/appi.psychotherapy.2016.70.2.203. Accessed 5.25.23.

6. Lanius RA, Terpou BA, McKinnon MC. The sense of self in the aftermath of trauma: lessons from the default mode network in posttraumatic stress disorder. Eur J Psychotraumatol. 2020 Oct 23;11(1):1807703. doi: 10.1080/20008198.2020.1807703. PMID: 33178406; PMCID: PMC7594748.

7. Bush, Ryan A. Designing the Mind: The Principles of Psychitecture.

2021.

8. Nietzsche, Friedrich. Beyond Good and Evil. Penguin, 2003.

9. Hunt, Lester. Nietzsche and the Origin of Virtue. Routledge, 2005.

10. Nietzsche, Friedrich. Nietzsche: Untimely Meditations. Cambridge University Press, 1997.

11. Robertson, Donald. Stoicism and the Art of Happiness. Teach Yourself, 2018.

12. Plato's Ethics: An Overview (Stanford Encyclopedia of Philosophy). https://plato.stanford.edu/entries/plato-ethics/. Accessed 25 May 2023.

13. Grudem, Wayne. Christian Ethics. Crossway, 2018.

14. Rahula, Walpola. What the Buddha Taught. Open Road + Grove/Atlantic, 2007.

15. Nietzsche, Friedrich. Anti-Christ. See Sharp Press, 2015.

16. Friedrich Nietzsche (Stanford Encyclopedia of Philosophy). https://plato.stanford.edu/entries/nietzsche/. Accessed 25 May 2023.

17. Aristotle's Ethics (Stanford Encyclopedia of Philosophy). https://plato.stanford.edu/entries/aristotle-ethics/. Accessed 25 May 2023.

18. Swanton, Christine. The Virtue Ethics of Hume and Nietzsche. John Wiley & Sons, 2015.

19. Nietzsche, Friedrich. Thus Spoke Zarathustra. Penguin UK, 1974.

20. Mikael Rostila and others, Birth Order and Suicide in Adulthood: Evidence From Swedish Population Data, American Journal of Epidemiology, Volume 179, Issue 12, 15 June 2014, Pages 1450–1457, https://doi.org/10.1093/aje/kwu090

21. Krauss S, Orth U, Robins RW. Family environment and self-esteem development: A longitudinal study from age 10 to 16. J Pers Soc Psychol. 2020 Aug;119(2):457-478. doi: 10.1037/pspp0000263. Epub 2019 Sep 19. PMID: 31535888; PMCID: PMC7080605.

22. Rohrer, Julia M., et al. "Examining the Effects of Birth Order on Personality." PSYCHOLOGICAL AND COGNITIVE SCIENCES, https://www.pnas.org/doi/10.1073/pnas.1506451112. Accessed 5.25.23.

23. Dahlgreen, Will. "It's True: Birth Order Shapes Personality |

YouGov." YouGov, 17 Jan. 2015, https://yougov.co.uk/topics/society/articles-reports/2015/01/17/birth-order-personality.

24. Janus, Samuel S. "The Great Comedians: Personality and Other Factors." The American Journal of Psychoanalysis, https://emilkirkegaard.dk//en/wp-content/uploads/The-great-comedians-Personality-and-other-factors.pdf. Accessed 5.25.23.

25. Stewart S, Thompson DR. Does comedy kill? A retrospective, longitudinal cohort, nested case-control study of humour and longevity in 53 British comedians. Int J Cardiol. 2015 Feb 1;180:258-61. doi: 10.1016/j.ijcard.2014.11.152. Epub 2014 Nov 26. PMID: 25463379.

26. Gotlib, Ian. Handbook of Depression, Third Edition. Guilford Publications, 2015.

27. Rottenberg, Jonathan. The Depths. Basic Books, 2014.

28. Castelnuovo, Gianluca. "Depression and Identity: Are Self-Constructions Negative or Conflictual?" Frontiers, 3 Apr. 2016, https://www.frontiersin.org/articles/10.3389/fpsyg.2017.00877/full.

29. Clear, James. Atomic Habits. Penguin, 2018.

30. "Signature Strengths | VIA Institute." VIA Institute On Character, https://www.viacharacter.org/research/findings/signature-strengths

31. Bregman, Peter. "Diversify Your Self." Harvard Business Review, 21 Oct. 2009, https://hbr.org/2009/10/diversify-yourself.

32. Seligman, Martin. Authentic Happiness Using the New Positive Psychology to Realise Your Potential for Lastin. 2017.

33. Seligman, Martin. "Authentic Happiness." Authentic Happiness, https://www.authentichappiness.sas.upenn.edu/. Accessed 26 May 2023.

34. Tehranchi A, Neshat Doost HT, Amiri S, Power MJ. The Role of Character Strengths in Depression: A Structural Equation Model. Front Psychol. 2018 Sep 6;9:1609. doi: 10.3389/fpsyg.2018.01609. PMID: 30237776; PMCID: PMC6135893.

35. Traeger, Lara. "Cognitive Restructuring." Encyclopedia of Behavioral Medicine, https://link.springer.com/referenceworkentry/10.1007/978-1-4419-1005-9_166. Accessed 5.26.23.

36. "Rumination: A Cycle of Negative Thinking." American Psychiatric Association, https://www.psychiatry.org/news-room/apa-blogs/rumination-a-cycle-of-negative-thinking. Accessed 5.26.23.

37. "Cognitive Therapy for Depression | Society of Clinical Psychology." Society of Clinical Psychology | Division 12 of the American Psychological Association, 6 Mar. 2017, https://div12.org/treatment/cognitive-therapy-for-depression/.

38. Pouget A, Beck JM, Ma WJ, Latham PE. Probabilistic brains: knowns and unknowns. Nat Neurosci. 2013 Sep;16(9):1170-8. doi: 10.1038/nn.3495. Epub 2013 Aug 18. PMID: 23955561; PMCID: PMC4487650.

39. Nesse RM. The smoke detector principle. Natural selection and the regulation of defensive responses. Ann N Y Acad Sci. 2001 May;935:75-85. PMID: 11411177.

40. Li, N. P., van Vugt, M., & Colarelli, S. M. (2018). The evolutionary mismatch hypothesis: Implications for psychological science. Current Directions in Psychological Science, 27(1), 38–44. https://doi.org/10.1177/0963721417731378.

41. Lim AJ, Lau C, Li NP. The Moderating Role of Social Network Size on Social Media Use and Self-Esteem: An Evolutionary Mismatch Perspective. Front Psychol. 2021 Sep 27;12:734206. doi: 10.3389/fpsyg.2021.734206. PMID: 34646214; PMCID: PMC8503551.

42. Greenberger, Dennis. Mind Over Mood, Second Edition. Guilford Publications, 2015.

43. Burns, David. Feeling Good. Harper Collins, 2012.

44. Segal, Zindel. Mindfulness-Based Cognitive Therapy for Depression, Second Edition. Guilford Publications, 2018.

45. Harris, Russ. ACT Made Simple. New Harbinger Publications, 2019.

46. Wells, Adrian. Metacognitive Therapy for Anxiety and Depression. Guilford Press, 2011.

47. Beck, Aaron. Cognitive Therapy and the Emotional Disorders. Penguin, 1979.

# Chapter 11

1. Kirsch I, Deacon BJ, Huedo-Medina TB, Scoboria A, Moore TJ, Johnson BT. Initial severity and antidepressant benefits: a meta-analysis of data submitted to the Food and Drug Administration. PLoS Med. 2008 Feb;5(2):e45. doi: 10.1371/journal.pmed.0050045. PMID: 18303940; PMCID: PMC2253608.

2. Chu A, Wadhwa R. Selective Serotonin Reuptake Inhibitors. [Updated 2023 Feb 12]. In: StatPearls [Internet]. Treasure Island (FL): StatPearls Publishing; 2023 Jan-. Available from: https://www.ncbi.nlm.nih.gov/books/NBK554406/

3. Targum SD. Identification and treatment of antidepressant tachyphylaxis. Innov Clin Neurosci. 2014 Mar;11(3-4):24-8. PMID: 24800130; PMCID: PMC4008298.

4. Gabriel M, Sharma V. Antidepressant discontinuation syndrome. CMAJ. 2017 May 29;189(21):E747. doi: 10.1503/cmaj.160991. PMID: 28554948; PMCID: PMC5449237.

5. O'Connor, Richard. Undoing Depression. Berkley Publishing Group, 1999.

6. Ilardi, Stephen. The Depression Cure. Da Capo Lifelong Books, 2009.

7. Seligman, Martin. Flourish. Simon and Schuster, 2012.

8. Hofmann SG, Asnaani A, Vonk IJ, Sawyer AT, Fang A. The Efficacy of Cognitive Behavioral Therapy: A Review of Meta-analyses. Cognit Ther Res. 2012 Oct 1;36(5):427-440. doi: 10.1007/s10608-012-9476-1. Epub 2012 Jul 31. PMID: 23459093; PMCID: PMC3584580.

9. Cuijpers P, Miguel C, Harrer M, Plessen CY, Ciharova M, Ebert D, Karyotaki E. Cognitive behavior therapy vs. control conditions, other psychotherapies, pharmacotherapies and combined treatment for depression: a comprehensive meta-analysis including 409 trials with 52,702 patients. World Psychiatry. 2023 Feb;22(1):105-115. doi: 10.1002/wps.21069. PMID: 36640411; PMCID: PMC9840507.

10. Kirsch, Irving. The Emperor's New Drugs. ReadHowYouWant.com, 2010.

11. Hasselmann HW. Ketamine as antidepressant? Current state

and future perspectives. Curr Neuropharmacol. 2014 Jan;12(1):57-70. doi: 10.2174/1570159X113119990043. PMID: 24533016; PMCID: PMC3915350.

12. Fuller, Kristen. "Ketamine for Treatment-Resistant Depression." Verywell Mind, https://www.verywellmind.com/ketamine-to-treat-depression-5114938. Accessed 5.26.23.

13. Li M, Woelfer M, Colic L, Safron A, Chang C, Heinze HJ, Speck O, Mayberg HS, Biswal BB, Salvadore G, Fejtova A, Walter M. Default mode network connectivity change corresponds to ketamine's delayed glutamatergic effects. Eur Arch Psychiatry Clin Neurosci. 2020 Mar;270(2):207-216. doi: 10.1007/s00406-018-0942-y. Epub 2018 Oct 23. PMID: 30353262.

14. Hamilton JP, Farmer M, Fogelman P, Gotlib IH. Depressive Rumination, the Default-Mode Network, and the Dark Matter of Clinical Neuroscience. Biol Psychiatry. 2015 Aug 15;78(4):224-30. doi: 10.1016/j.biopsych.2015.02.020. Epub 2015 Feb 24. PMID: 25861700; PMCID: PMC4524294.

15. Garrison, K. A., Zeffiro, T. A., Scheinost, D., Constable, R. T., & Brewer, J. A. (2015). Meditation leads to reduced default mode network activity beyond an active task. Cognitive, affective & behavioral neuroscience, 15(3), 712–720. https://doi.org/10.3758/s13415-015-0358-3

16. Woo, David. "Why You Shouldn't Stop Taking Your Antidepressant without Talking to Your Doctor | Madison Avenue TMS." Madison Avenue TMS, 7 Apr. 2022, https://www.madisonavetms.com/blog/why-you-shouldnt-stop-taking-your-antidepressant-without-talking-to-your-doctor/..

17. von Goethe, Johann. Maxims and Reflections. Library of Alexandria, 1893.

18. "Behavioral Activation: How It Works, Examples, and More." Medical News Today, https://www.medicalnewstoday.com/articles/behavioral-activation. Accessed 26 May 2023.

19. "Behavioral Activation for Depression | Society of Clinical Psychology." Society of Clinical Psychology | Division 12 of the American Psychological Association, 6 Mar. 2017, https://div12.org/treatment/behavioral-activation-for-depression/.

20. Dimidjian S, Hollon SD, Dobson KS, Schmaling KB, Kohlenberg RJ,

Addis ME, Gallop R, McGlinchey JB, Markley DK, Gollan JK, Atkins DC, Dunner DL, Jacobson NS. Randomized trial of behavioral activation, cognitive therapy, and antidepressant medication in the acute treatment of adults with major depression. J Consult Clin Psychol. 2006 Aug;74(4):658-70. doi: 10.1037/0022-006X.74.4.658. PMID: 16881773.

21. Jacobson, N. S., Martell, C. R., & Dimidjian, S. (2001). Behavioral activation treatment for depression: Returning to contextual roots. Clinical Psychology: Science and Practice, 8(3), 255–270. https://doi.org/10.1093/clipsy.8.3.255..

22. Greenberger, Dennis. Mind Over Mood, Second Edition. Guilford Publications, 2015.

23. Burns, David. Feeling Good. Harper Collins, 1999.

24. "Behavioral Activation for Depression." University of Michigan Medicine, https://medicine.umich.edu/sites/default/files/content/downloads/Behavioral-Activation-for-Depression.pdf. Accessed 26 May 2023.

25. "Why New Year's Resolutions Fail | News Direct." News Direct, https://newsdirect.com/news/why-new-years-resolutions-fail-739787570. Accessed 26 May 2023.

26. Huddleston, Andrew. "Nietzsche on the Health of the Soul." Inquiry, https://www.tandfonline.com/doi/full/10.1080/0020174X.2016.1258147. Accessed 5.26.23.

27. Korb, Alex. The Upward Spiral. New Harbinger Publications, 2015.

28. Kesebir, P., & Diener, E. (2014). A virtuous cycle: The relationship between happiness and virtue. In N. Snow & F. Trivigno (Eds.), The philosophy and psychology of character and happiness. (pp. 287-306). New York: Routledge.

29. Gander F, Proyer RT, Ruch W. Positive Psychology Interventions Addressing Pleasure, Engagement, Meaning, Positive Relationships, and Accomplishment Increase Well-Being and Ameliorate Depressive Symptoms: A Randomized, Placebo-Controlled Online Study. Front Psychol. 2016 May 20;7:686. doi: 10.3389/fpsyg.2016.00686. PMID: 27242600; PMCID: PMC4873493.

30. Peterson TD, Peterson EW. Stemming the tide of law student depression: what law schools need to learn from the science of positive psychology.

Yale J Health Policy Law Ethics. 2009 Summer;9(2):357-434. PMID: 19725388.

31. Schutte, N. S., & Malouff, J. M. (2019). The impact of signature character strengths interventions: A meta-analysis. Journal of Happiness Studies: An Interdisciplinary Forum on Subjective Well-Being, 20(4), 1179–1196. https://doi.org/10.1007/s10902-018-9990-2

32. Duan , Wenjie, and He Bu. "Randomized Trial Investigating of a Single-Session Character-Strength-Based Cognitive Intervention on Freshman's Adaptability." Research on Social Work Practice, https://journals.sagepub.com/doi/10.1177/1049731517699525. Accessed 5.26.23.

33. Koydemir, Selda Z., and Eda Sun-Selışık. "Well-Being on Campus: Testing the Effectiveness of an Online Strengths-Based Intervention for First Year College Students." British Journal of Guidance & Counselling, https://www.tandfonline.com/doi/abs/10.1080/03069885.2015.1110562?journalCode=cbjg20. Accessed 5.26.23.

34. Steger , Michael F., et al. "Being Good by Doing Good: Daily Eudaimonic Activity and Well-Being." Journal of Research in Personality, https://www.sciencedirect.com/science/article/abs/pii/S0092656607000396?via%3Dihub. Accessed 5.26.23.

35. Emmons, R. A. (2003). Personal goals, life meaning, and virtue: Wellsprings of a positive life. In C. L. M. Keyes & J. Haidt (Eds.), Flourishing: Positive psychology and the life well-lived (pp. 105–128). American Psychological Association. https://doi.org/10.1037/10594-005

36. Seligman ME, Steen TA, Park N, Peterson C. Positive psychology progress: empirical validation of interventions. Am Psychol. 2005 Jul-Aug;60(5):410-21. doi: 10.1037/0003-066X.60.5.410. PMID: 16045394.

37. Khanna, P., Singh, K. & Proctor, C. Exploring the Impact of a Character Strengths Intervention on Well-Being in Indian Classrooms. School Mental Health 13, 819–831 (2021). https://doi.org/10.1007/s12310-021-09450-w

38. "Cognitive Behavioral Therapy (CBT): What It Is & Techniques." Cleveland Clinic, https://my.clevelandclinic.org/health/treatments/21208-cognitive-behavioral-therapy-cbt. Accessed 26 May 2023.

39. Lyubomirsky, Sonja. The How of Happiness. Penguin, 2007.

# Chapter 12

1. Nietzsche, Friedrich. Thus Spoke Zarathustra. BoD – Books on Demand, 2015.
2. Janaway, Christopher. "Attitudes to Suffering: Parfit and Nietzsche." OUP Academic, 1 Oct. 2022, https://academic.oup.com/book/44613/chapter/378600073.
3. Kail, Peter. Simply Nietzsche. 2018.
4. Aurelius, Marcus. Meditations. Oxford University Press, 2011.
5. "Daily Stoic Store." THE OBSTACLE IS THE WAY (PREMIUM LEATHER EDITION BOOK), https://store.dailystoic.com/products/the-obstacle-is-the-way-premium-leather-edition-book. Accessed 5.26.23.
6. Hunt, Lester. Nietzsche and the Origin of Virtue. Routledge, 2005.
7. Nietzsche, Friedrich. Nietzsche: The Gay Science. Cambridge University Press, 2001.
8. Seneca. On Providence. 2017.
9. Holiday, Ryan. "Daily Stoic." Wishing You Betrayal and Bad Luck, https://dailystoic.com/wishing-you-betrayal-bad-luck. Accessed 5.26.23.
10. Nietzsche, Friedrich. The Will to Power. Jovian Press, 2018.
11. Seligman, Martin. Flourish. Simon and Schuster, 2012.
12. Doman, Fatima. "How Character Strengths Help Us Through Trying Times | VIA Institute." VIA Institute On Character, 18 June 2020, https://www.viacharacter.org/topics/articles/how-character-strengths-help%20us-through-trying-times.
13. Nietzsche, Friedrich. Human, All Too Human. 1915.
14. Designing The Mind. Designing the Mind: The Principles of Psychitecture. 2021.
15. Baumeister, R. F., & Exline, J. J. (1999). Virtue, personality and social relations: Self-control as the moral muscle. Journal of Personality, 67, 1165-1194. doi:10.1111/1467-6494.00086.
16. Sandstrom, G. M., & Dunn, E. W. (2011). The virtue blind spot: Do affective forecasting errors undermine virtuous behavior? Social and Per-

sonality Psychology Compass, 5(10), 720–733. https://doi.org/10.1111/j.1751-9004.2011.00384.x

17. Stanovich, Keith. The Robot's Rebellion. University of Chicago Press, 2005.

18. Nietzsche, Friedrich. Schopenhauer as Educator. Good Press, 2021.

19. "Quotes of Michelangelo." Michelangelo.Org, https://www.michelangelo.org/michelangelo-quotes.jsp. Accessed 5.26.23.

20. Maslow, Abraham. Toward a Psychology of Being. John Wiley & Sons, 1998.

21. Maslow, Abraham. The Farther Reaches of Human Nature. Penguin Books, 1993.

22. Nietzsche, Friedrich. Unpublished Fragments from the Period of Dawn (Winter 1879/80-Spring 1881). 2023.

Made in United States
North Haven, CT
26 May 2025